Henry Van Boynton

The National Military Park, Chickamauga -- Chattanooga

A Historical Guide

Henry Van Boynton

The National Military Park, Chickamauga -- Chattanooga
A Historical Guide

ISBN/EAN: 9783337203245

Printed in Europe, USA, Canada, Australia, Japan

Cover: Foto ©ninafisch / pixelio.de

More available books at **www.hansebooks.com**

Lookout Mountain from the Mouth of Chattanooga Creek. (See page xi.)

THE NATIONAL MILITARY PARK

CHICKAMAUGA—CHATTANOOGA.

AN HISTORICAL GUIDE,

WITH MAPS AND ILLUSTRATIONS.

BY
H. V. BOYNTON.

CINCINNATI:
THE ROBERT CLARKE COMPANY.
1895.

Copyright, 1895,
By H. V. BOYNTON.

PREFACE.

Chattanooga was an objective of the Union armies of the central west from an early period of the war. Gen. Thomas, in November, 1861, asked for a force of 20,000 with which he designed to advance through Cumberland Gap on Knoxville, and thence to Chattanooga. Gen. Buell, after having been turned aside from Nashville to co-operate with Gen. Grant toward Corinth, was sent eastward from the latter point against Chattanooga. The objects of Gen. Rosecrans' advance from Nashville were to clear Tennessee and occupy Chattanooga. While other elements, such as securing Nashville, and re-establishing a Union State Government there, entered into previous campaigns, Chattanooga was the direct objective of the Chickamauga campaign.

The battle of Chickamauga was one of the best illustrations of the pluck, endurance, and prowess of the American soldier which the war afforded. Measured by the percentages of losses, and the duration of the fighting for the various portions of each army, it was the deadliest battle of modern times. Its strategy will always be notable in the history of wars. So far as the occupation of the field is concerned it was a Confederate victory. Considering the objects of the campaign it was a Union triumph.

The battle of Chattanooga was the grandest spectacular engagement of the war. Its features appear in as bold relief as do Lookout Mountain and Missionary Ridge upon the fields which they dominate.

Twenty-nine of the thirty-three States east of the Rocky Mountains, which comprised the Union at the outbreak of the war, had troops engaged in these campaigns, and five of these were represented on both sides. The latter were Kentucky, Missouri, Tennessee, West Virginia, and Maryland. Three Union armies took part in the campaign for Chattanooga, the Army of the Cumberland in its entirety, four divisions from the Army of the Tennessee under Gen. Sherman, and four from the Army of the Potomac under Gen. Hooker. On the Confederate side Gen. Bragg was re-enforced by Gen. Longstreet's Corps from the Army of North Virginia, by troops from Gen. Johnson in Mississippi, and by Gen. Buckner's Corps from East Tennessee. Thus the whole country was directly and largely interested in the campaign and battles for Chattanooga, while on each side were many of the most distinguished and prominent officers of the war.

It was this universal interest of the country and its armies in these battles, the brilliancy of the strategy, the unsurpassed pluck of the fighting, and the wonderful natural features of the fields of battle, which made it possible to secure the unanimous support of Congress for the project of establishing the Chickamauga and Chattanooga National Military Park.

It was the pioneer project in giving impartial representation to both sides in preserving the history of the fields and marking the lines of battle. The Gettysburg Memorial Association soon followed and the act establishing a Park at Shiloh, the work of preserving the field at Antietam, and the proposed completion of Gettysburg under the Government are proceeding upon the methods inaugurated at Chickamauga and Chattanooga.

It is proposed in this volume to present such concise history of the Park project, and the battles for Chattanooga, as its limits will admit; also a comprehensive guide to all parts of these fields.

The great extent of the Park, the fact that it can be visited from several directions, each of which requires a different route, and that many visitors will have time only to make themselves familiar with the more prominent features of the movements and battles, render repetitions necessary in describing the general features for the benefit of all visitors.

In order to fix the field in mind as it was at the time of the battle it is well to remember:

1. All the roads were surface roads, without cuts or fills.
2. Most of the forest was thickly obstructed with underbrush.
3. Some of the present fields were woods.

A list of the fields cleared since the battle will be found in the body of the book.

Owing to the intricacies of movements, and the absence of many important reports, the studies of these extended fields are far from complete. The valuable aid of state commissions has supplied many of these lacks, and greatly facilitated this branch of the work. The author will regard it as a special favor if those who discover errors in this volume will notify him.

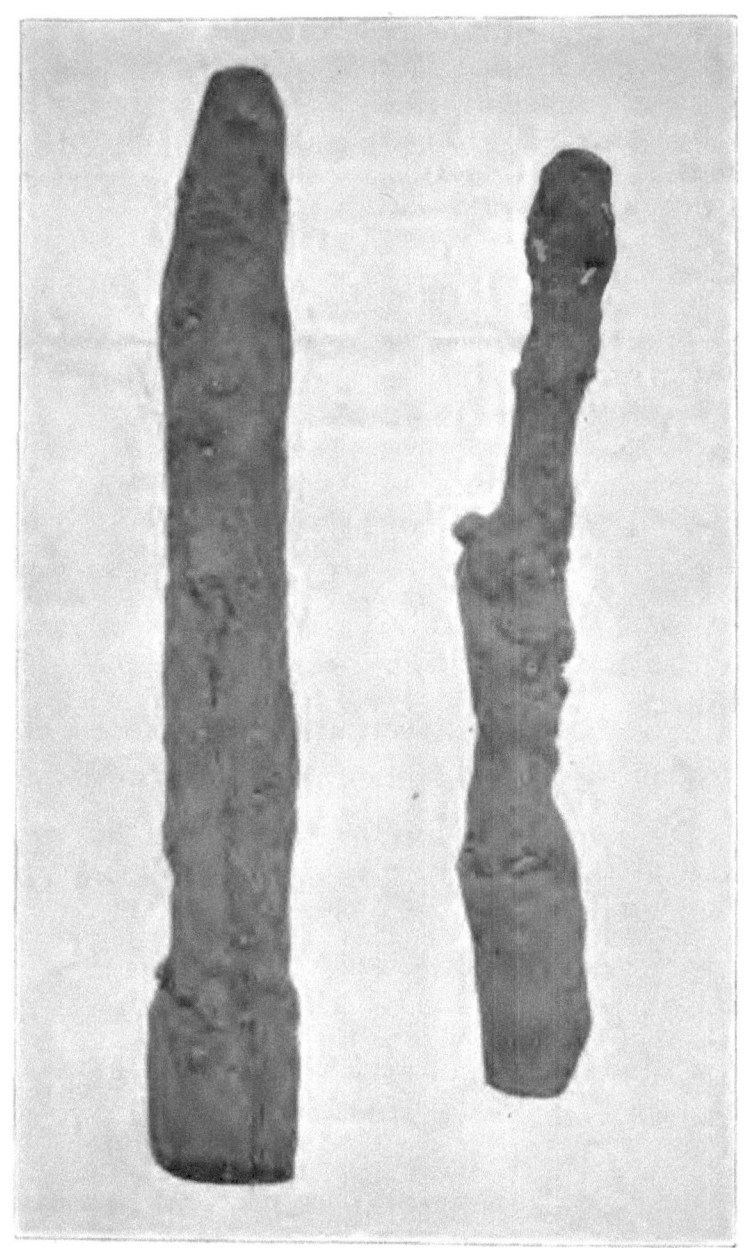

WAR RELICS FROM SNODGRASS HILL. (See page xi.)

CONTENTS.

	PAGE
GUIDE TO THE CHICKAMAUGA FIELD	167
VISITING CHICKAMAUGA FROM CHATTANOOGA	195
GUIDE TO THE CHATTANOOGA FIELDS	207

CHAPTER I.

General Description of the Park	1
Table of Distances	12

CHAPTER II.

The Chickamauga Campaign—Rosecrans' Strategy	15

CHAPTER III.

Bragg in McLemore's Cove—Rosecrans' Concentration	21

CHAPTER IV.

Battle of Chickamauga—First Day, Saturday, Sept. 19, 1863	29

CHAPTER V.

Battle of Chickamauga—Second Day, Sunday, Sept. 20, 1863	41

CHAPTER VI.

Roster of the Union and the Confederate Armies at Chickamauga	60

CHAPTER VII.

Rosecrans at Chattanooga—Bragg's Investment	89

CHAPTER VIII.

The Chickamauga Campaign Skeletonized	95

CHAPTER IX.

Re-opening the Tennessee River—The Brown's Ferry Affair.. 99

CHAPTER X.

Re-opening the Tennessee River—Battle of Wauhatchie....... 105

CHAPTER XI.

Battle of Chattanooga—Orchard Knob—Lookout Mountain—Missionary Ridge.. 109

CHAPTER XII.

Rosters of the Union and Confederate Armies at Chattanooga. 140

CHAPTER XIII.

Guide to the Chickamauga Field—Approaching from Crawfish Springs 167

CHAPTER XIV.

Visiting Chickamauga from Chattanooga..................... 195

CHAPTER XV.

Guide to the Chattanooga Fields............................ 207

CHAPTER XVI.

Origin and Development of the Park Project—The Chickamauga Memorial Association................................ 219

CHAPTER XVII.

Development of the Park Project—The Plan Changed—A National Military Park Supplants the Memorial Association 251

CHAPTER XVIII.

                                                                PAGE
Establishing the Park—Organization and Prosecution of the
    Work—The Park Commission............................ 272

CHAPTER XIX.

State Commissioners and State Troops..................... 275
The Friendly Governors................................... 275

CHAPTER XX.

Points of Discussion and Dispute.......................... 287

LIST OF MAPS.

                                                                PAGE
THE NATIONAL PARK AND ITS APPROACHES..................   1
THEATER OF THE CAMPAIGN FOR CHATTANOOGA..........   14
MOVEMENTS IN MCLEMORE'S COVE.........................   22
BATTLE OF CHICKAMAUGA—FIRST DAY......................   30
BATTLE OF CHICKAMAUGA—SECOND DAY.....................   42
KELLY FIELD, SNODGRASS HILL, AFTERNOON SECOND DAY.   51
CHATTANOOGA, LOOKOUT, MISSIONARY RIDGE...............   88
CHICKAMAUGA CAMPAIGN SKELETONIZED....................   96
BROWN'S FERRY MOVEMENT—BATTLE OF WAUHATCHIE..   100
CHATTANOOGA, LOOKOUT, MISSIONARY RIDGE...............   110

Specimen of Shell Monuments. (See page xi.)

LIST OF ILLUSTRATIONS.

WITH DESCRIPTIONS.

PAGE

LOOKOUT MOUNTAIN FROM THE MOUTH OF CHATTA-
NOOGA CREEK............................... Frontispiece.
 This view is from the Chattanooga or eastern side of
the mountain. The slope shown against the sky at the
right of the picture is the line along which Hooker's flags
first came into view from the city as his troops advanced
from the west side of the mountain. The high ground to
the right, in the foreground, is on Moccasin Point.

RELICS FROM SNODGRASS HILL................................ 6
 These limbs of oak trees were cut on Snodgrass Hill
in 1888, two years before the Park was established. The
trees from which they were taken stood at the foot of the
slope where Steedman's Division went into action when
it reached Thomas' line Sunday afternoon. The firing
was from Confederate batteries at Steedman's lines.

PYRAMIDAL MONUMENTS OF EIGHT INCH SHELL.......... 10
 These are erected to mark the spots where those exercising the command of general officers were killed or
mortally wounded. There were four of these on each side,
all commanding bridges: Brig.-Gen. W. H. Lytle and
Cols. P. P. Baldwin, H. C. Heg, and E. A. King, on the
Union side; and Brig.-Gens. Jas. Deshler, B. H. Helm and
Preston Smith and Col. P. H. Colquitt, of the Confederates.

LEE AND GORDON'S MILL................................. 33
 The La Fayette Road runs upon high ground which
looks down upon the front of the Mill at a distance of
about 300 yards, and crosses the Chickamauga a little
to the right (above) the Mill.

(xi)

KELLY FIELD, LOOKING NORTH.......................... 46
    The telegraph poles at the left are on the La Fayette Road, the west side of the field. Breckinridge's Division, after turning the Union left, marched out of the woods on the north full into the Union rear. John Beatty's Brigade resisted Breckinridge on the La Fayette Road beyond the break in the forest, Stanley's Brigade in the forest to the left of the field, and Van Derveer's, which finally repulsed him after Stanley's Brigade had been sent to Snodgrass Hill, advanced from the forest on the west side into the field, wheeled north, and pressed Breckinridge back over the ground of his advance.

THE BROTHERTON HOUSE............................ 48
    This house fronts on the La Fayette Road. The Union line Sunday morning was parallel to the road and in the edge of the woods back of the house. Longstreet's column of three divisions was in the woods in front of the house. Negley's Division first held the line back of the house, and was relieved by Wood's. As the latter was moving to his left under orders, and before the gap was filled, Longstreet's column pressed into it, broke the Union center and forced its lines back to Snodgrass Hill.

DYER'S FIELD, LOOKING NORTH........................ 50
    The flag marks the present Park Headquarters, which are at the Dyer House. The tower to the right of it is back of the first ridge, and stands at the high point of Snodgrass Hill, on the ground which was Brannan's right before Granger's troops arrived. The woods to the right skirt the eastern side of the field. The La Fayette Road runs parallel to this line of forest, and a quarter of a mile east of it. The Brotherton House where Longstreet's center pierced the Union line, is directly east of the monument at the right. The ridge at the extreme north end of the field in the center of the picture, is where Harker's Brigade checked Law's advance. Over the same ridge Kershaw's Brigade, forcing Harker back, advanced to the assault of Snodgrass Hill with Humphrey's Brigade on its right. Upon the ridge to the left, Bushrod Johnson's Division captured fifteen guns, and went on to the assault of Snodgrass Hill from the Viditoe House. The tablet in

the center of the field marks the point at the site of the old Tan Yard to which Clayton's Brigade of Stewart's Division penetrated Saturday at 4:30 p. m., after forcing Van Cleve's two brigades back from their line in front of Brotherton's, and subsequently breaking the Union line at the latter point. The line was restored by the advance of Negley's Division into the south end of the field, and of Brannan's into its northern extremity.

VIDITOE HOUSE—LINE OF JOHNSON AND HINDMAN'S ASSAULT ON SNODGRASS HILL...................... 54

The Viditoe House stands at the left near the gorge through which the Crawfish Springs Road passes toward McFarland's Gap. In the assault on the Ridge, the left of Hindman's Division extended into the gorge, and his right about to the middle of the picture. There Bushrod Johnson's line began, and ran along the road at the base of the Ridge for a considerable distance to the right.

CHATTANOOGA IN 1863......... ... .,...... 91

The arched railroad depot still stands. To its right, the long low building with chimneys is the Crutchfield House, where a deposit of a dollar was required to secure a towel and a piece of soap. The cluster of white buildings on the hill in the direction of Lookout are the thirteen hospitals which were used in succession by both armies.

CHATTANOOGA AND BROWN'S FERRY FROM LOOKOUT MOUNTAIN....... 102

Brown's Ferry, where the bridge was thrown as the preliminary move in opening the lines of supply, lies near the lower point of the low range parallel to the river at the left of the picture. The point of landing was just opposite the line of trees which run down to the bank perpendicular to the direction of the stream and just above the lower point of the range. The large island below Brown's Ferry is William's Island. The center of the picture is occupied by Moccasin Point. The toe is at the right, the heel at the left, and the ankle is the narrow neck between Brown's Ferry and Chattanooga. Sherman's troops crossed first at Brown's Ferry, and again, the night of November 23d, at the last bend where a glimpse of the river is seen at the right. The slope of Lookout in the foreground extends from the foot of the palisades to the river bluff a width of a mile and a half. The Craven House, which was Gen. Walthall's Headquarters, stands at the right end of the heavy clump of trees close to and over the word "Lookout Mt." in the title. The highest point in the woods near the toe of the Moccasin was occupied by Union batteries, which raked the entire Craven House slope.

ORCHARD KNOB—HEADQUARTERS OF GRANT AND
    THOMAS, NOVEMBER 25TH............................. 115
    The view is from the Chattanooga side looking toward Missionary Ridge. It stands half way between the eastern limits of the city and the Ridge. It was carried by the Union forces in the first day's operations. It commands a view of both Union and Confederate lines from Lookout Mountain to Sherman Heights. It was the headquarters of Grant, Thomas, and Gordon Granger during the last day's battle. The monument to the left was erected by Massachusetts to her Second and Thirty-third regiments. The western portion of the Knob, the whole of which is part of the National Park, is set apart for monuments to such troops as served in the campaign, but were not engaged within the legal limits of the Park.

HOOKER'S BATTLE FIELD ON LOOKOUT MOUNTAIN 118
    Hooker's troops formed about two miles south of the point of the mountain on such ground as is shown in the cut, his lines reaching from the palisades to the base. They then moved north and swept around the point of the mountain and over the lower slope shown to the left. Across the river at the left is Moccasin Point.

TUNNEL HILL AND SHERMAN HEIGHTS... 124
    The high ground to the right, now marked by the Trueblood House, is Tunnel Hill. The Tunnel is a little over a quarter of a mile to the right. The house on the lower bench of the ridge to the left of Tunnel Hill is Moon's. The woods at the extreme left of the picture are the foot of the slope of the detached range occupied by Gen. Sherman in his first day's advance. In the battle of Novem-

ber 25th, Cleburne held Tunnel Hill, and the Confederate line extended beyond the Tunnel. Corse's Brigade assaulted from the ravine at the left and effected a lodgment on the extreme point; Loomis', Raum's, Matthies', and Bushbeck's Brigades on the line from the north point of the Ridge to the Tunnel; and Giles A. Smith's Brigade, assisted by three regiments of Lightburn's, from the ravine to the left of Corse. The Crest Road, which terminates just to the left of the Moon House, marks the north point of Missionary Ridge. This Park road, constructed on a fifty-foot right of way, extends twenty miles to Crawfish Springs. There were no houses at the base in 1862. The whole of the crest shown in the picture now belongs to the Park.

MISSIONARY RIDGE FROM ORCHARD KNOB............... 135

The view is taken from the eastern base of Orchard Knob. It takes in that portion of the Ridge which was carried November 25th by Baird's and Wood's Divisions, and extends on the right slightly over the left of Sheridan's Division. The tower at the left is at the De Long Place, and marks the point where the center of Baird's Division gained the crest. At this point the Government owns between five and six acres on the crest.

KELLY HOUSE AND FIELD, LOOKING EAST................ 171

The La Fayette Road was immediately in front of the tree to the left in the foreground, and parallel to the fence. On this ground, and in a field directly opposite the house, Brannan's Division halted at sunrise, September 19th, in its march from Pond Spring, and almost at once proceeded northward to the McDonald House and eastward to the vicinity of Jay's Mill, where it opened the battle. On Sunday, Gen. Reynolds' Division reached from the La Fayette Road around the south-east corner of the field. Palmer's held the line 150 yards inside the woods to about the center of the picture, and Johnson's, the ground thence nearly to the left of the picture. There Baird's line began and ran around the north-east corner of the field, and half way back to the La Fayette Road.

BLOODY POND—WIDOW GLENN'S.............................. 174
 This Pond lies on the Crawfish Springs Road a few hundred yards north of Widow Glenn's, which is on the higher ground in the woods to the right. It was the only water for a considerable distance in either direction, and its banks during the battle were covered with wounded men and animals. The low line of forest on the right in the distance is just beyond and parallel to the La Fayette Road. Viniard's is on that road a few hundred yards south of the high timber on the right of the picture. Lytle Hill is a short distance to the left of the line of woods at the left of the picture.

JAY'S MILL, LOOKING NORTH-WEST............................. 180
 The site of the steam saw mill is marked by the small tablet toward the left. At the time of the battle the field did not extend quite to the large cedar in its center. The spring which Dan McCook's Brigade of J. D. Morgan's Division tried to reach at daylight is at the loose pile of stones in front of the fence. Forrest's Cavalry formed parallel to this fence to meet Croxton's Brigade of Brannan's Division, which was advancing through the woods on the left, and came within a few hundred yards of the spring. The left brigade of Brannan (Van Derveer's) fought on the high ground in the woods west and north of the field. Dibbrell's Cavalry Brigade, dismounted, and Ector's Infantry Brigade advanced to the attack from the line of the spring. At 6 P. M., Cleburne's Division formed with its right at the Mill and advanced westward to the night attack on Baird's and Johnson's Divisions.

SNODGRASS HOUSE—FRONT VIEW............................. 191
 The Union line was re-formed in front of this house after Longstreet had broken it at Brotherton's Sunday morning. Gen. Thomas' Headquarters were under the crest to the right and rear of it throughout the afternoon. Horeshoe Ridge begins a short distance to the left of the house.

BRAGG'S HEADQUARTERS, MISSIONARY RIDGE, AND OBSERVATION TOWER... 196
 The tall poplars at the right mark the site of the small house which was Bragg's Headquarters. The steel ob-

servation tower is seventy feet to the upper platform. There are five of these in the Park. A section of the Crest Road shows in the foreground.

REAR OF SNODGRASS HOUSE—GEN. THOMAS' HEADQUARTERS 205

The Union left, on Sunday afternoon, September 20th, ran on the open crest to the left of the barn, past the Snodgrass House, and along the Ridge to the right for about a quarter of a mile. Granger's troops arrived from the left, passed to the right in front of the fence, and, ascending the Ridge from the rear, carried it, and prolonged Thomas's right something over half a mile. Gen. Thomas' Headquarters were to the left of and a little below the tree in the field at the left.

CHATTANOOGA AND SHERMAN HEIGHTS, FROM LOOKOUT 210

Moccasin Point is in the bend of the river to the right. The high ground in the city to the left is Cameron Hill. The prominent white building to the right of the center of the city is the post-office and custom house. It stands a short distance to the left and rear of the site of Fort Negley. The faint column of steam near the bend of the river to the right is Citico Furnace. The second bend in the river marks the point of Sherman Crossing, and the first low range seen beyond the first bend above the city marks the line of Missionary Ridge near Sherman Heights.

SCALING THE PALISADES, DAYLIGHT, NOVEMBER 25, 1863 212

The cliff shown in the picture is west of and immediately south of the point of the mountain as seen from Chattanooga. The ladders to the left, over which soldiers are seen climbing, are on a line where a detachment of the Eighth Kentucky scaled the cliff at daylight after Hooker's occupation of the Craven House plateau, and at sunrise unfurled their flag on the point shown in the illustration described in the preceding paragraph.

LIST OF ILLUSTRATIONS.

MISSIONARY RIDGE—BAIRD'S ASSAULT................ 217
  The tower on the Ridge stands on the jutting point
  (now De Long place) where Van Derveer's Brigade, the
  center of Baird's Division, scaled the Ridge in the assault
  of the Army of the Cumberland. Phelps' Brigade assaulted through the ravine to the left, where the ground is
  still more precipitous, and Turchin's Brigade along the
  open slope to the right. The Crest Road of the Park is
  seen at the right, just in front of the houses on the summit.

REED'S BRIDGE, LONGSTREET'S CROSSING PLACE.......... 185
  By this bridge, coming from the east (left), the first Confederate troops, Bushrod Johnson's, with a portion of
  Longstreet's, reached the battle field, Friday afternoon,
  September 18th. The crossing was resisted by Minty's
  Cavalry Brigade, assisted by troops from Wilder's Brigade of Mounted Infantry. The bridge is as it was at the
  time of the battle. Alexander's Bridge was a similar
  structure three miles up the stream. The latter was successfully defended by Wilder on the 18th and dismantled but
  restored and used by the Confederates on the 19th and 20th.

CRAWFISH SPRINGS—THE OLD WHEEL AND MILL...... 168
  Nearly the whole of the Fourteenth and Twentieth
  Corps of Rosecrans' army filled their canteens at this
  spring, or the stream below it, as they passed during the
  night march of September 18th from McLemore's Cove
  to Kelly's. The road ran upon the high bank a short distance back of the spring. The stream from the spring
  was about twenty-five feet wide and six inches deep, and
  the flow rapid. After the battle, it furnished water to a
  large proportion of the wounded of both armies.

CRAVEN HOUSE, LOOKOUT MOUNTAIN—WALTHALL'S
    HEADQUARTERS............ 130
  The Craven, or White House, was Gen. Walthall's
  Headquarters at the time of Hooker's assault. Its relative
  position is best shown in the Frontispiece, under the branch
  which hangs below the summit. The palisades range
  from 75 to 150 feet high. The Union flag was unfurled at daylight, November 25th, from the top of the
  cliff to the right. The slope is very steep from the foot of
  the palisades and is accurately shown in the view of
  Hooker's battle field, page 118.

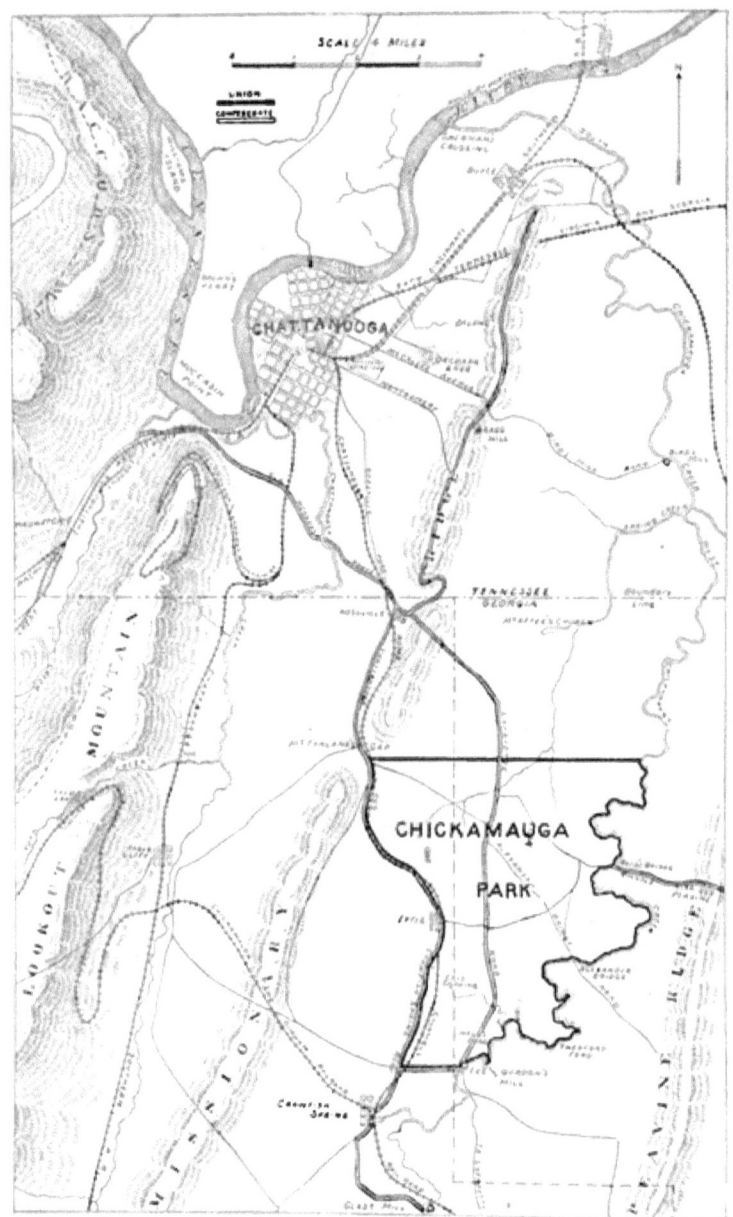

THE NATIONAL PARK AND ITS APPROACHES.

THE NATIONAL MILITARY PARK.

CHAPTER I.

GENERAL DESCRIPTION OF THE PARK.

The Chickamauga and Chattanooga National Military Park consists of two distinct parts, as shown by the map on the opposite page, the Park proper, which embraces the entire battle field of Chickamauga, and the Approaches. The area within the legal limits of the Park is about fifteen square miles. The aggregate length of the roads forming the Approaches is thirty-six miles, made up as follows:

	MILES.
Missionary Ridge Crest Road from Rossville	8.46
Crest Road to La Fayette Road	1.00
Rossville to Lookout Mountain	3.30
East base of Lookout to Lookout Creek	2.40
Rossville to Northern Line of Park	3.00
Rossville to McFarland's Gap	2.77
McFarland's Gap to Crawfish Springs	6.23
Reed's Bridge to Ringgold	6.00
Crawfish Springs to Glass' Mill	2.75
	35.91

Aside from the Approaches, the legal boundaries of the Park are these: An east and west line, crossing the La Fayette Road at a point about 600 yards north of the Cloud House, and extending from the McFarland's Gap road to the Chickamauga River, forms the northern boundary. The

Chickamauga River bounds it on the east, the road from Lee and Gordon's Mill to the Crawfish Springs road is its southern limit, and the Crawfish Springs road from the Lee & Gordon's Mill road to McFarland's Gap is its western boundary.

The Approaches in the vicinity of Chickamauga are mainly roads over which the armies reached and left the field. Those about Chattanooga lie mainly along lines of battle. Those over Lookout cross Hooker's battle field and lie near Walthall's, while the Crest Road along Missionary Ridge follows Bragg's line of battle in front of Gen. Thomas' Army of the Cumberland and Gen. Sherman's Army of the Tennessee.

Nearly all these Approaches, as well as the roads within the Park, have been rebuilt by the government in the most solid manner. The Crest Road and the La Fayette, or State road from Rossville to Lee and Gordon's Mill, are both constructed on a fifty foot right of way. The drive over this magnificent boulevard from Sherman Heights to Glass' Mill, which was the Confederate left flank in the battle of Chickamauga, is twenty miles. The scenery alone, over eight miles of its extent, from the northern extremity of Missionary Ridge to Rossville, is such as will give the drive a national reputation. When to these remarkable charms of valleys, city, river, and bold mountains, we add a comprehensive and distinct view of the battle fields of Lookout Mountain, Orchard Knob, and Missionary Ridge, this drive becomes one that is without parallel. The remaining twelve miles of the boulevard run through the center, and touch both flanks of the Chickamauga field, and the whole passes through or in plain sight of the hot fighting ground of five day's battle between great armies. The boulevard, when completed, like the other roads and approaches of the Park, will have historical tablets or monuments, or both, to illustrate every important point of action on each side in these battles.

The government has acquired the site of Bragg's Headquarters on Missionary Ridge and about three acres surrounding it. It has also purchased a spur of the Ridge which juts out toward Chattanooga, opposite the left of the line of assault of the Army of the Cumberland. This tract contains five and a half acres, and from it the face of the Ridge to a point within a division front of the right of the line of assault can be seen. Upon each of these tracts stands one of the five observation towers which have been erected in the Park. Besides these, the whole of Orchard Knob has been acquired. This was the headquarters of Gens. Grant, Thomas, and Gordon Granger during the battle of Missionary Ridge. It is an isolated knoll about six acres in extent and about sixty feet above the plain, standing half way between Chattanooga and the Ridge. The Confederate works, and those erected after the Union forces captured it, are still well defined, and the general appearance of the knoll remains unchanged. See note, page 13.

Except in the growth of timber, the features of the Chickamauga field have changed but little since the battle. There have been few clearings in the extensive woods where the heavy fighting occurred, but several of the fields in these forests had grown up with heavy timber, and, in consequence, the first studies of the lines were quite puzzling.

The plan of establishing the Park contemplates a restoration of the whole field, as near as may be, to its condition at the time of the battle. This involves clearing out the recent growths of timber and replanting clearings so that they may grow up to forest.

The old roads, which were those of the battle, have been re-opened and improved, and roads opened since the battle have been closed and abandoned. The only natural feature existing at the time of the fight, which has been changed, is the cutting out of the underbrush. This was absolutely necessary in order to bring the lines of battle into view, and to show the topography of the field. As a result of this work, carriages can now drive in all directions through the great forests and along the various lines of battle.

Thus far five iron and steel observation towers, each seventy feet to the upper platform, have been erected at prominent points of the Park. Three of these are on the Chickamauga field, and two on Missionary Ridge. Of the former, one is near Hall's Ford, on the ground where Bragg's army first formed for battle, one is near Jay's saw-mill, where the battle actually began, and the third is on Snodgrass Hill. All the towers are in sight of each other, and they thus serve to indicate the relative positions of the various points of the fields of Chickamauga and Chattanooga. The strategy of the campaigns and the movements of the battles are readily understood by the views afforded from them.

The plan of marking the lines of battle is to designate them both by monuments and historical tablets. The government erects the monuments to the regular regiments and batteries and the tablets. The erection of monuments to mark the positions of volunteer organizations is left to the States.

The historical tablets are of iron with the lettering cast as part of the plate. They are each four feet by three. They are of several classes—as, those for army headquarters, corps, divisions, and brigades. The first named show the corps which make up the armies with their commanders; the corps tablets show the divisions and their commanders; the division tablets show the brigades which compose them and their commanders; while the brigade tablets carry the organization to the individual regiments and batteries and their commanders in the battle. There are also staff tablets of uniform size with the others giving the names of the respective staff officers. The historical tablets each present from 200 to 300 words of text setting forth in condensed yet comprehensive form the movements at the points where they are erected. Both sides have equal attention in the erection of these tablets. The only distinctive mark is the letter " U " for Union in the upper right hand corner, and the letter " C " for Confederate. Following are specimens of several hundred tablets erected on the field:

No. 28.

FIELD HEADQUARTERS, ARMY OF TENNESSEE.

GEN. BRAXTON BRAGG.

[Sept. 19, 1863.]

Polk's Corps—Lieut.-Gen. LEONIDAS POLK.
Hill's Corps—Lieut.-Gen. DANIEL H. HILL.
Reserve Corps—Maj.-Gen. W. H. T. WALKER.
Buckner's Corps—Maj.-Gen. SIMON BOLIVAR BUCKNER.
Longstreet's Corps—Maj.-Gen. JOHN B. HOOD.
Wheeler's Corps (Cavalry)—Maj.-Gen. JOSEPH WHEELER.
Forrest's Corps (Cavalry)—Brig. Gen. NATHAN BEDFORD FORREST.

By reason of Rosecrans' flanking movement over Lookout Mountain south of Chattanooga, Bragg withdrew from that city, Sept. 7th and 8th, and on the 9th established headquarters at Snow Hill, near Lee and Gordon's Mill, his lines extending from that point to LaFayette, fronting the gaps in Pigeon Mountain and Lookout Mountain beyond. Orders were issued at midnight of the 9th to Hindman and Hill for an attack by way of Davis' Cross Roads upon Gen. Thomas' Corps at Stevens' Gap. These were repeated at midnight of the 10th from Bragg's Headquarters, then at LaFayette. The movement miscarried. Sept. 12th, Gen. Polk was ordered with his own and Walker's Corps, supported by Buckner's, to attack Crittenden's Corps, then supposed to be divided in the region between Lee and Gordon's Mill and Ringgold. This movement also miscarried. The night of the 17th, Bragg, from his headquarters at Leet's Tan-yard, ordered a crossing of the Chickamauga at Reed's and Alexander's Bridges and the fords above them, with the design of attacking Crittenden's Corps, which was then the Union left, at Lee and Gordon's Mill. The crossing was accomplished on the afternoon and night of the 18th and early on the 19th, and orders were given for attack at about 8 o'clock of the 19th. Bragg's Headquarters were established at Thedford's Ford.

(5)

RESERVE CORPS.

MAJ.-GEN. GORDON GRANGER.

[Sept. 20, 1863, 1 P. M.]

1st Division—Brig.-Gen. JAMES B. STEEDMAN.
2d Brigade, 2d Division—Col. DANIEL McCOOK.

On the morning of the 20th of September, the Reserve Corps was in the vicinity of McAfee's Church, 2¼ miles north-east of this point. Gen. Granger, about noon, judging by the firing that Gen. Thomas was hard pressed, marched in haste with Steedman's Division to his assistance, guided by the sound of the guns, and without orders. While passing this point at 1 o'clock, Forrest's Cavalry attacked his flank without delaying him. He deployed Whitaker's Brigade upon the high ground west of this road and drove the enemy's cavalry away from the Union hospital at Cloud's Spring. He then sent back for McCook's Brigade, of Gen. J. D. Morgan's Division, and, posting it on the crest next south of Cloud's House and west of McDonald's, rapidly pressed on with the rest of his command to the Snodgrass House, where he reported to Gen. Thomas. There Steedman's Division went immediately into action on the right of Thomas' line, repulsing the enemy's troops who were in the act of turning that flank. At 6 P. M., the division withdrew under orders to the next ridge, in the the rear, followed by the enemy to the foot of that ridge. Loss in the battle, all but 34 of which was in Steedman's two brigades, during the afternoon of September 20th: Killed, 215; wounded, 976; missing, 631; total, 1,822. Strength of Steedman's two brigades in action, 3,943. Between 1 o'clock and 6 P. M., the killed and wounded numbered 1,732. Percentage of loss, 44. Of 216 officers, 109 were killed or wounded. Percentage, 45.8.

No. 62.

JOHNSON'S DIVISION—McCOOK'S CORPS.

BRIG.-GEN. RICHARD W. JOHNSON.

[Sept. 20, 1863, until 6 P. M.]

1st Brigade—Brig.-Gen. AUGUST WILLICH.
2d Brigade—Col. JOSEPH B. DODGE.
3d Brigade—Col. WILLIAM W. BERRY.

This division was established on this line before daylight of Sept. 20th, having withdrawn the evening before from the vicinity of Winfrey's House in the face of Cleburne's attack. Berry's Brigade was on the front line and Willich in reserve. Baird's Division was on the left and Palmer's on the right. Dodge's Brigade was transferred before the attack to the left of Baird's Division. The front was protected by a breastwork of logs. About 10 A. M., Cleburne's division attacked the fronts of Johnson and Palmer, but after desperate fighting for about an hour it was repulsed with heavy loss. Thereafter, there was little fighting on this front until late in the afternoon. Meantime part of Berry's and all of Willich's Brigades assisted in repelling the persistent attacks on Baird's left. At 4 P. M., Willich's Brigade moved in rear of Baird's line and skirting the woods advanced southwards and cleared them of scattered forces of the enemy and took position in the south-west corner of the Kelly Field to the right of Reynolds' Division. Soon after 5:30 P. M., Johnson was ordered to follow Palmer in withdrawing. Being heavily attacked at this moment, Johnson and Baird maintained their lines for a short time and then withdrew in haste and in disorder to the woods west of the Kelly Field. They were not pursued into the forest, and thence moved to Rossville by way of McFarland's Gap. Loss during the two days: Killed, 148; wounded, 940; missing, 554; total, 1,642.

(7)

LIDDELL'S DIVISION—WALKER'S CORPS.

BRIG.-GEN. ST. JOHN R. LIDDELL.

[Sept. 19, 1863, 11 A. M.]

Liddell's Brigade—Col. DANIEL C. GOVAN.
Walthall's Brigade—Brig.-Gen. EDWARD CARY WALTHALL.

At 10:30 A. M., Gen. Walker ordered this division, then halted on the road from Alexander's Bridge to Lee & Gordon's Mill in rear of Gen. Hood's line, to proceed rapidly to the right to the assistance of the forces then desperately engaged in front of Jay's Mill. Moving quickly toward the sound of battle with Walthall's Brigade on the right and Govan's Brigade on the left, the division struck the flank of Scribner's and King's Brigades of Baird's Division, threw them into confusion and captured Battery A, 1st Michigan, and Battery H, 5th U. S. Artillery, thus relieving the pressure on Ector's and Wilson's Brigades. While pressing with great vigor the advantage gained, Liddell's line was first checked by Brannan's Division, and then taken in flank by Johnston's Division of McCook's Corps. Narrowly escaping capture, it followed Walker's Division, all in considerable confusion to a position with Forrest's Corps in rear of Jay's Mill. The fighting was terrific on both sides throughout the action over all this portion of the field.

No. A. 3.

WILDER'S BRIGADE.
REYNOLDS' DIVISION—THOMAS' CORPS.

COL. JOHN T. WILDER.

[Sept. 18 and 19, 1863.]

92d Ill.—Col. SMITH D. ATKINS.
98th Ill.—Col. JOHN J. FUNKHOUSER.
123d Ill.—Col. JAMES MONROE.
17th Ind.—Maj. WILLIAM T. JONES.
72d Ind.—Col. ABRAM O. MILLER.
Ind. Light, 18th Battery—Capt. ELI LILLY.

On the 17th of September, this brigade of mounted infantry took position here with troops thrown forward to hold Alexander's Bridge. At noon, reinforcements from the 72d Ind. and 123d Ill., with two guns of Lilly's (18th Ind.) Battery, were sent to Minty at Reed's Bridge. At 2 P. M., Walthall's Brigade of Liddell's Division of Walker's Corps attempted to force a crossing at Alexander's Bridge, but was repulsed with a loss of 105 men, and the bridge was dismantled. Wilder's four brigades then moved down the river, and crossed at Byram's (Lambert's) Ford at dark. Wilder's Brigade, being threatened in the rear by Hood's column advancing from Reed's Bridge, withdrew slowly, skirmishing heavily, to a point east of the LaFayette Road near Viniard's House. Here he was rejoined by the troops which he had dispatched to Minty's assistance, and held his brigade in close contact with Hood's forces throughout the night.

(9)

BAIRD'S DIVISION.

BRIG.-GEN. ABSALOM BAIRD.

[Sept. 19-20, 1863.]

STAFF ON THE FIELD.

Capt. BURR H. POLK, U. S. V., Assistant Adjutant-General.
Maj. MICHAEL H. FITCH, 21st Wis. Inf., Inspector-General.
Surg. SOLON MARKS, 10th Wis. Inf., Medical Director.
Capt. ENOCH F. DEATON, U. S. V., Commissary of Subsistence.
Capt. CHARLES K. SMITH, Jr., U. S. V., Assistant Quartermaster.
Capt. MORRIS D. WICKERSHAM, 79th Pa. Inf., Acting Assistant Quartermaster.
Capt. EUGENE CARY, 1st Wis. Inf., Judge Advocate.
Capt. THOMAS C. WILLIAMS, 19th U. S. Inf., Provost Marshal.
Lieut. WILLIAM R. LOWE, 19th U. S. Inf., Ordnance Officer.
Lieut. LOUIS T. MORRIS, 19th U. S. Inf., Assistant Commissary of Musters.
Lieut. HOWARD M. BURNHAM, 5th U. S. Art., Chief of Artillery.
Lieut. THOMAS A. ELKIN, 19th Ky. Inf., Aide-de Camp.

Besides the large historical tablets, there are guide tablets at every crossroads giving distances and direction to the prominent points of the field, and many locality tablets marking the sites of houses and fields which were landmarks in the battle, points where prominent officers were wounded, and where notable captures of prisoners or guns occurred.

The fighting positions of all batteries will be marked, as they are identified, by guns of the same kind used in the battle by the battery, mounted upon cast iron carriages painted so as to be an exact representation of the carriage of 1861. The Chief of Ordnance, Gen. D. W. Flagler, and his assistant, Capt. V. McNally, took every pains to procure from the stock of old guns on hand in the various arsenals, enough of the kinds used by the thirty-five Union and the thirty-nine Confederate batteries engaged, to carry out the plan.

The spots where general officers, or those exercising the command of a general officer, were killed or mortally wounded, are marked by triangular pyramids of eight inch shells, ten feet in height. A tablet on each gives name, rank, and army of the officer killed. There were four of these on each side, all commanding brigades, namely: Col. Philemon P. Baldwin, Col. Hans C. Heg, Col. Edward A. King, and Brig.-Gen. William H. Lytle, on the Union side; and Col. Peyton H. Colquitt, Brig.-Gen. Ben Hardin Helm, Brig.-Gen. James Deshler, and Brig.-Gen. Preston Smith, on the Confederate.

The lines of the rude works used by each side in various parts of the field have been found and are to be restored.

All the lines of each day's battle are being marked. As a rule, the regimental monuments are erected where the representatives of the regiments think the organizations made the most notable record. Other positions are then to be designated by granite markers. Those adopted by the Ohio Commission, the first to erect them, are fifteen inches square, and three feet high, one face being polished to receive the designation of the organization, and the day and time it occupied the position.

It will thus be seen that the field is being thoroughly marked, and that not only general movements, but those of every regiment and battery can be followed through the battle, and that the Park, when fully established, will be a most complete object lesson in war.

Table of Distances.

	MILES.
Chattanooga to Rossville	4.00
" Cloud House	7.20
" Kelly's	8.54
" Viniard's	10.52
" Lee and Gordon's Mill	12.04
" Snodgrass House	9.94
" Crawfish Springs via Lee and Gordon's	14.01
" La Fayette	25.29
Rossville to McFarland's Gap	2.77
Rossville via McFarland's Gap to Widow Glenn's	6.00
" " " " Crawfish Springs	9.00
Rossville to Kelly's	4.54
" Bragg's Headquarters, Missionary Ridge	3.80
" De Long's place (Tower)	5.50
" Tunnel	7.82
" North end Missionary Ridge	8.46
" West foot of Lookout	3.33
" Lookout Creek	5.73
Crawfish Springs to Glass' Mill	2.75
" " Widow Glenn's	3.00
" " Lee and Gordon's Mill	1.97
Ringgold to Reed's Bridge	6.25
Distances on the Chickamauga Field:	
Clouds' to McDaniel's	.52
McDaniel's to Kelly's	.82
Kelly's to Poe's	.72
Poe's to Brotherton's	.24
Brotherton's to Viniard's	1.02
Viniard's to Lee and Gordon's Mill	1.52
Lee and Gordon's to La Fayette	13.25

Lee and Gordon's to Crawfish Springs Road........ .97
Lee and Gordon's to Crawfish Springs.............. 1.97
McDonald's to Reed's Bridge....................... 2.50
       "   Jay's Mill......................... 2.12
Kelly's to   " 2.09
Brotherton's to " 2.00
Viniard's to Hall's Ford........................... 1.09
       "   Jay's Mill......................... 2.80
       "   Alexander's Bridge................. 2.45
Alexander's Bridge to Jay's Mill................... 1.55
       "   "   McDonald's.................. 3.15
McDonald's to McFarland's Gap...................... 2.25
Snodgrass Hill to "   " 2.45
Hall's Ford to Jay's Mill.......................... 2.80
Widow Glenn's to Kelly's........................... 2.00
Kelly's to Snodgrass House......................... .62
Brotherton's to Snodgrass House.................... 1.30
McDonald's to   "   " 1.34

NOTE.—Since the plates for this chapter were electrotyped the Park Commission has purchased 44 acres at the north end of Missionary Ridge, including the Tunnel Hill position defended by Gen. Hardee, and the points assaulted by the Army of the Tennessee under Gen. Sherman.

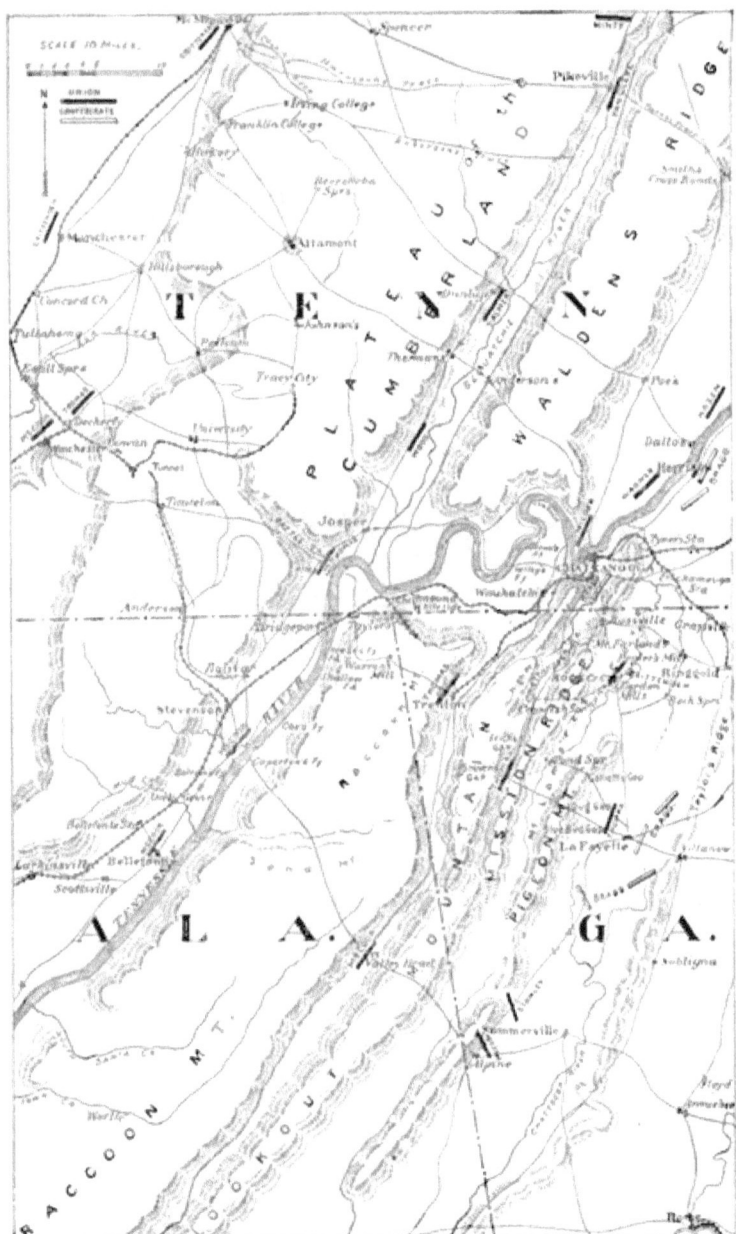

Theater of the Campaign for Chattanooga.

CHAPTER II.

THE CHICKAMAUGA CAMPAIGN—GEN. ROSECRANS' STRATEGY.

To understand the full value and significance of the military history preserved at the National Park, a study of the campaigns and battles which occurred in and about it becomes necessary.

At the opening of the Chickamauga campaign, the objective of which was Chattanooga, Gen. Rosecrans' army lay along the western base of the Cumberland Mountains, while Gen. Bragg's forces held Chattanooga, the south bank of the Tennessee, and the mountain passes above and below the city.

The Union army was composed of three corps of infantry: the Fourteenth, Maj.-Gen. George H. Thomas; the Twentieth, Maj.-Gen. Thomas L. Crittenden; and the Twenty-first, Maj.-Gen. Alexander McD. McCook; and one corps of cavalry, Maj.-Gen. David S. Stanley, Chief of Cavalry, Army of the Cumberland.

The Confederate army consisted of three corps of infantry: Polk's Corps, Lieut.-Gen. Leonidas Polk; Hill's Corps, Lieut.-Gen. Daniel H. Hill; and Buckner's Corps, Maj.-Gen. Simon Bolivar Buckner; and two corps of cavalry: Forrest's Corps, Brig.-Gen. Nathan B. Forrest; and Wheeler's Corps, Maj.-Gen. Joseph Wheeler. Before Bragg's withdrawal from Chattanooga, he was reinforced by Walker's Corps, mainly from Mississippi; and at the battle of Chickamauga, by Longstreet's Corps, from Virginia.

Gen. Rosecrans' Headquarters were at Winchester, where the Twentieth Corps was established. The Fourteenth Corps was at Decherd, and the Twenty-first Corps at

McMinnville. The Union army was 113 miles from its secondary base at Nashville. The Tullahoma campaign, by which Bragg had been forced out of Central Tennessee by a campaign of strategy involving a loss to the Union army of only 570 killed and wounded, ended July 4, 1863. The order of that day, halting the army, contained directions to immediately prepare for a forward campaign. The most vigorous efforts to that end continued day and night unremittingly until August 16th, when the Chickamauga campaign began.

Gen. Rosecrans had decided to make an imposing feint on his left, by throwing Crittenden's Corps over the Cumberland Mountains and Walden's Ridge into the Tennessee Valley, opposite and above Chattanooga, to create the belief that he intended to attack the city from that direction, while he threw the main body of his army over the river in the vicinity of Bridgeport, thirty-five miles below the city, and thence in succession over the Raccoon Mountains and the Lookout Range into the rear of Chattanooga, whence he could advance upon the city, and either shut Bragg up in it, or compel him to come out of it to protect his lines of communication.

The success of such a diversion was rendered the more probable from the fact that any movement in that direction would naturally be construed to indicate a purpose to effect a junction with Gen. Burnside's forces, which were then advancing from Kentucky toward East Tennessee.

The map will disclose both the strength of Gen. Bragg's position, and the serious character of the natural obstacles to military movements which lay in Gen. Rosecrans' path.

He must first cross the Cumberland Mountains, having a general elevation of 2,200 feet. These, and all the other ranges in his path, were very steep and rugged, and devoid of roads that were more than mountain trails, and their summits at all points terminated in palisades of formidable proportions. Next, for the main body of the army, came the Tennessee River, a deep stream, 1,254 feet wide at Caperton's and 2,700 feet at Bridgeport, where the bridges for crossing it were to be thrown. Crittenden's Corps, which was the diverting column on the north side of the river, after crossing the Cumberlands, had still to cross the precipitous range of Walden's Ridge, 1,300 feet high, before it could reach the Tennessee above Chattanooga.

South of the Tennessee, before the main body, rose Raccoon Mountains, and beyond them the formidable Lookout Range. Both had the same general altitude of the Cumberlands, namely, 2,200 feet. The Cumberlands averaged about thirty miles in width on the roads traveled, Walden's Ridge about fifteen, Raccoon Mountains about twenty, and Lookout about fifteen.

The campaign involved cutting loose from the base at Stevenson, carrying twenty-five days' rations and ammunition sufficient for two battles, crossing a wide river with most inadequate facilities into the enemy's country, and throwing an army over two precipitous and exceedingly difficult mountain ranges into the rear of Chattanooga.

The campaign for Chattanooga opened August 16th. Crittenden's Corps moved from Hillsboro, Manchester, and McMinnville for the Tennessee Valley above Chattanooga. Minty's cavalry operated on the extreme left through Sparta and Pikeville, and pushed a force of the enemy's cavalry under Gen. Dibrell across the river at Kingston. Minty then proceeded to make most energetic commotion along the river for thirty miles above Blythe's Ferry. Crittenden, who had occupied the Sequatchee Valley with Wood's Division at Anderson, Palmer's at Dunlap, and Van Cleve's at Pikeville, threw Hazen's Brigade of Palmer's Division, and Wagner's of Wood's, over Walden's Ridge into the Tennessee Valley, where Wilder's Brigade of mounted infantry of Reynolds' Division of the Fourteenth Corps joined them. Tents were pitched for many miles along the edge of the escarpment of the ridge, and fires lighted nightly along the crest. Bugles were blown at evening and morning near all fords for a long distance up the river, ends of boards and timbers were sawed off and allowed to float out of the larger streams, to create the impression that bridges were under construction. A few batteries, by continuous circling from the forests through open spaces visible from the enemy's side of the river, strengthened the idea of an army moving to occupy the other side. On August 21st, Wilder's Brigade appeared on Stringer's Ridge, within easy range of the city, and opened fire upon it with his battery.

The diversion proved entirely successful. Bragg was completely deceived. He withdrew from below the city his only infantry brigade, which was watching the river at Bridgeport, and sent his forces up the river to fortify and defend its crossings against Rosecrans, and Buckner's Corps was ordered toward these positions from East Tennessee.

Meantime the Fourteenth and Twenty-first Corps, and the cavalry, had crossed the Cumberlands to the Tennessee, awaiting the full development of Crittenden's diversion. Reynolds' and Brannan's Divisions were at the mouth of Battle Creek, Baird and Negley near Bridgeport, McCook's Corps near Stevenson, with the cavalry on its right below that point. The train which brought the bridge to be thrown at Caperton's was halted in the forest out of sight where the troops that were to lay it practiced in their work. The cavalry was extended well into the plain country below. The front of Rosecrans' movement as it reached the Tennessee Valley was 150 miles, and no mistake or delay had attended any part of it.

At daybreak, August 29th, fifty boats, each with a capacity for fifty men, were rushed across the open fields back of Caperton's, launched, and rapidly rowed to the south bank of the Tennessee, the small cavalry picket of the enemy driven off, and the bridge promptly laid without opposition. Davis' Division crossed and camped at the foot of Raccoon Mountains. September 2d he had crossed this range with Johnson's Division following, and two days later he had seized the pass at Winston's over Lookout Mountain, forty-two miles south of Chattanooga. The same day Stanley's cavalry crossed Lookout, and on the 5th descended into Broomtown Valley. Sheridan had thrown pontoons at Bridgeport, crossed, and followed to Valley Head.

Negley's Division of Thomas' Corps crossed with McCook, and Baird's with Sheridan. Brannan and Reynolds crossed August 31st at Battle Creek and Shellmound, chiefly on rafts and in canoes, while such of the men as could swim made light rafts of rails to hold part of their clothes and equipments and swam over. The moment the crossing of the main force was effected, Crittenden withdrew that part of his column in the Sequatchee Valley to Battle Creek, and crossed September 3d and 4th with the rafts and canoes used by Brannan and Reynolds.

The head of Thomas' Corps was over Lookout September 8th, crossing twenty-six miles south of Chattanooga by Johnson's Crook to Stevens' Gap, and Crittenden was nearing Wauhatchie, September 6th.

September 7th Bragg evacuated Chattanooga, and set all his columns from the city and the valley of the river above it in motion toward La Fayette behind Pigeon Mountains.

Of the Union troops in the Tennessee Valley, Wilder's Brigade crossed the river at Friar's Island September 8th, followed by Hazen's Brigade at the same crossing on the 10th, while Wagner's Brigade crossed directly into the city on the afternoon of the 9th.

Crittenden on the 9th had pushed a small force to the top of Lookout, and discovered that Bragg had left Chattanooga. The remainder of Woods' Division, preceded by the Ninety-second Illinois Mounted Infantry of Wilder's Brigade—Col. Smith D. Atkins commanding—marched into the city, while Palmer's and Van Cleve's Divisions passed around the north point of Lookout, and, leaving Chattanooga three miles to the left, followed after Bragg, and camped at night in Rossville Gap. The first Union troops to enter Chattanooga were those of the Ninety-second Illinois. Wagner's followed immediately from the north side of the river.

Thus, in three weeks, Rosecrans had repeated his Tullahoma campaign on a greater scale, through a well-nigh barren country, crowded with military obstacles of the most formidable character, and compelled the enemy to evacuate its mountain stronghold. This, too, had been accomplished with a total loss of less than 100 men, most of this occurring in the cavalry operations, and mainly in Minty's command.

Upon leaving Chattanooga, Polk's and Hill's Corps marched by Rossville and Lee and Gordon's Mill to La Fayette, reaching the latter point on the 8th. Walker's and Buckner's Corps withdrew from Tyner's Station and points on the river above it, by way of Graysville, toward La Fayette, while the forces at Hiwassee and Chickamauga Station moved by way of Ringgold. Cleburne's Division was thrown forward into the gaps of Pigeon Mountain. Gen. Bragg had not moved his headquarters beyond Lee and Gordon's, and on the night of the 9th he issued orders for an advance of Hindman's and Cleburne's Divisions to begin at midnight against the head of Gen. Thomas' column, which had reached Davis' Cross-roads from Stevens' Gap.

CHAPTER III.

BRAGG IN McLEMORE'S COVE.—ROSECRANS' CONCENTRATION.

The generalship of Bragg in withdrawing from Chattanooga was speedily developed. The strategy of Rosecrans had compelled the abandonment of the city, but the method of executing it gave promise of serious work for the Union forces. With his main body at La Fayette, and his right behind the point of Pigeon Mountain, a few miles south of Lee and Gordon's Mill, Bragg looked out through Blue Bird, Dug, and Catlett's Gaps directly upon the head of Rosecrans' center column, then descending Lookout at Stevens' Gap. It was twenty miles to Crittenden's Corps at Rossville, while McCook's Corps, in the vicinity of Alpine and Summerville, was altogether beyond supporting distance. Crook's Cavalry Division with this column had pushed to within three miles of La Fayette. As has been heretofore noted, the positions of the only roads, or rather trails, over Lookout, practicable for an army, compelled this separation of the several corps while crossing.

At midnight of September 9th, Bragg ordered Hindman's Division, then at Lee and Gordon's Mill, to march at daylight to Davis' Cross-roads, at the intersection of the road from La Fayette through Dug Gap to Stevens' Gap. Gen. Hill was at the same time ordered to send Cleburne's Division, then in the gaps in front of La Fayette, to make a junction with Hindman at the cross-roads, and both were to attack the troops of Gen. Thomas, then advancing from Stevens' Gap.

Had these orders been promptly and vigorously executed, Negley's Division would have been met at that point, and in

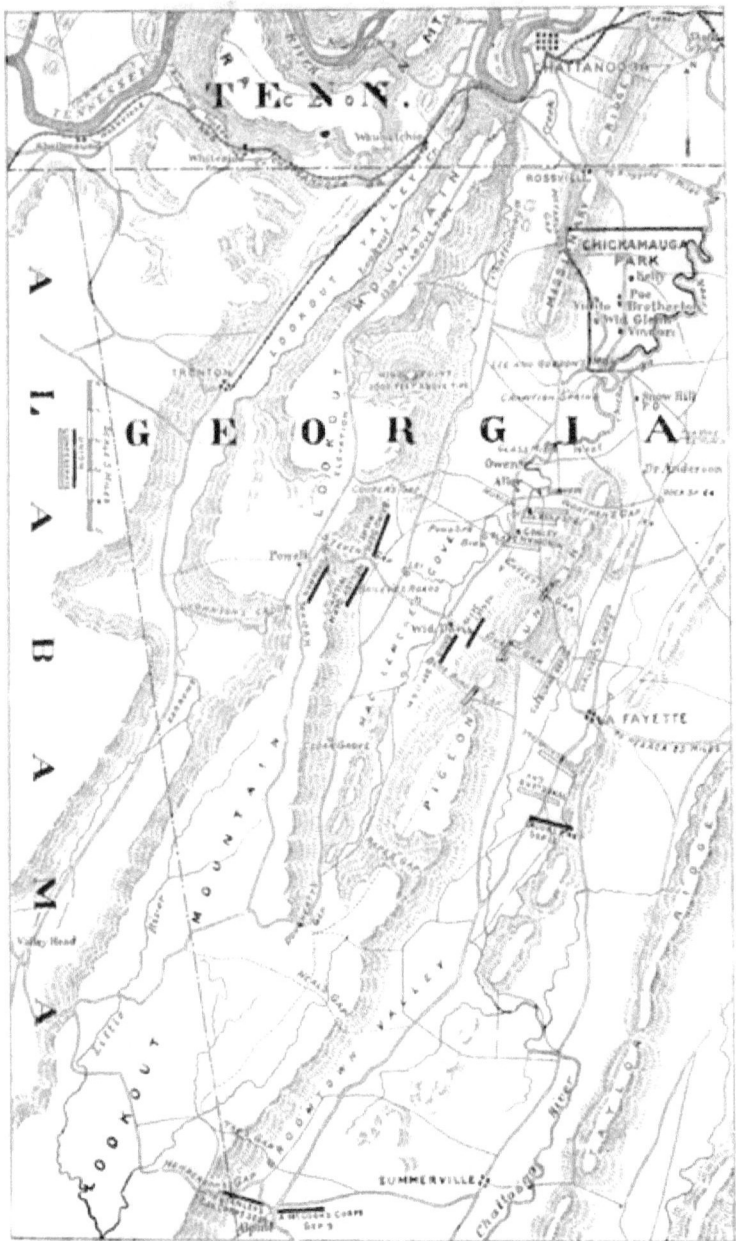

MOVEMENTS IN McLEMORE'S COVE.

all probability overwhelmed, since his nearest support, Baird's Division, only succeeded after a very hard day's work in reaching the foot of the mountain at 10 P. M. of the 10th.

But Hill sent word that the gaps had been so obstructed by felled timbers that they could not be cleared in less than twenty-four hours. Bragg then, at 10 o'clock of September 10th, ordered Buckner's Corps of two divisions to follow Hindman and attack with him. Hindman, however, halted his command at Morgan's, three miles north of Davis' Cross Roads, and Buckner joined him there on the afternoon of the 10th, the united column being in the immediate vicinity of Negley, who was isolated. To hasten the attack on the Union center, Gen. Bragg moved his headquarters to La Fayette, reaching there in person at midnight of the 10th, and at once directing Walker's Corps to join Cleburne's Division at Dug Gap and unite in the attack. At daylight of the 11th, Bragg himself proceeded to Cleburne's position. The day was spent till the middle of the afternoon in listening for Hindman's expected attack. Meantime, at 8 o'clock in the morning of the 11th, Gen. Baird's Division had joined Negley's at the cross-roads. Repeated orders from Bragg to Hindman's column to move forward did not secure an attack until the middle of the afternoon. Gen. Hindman was awaiting co-operation from Gen. Hill, and deemed the force reported in front of him too strong for his column. Under the skillful assistance of Gen. Baird, and the sagacious dispositions of Gen. Negley, their divisions were extricated after sharp fighting, and withdrew to the base of Lookout. The speedy arrival of Brannan's and Reynolds' Divisions rendered the Union center secure.

Gen. Bragg, deeply disappointed at the failure of his projected attack upon the Union center, turned promptly toward Crittenden's Corps, the Union left. Polk's and Walker's Corps were withdrawn to La Fayette, and moved immediately toward Lee and Gordon's Mill. At this time, Crittenden's Corps was divided, one division having been sent to Ringgold. On the evening of September 12th, Polk was directed to attack Crittenden at daylight of the 13th. At midnight of the 12th, Polk dispatched that he had taken a strong defensive position, and asked for reinforcements. He was informed that his force exceeded the enemy's, and again ordered to attack at daylight. In addition, he was notified that Buckner's Corps would early be moved within supporting distance. Promptly on the 13th, Gen. Bragg rode to the front, to find that no attack had been made on Crittenten, and that the latter had united his forces, recrossed the Chickamauga, and taken a strong position at Lee and Gordon's Mill. This result caused another keen disappointment to Gen. Bragg, but reinforcements having arrived from Mississippi and Virginia, he promptly decided to move down the Chickamauga to points well below Crittenden's position, cross the river, interpose between Rosecrans and Chattanooga, and attack Crittenden at Lee and Gordon's. This latter corps was then the left of Rosecrans, and Bragg's plan was to drive it back upon the Union center, which was still in McLemore's Cove in front of Stevens' Gap, and force the Union army into the mountains.

When Gen. Rosecrans discovered, September 11th, that the Confederate rear guard had not moved south of Lee and Gordon's, and that Bragg's left was firmly established near that point, he saw that the latter was concentrating for battle. He therefore abandoned his offensive movements against Bragg which had been in progress upon the theory that he was retreating to Rome, and began most active work to concentrate his own army between Bragg and Chattanooga. As he declared in his official report, it had become a matter of life and death to accomplish this. On this day, September 11th, when the supreme effort of his campaign began, he received a telegram from Gen. Halleck at Washington saying that it was there reported that a portion of Bragg's army was reinforcing Lee, and that it was important to ascertain the truth of the report. He was also informed that no troops had left the Army of Northern Virginia for the West. As a matter of fact, Longstreet's Corps had been for four days on its way South, and was nearing its junction with Bragg.

Crittenden's great activity east of the Chickamauga, and in the vicinity of Ringgold, where he was aided by Wilder's and Minty's mounted force fresh from their feint on the north side of the Tennessee, had enabled him to concentrate his corps at Lee and Gordon's. Thomas stretched toward him from Stevens' Gap, holding on to the latter point while awaiting the arrival of McCook's Corps, which Rosecrans had ordered to withdraw to Lookout Mountain, and move in haste along its top to Stevens' Gap. McCook, not being able to assure himself that there was a practicable road on the summit of the mountain, felt more confident of effecting a prompt junction with Thomas by recrossing Lookout to its western base, and taking the road which he knew thence to Stevens' Gap. After crossing the mountain, he heard of a good road along the top, and directed Davis' and Johnson's Divisions to reascend and move in haste to Stevens' Gap. These additional crossings of Lookout delayed the junction with Gen. Thomas until dusk of the 16th. Stanley's Cavalry Corps, now under the command of Gen. R. B. Mitchell, Stanley being sick, came into McLemore's Cove through Dougherty's Gap simultaneously with McCook's Corps. Meantime Crittenden had been moved toward Thomas, and put in strong position on the southern spur of Missionary Ridge to await the arrival of McCook. On the 17th Thomas moved toward Crittenden, and on the evening of that day the three corps of Rosecrans' army were within supporting distance.

On the night of the 17th Bragg issued the following order for crossing his army over the Chickamauga, turning up the stream on the opposite side, and attacking at Lee and Gordon's, the movement to begin at sunrise:

HEADQUARTERS ARMY OF THE TENNESSEE.
IN THE FIELD, LEET'S TAN YARD, *September* 18, 1863.

1. Johnson's column (Hood's) on crossing at or near Reed's Bridge will turn to the left by the most practicable route, and sweep up the Chickamauga toward Lee and Gordon's Mill.

2. Walker, crossing at Alexander's Bridge, will unite in this move, and push vigorously on the enemy's flank and rear in the same direction.

3. Buckner, crossing at Thedford's Ford, will join in the movement to the left, and press the enemy up the stream from Polk's front at Lee and Gordon's Mill.

4. Polk will press his forces to the front of Lee and Gordon's Mill, and if met by too much resistance to cross, will bear to the right and cross at Dalton's Ford, or at Thedford's, as may be necessary, and join in the attack wherever the enemy may be.

5. Hill will cover our left flank from an advance of the enemy from the Cove, and by pressing the cavalry in his front, ascertain if the enemy is re-inforcing at Lee and Gordon's Mill, in which event he will attack them in flank.

6. Wheeler's Cavalry will hold the gaps in Pigeon Mountain and cover our rear and left, and bring up stragglers.

7. All teams, etc., not with troops should go toward Ringgold and Dalton, beyond Taylor's Ridge. All cooking should be done at the trains. Rations, when cooked, will be forwarded to the troops.

8. The above movements will be executed with the utmost promptness, vigor, and persistence.

By command of Gen. Bragg.

GEORGE WM. BRENT,
Assistant Adjutant-General.

The narrow roads and the stubborn resistance of Minty's Cavalry Brigade from Pea Vine Creek to Reed's Bridge, and of Wilder's Mounted Brigade at Alexander's Bridge, also at

Reed's, in aiding Minty, so delayed Bragg's columns that no general attack was possible on the 18th.

On the night of that day, Crittenden's Corps was returned to Lee and Gordon's Mill, and took position along the La Fayette Road facing east toward Bragg's advance. During the same night, the main body of the Confederate army completed its crossing, and early on the 19th formed in line of battle confronting Crittenden, and at 7 o'clock stood ready to deliver its attack. Five divisions were thus formed, and two others were moving into position to drive Rosecrans' left back into McLemore's Cove upon his center and right, which were still supposed to be in the vicinity of Pond Spring and Stevens' Gap. Three brigades of Forrest's Cavalry had been sent at daylight from Alexander's House to Jay's Mill to guard Bragg's right and rear against Gordon Granger's forces further down the Chickamauga and in the vicinity of McAfee's Church.

Suddenly and unexpectedly, just as the Confederate lines of battle were about to advance on Crittenden's position, furious fighting broke out at Jay's Mill, two miles to Bragg's right and rear. The cause was not understood. Gen. Forrest soon appeared asking for infantry. The nearest brigade (Wilson's) was given him. Shortly after, he asked for and received another (Ector's). Then Walker's Division was dispatched as the resounding battle increased in intensity. Next, Bragg's reserve (Cheatham's Division) was hurried to the left, and soon after Stewart's Division was sent forward to assist this reserve. Bragg's plan of battle had been replaced by these unexpected movements which the emergency demanded. The explanation of the changed conditions is simple.

During the night Rosecrans had inverted his army, and soon after sunrise, Crittenden's Corps, which was the left at sundown, had become the right; Thomas, with the head of his column near Reed's Bridge, the left; and the Union army was between Bragg and Chattanooga.

Toward evening of the 18th, Thomas' Corps had left Pond Spring, followed by McCook's, moving toward Crittenden. As soon as dusk obscured the columns, they were pressed rapidly to the left. Upon reaching Crawfish Springs, Negley's Division was turned off to Glass' Mill to guard the flank of the movement, and Thomas with his three remaining divisions pushed on all night by way of Widow Glenn's to the La Fayette Road at the Kelly Farm. Here Baird's Division took position at daylight, while Brannan's, at sunrise, without taking time for breakfast, moved rapidly northward to McDonald's, then turned eastward toward Reed's Bridge, struck Forrest at Jay's Mill, at half after 7 o'clock, immediately became hotly engaged and opened the battle of Chickamauga. With Rosecrans between Bragg and Chattanooga, the dawning struggle resolved itself into a direct battle for that city.

CHAPTER IV.

BATTLE OF CHICKAMAUGA—FIRST DAY, SATURDAY, SEPTEMBER 19, 1863.

Before considering the movements of the opposing forces, it is well to remember that at the time of the battle, a number of the present fields were woods.

Beginning on the La Fayette Road at McDonald's, the present field east of that and north of the Ringgold Road was partially in forest.

The clearing on the east side of the road south of Brotherton's and north of Viniard's was thick woods.

The grove in the field directly east of Viniard's was dense, and extended from the present eastern limit to a point on the La Fayette Road opposite the house. There was also a strip of timber along the west of the road in the vicinity of the Heg Monument.

The tract, a quarter of a mile south of Viniard's and east of the road, was open forest, as was part of the fields on the west side near Lee and Gordon's Mill.

The northern portion of the Dyer field, about the old blacksmith shop, and the slope above it and north to the foot of the crest upon which Harker fought, was woods. The point of woods which surrounds the Snodgrass well at the foot of the latter crest extended with its present width to the forest east of it.

The Bloody Pond was surrounded with forest which extended eastward to a line running from the Widow Glenn's to the point of the woods which project into the present field south-east of Lytle Hill.

Riding eastward on the Brotherton-Jay's Mill Road, after

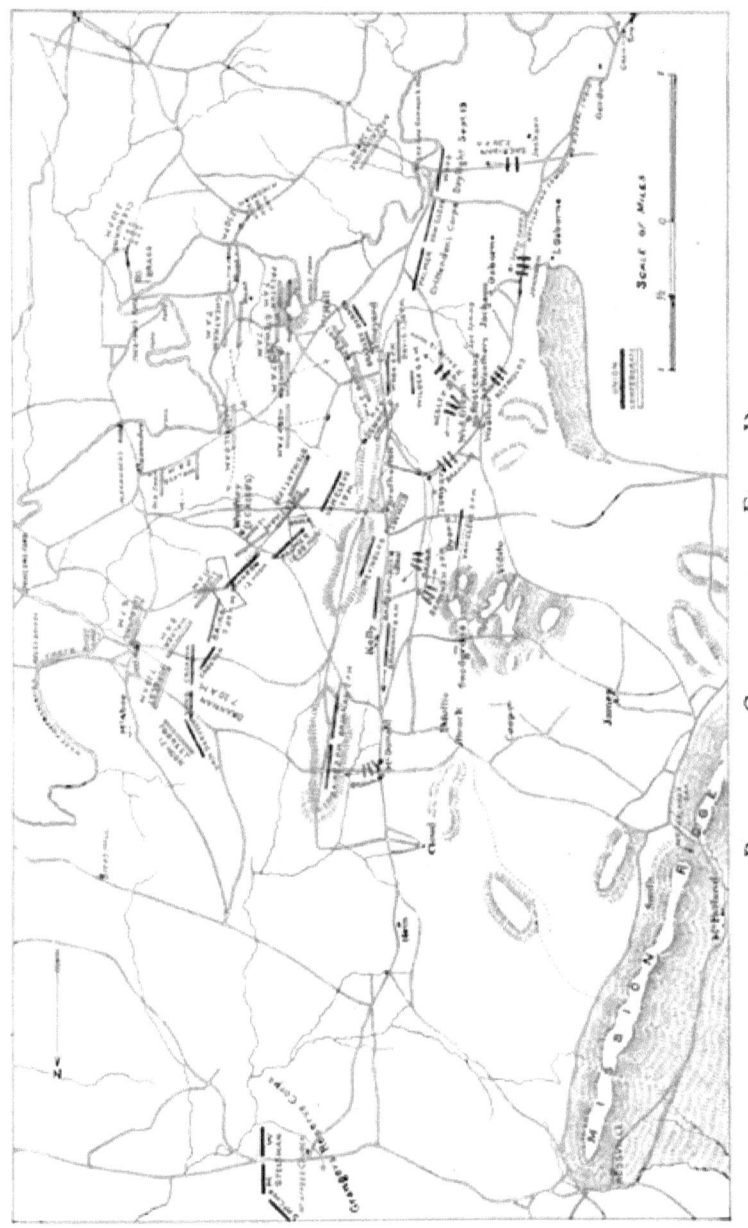

BATTLE OF CHICKAMAUGA—FIRST DAY.

passing the Brock field on the right, the growth of young trees on the left marks an area which was slashed timber. The present clearing beyond it through which the road passes was mostly woods, as was a considerable portion of the fields north of the Winfrey House in the vicinity of the shell monument to Baldwin. The field back of this pyramid was in woods, and a considerable part of that in front of it, while to the right of the road the clearing extended only to the line of the present fence running from a point near the Reed House (Winfrey's) parallel to the road.

The next long field entered in riding toward Jay's Mill was all forest.

The extensive field adjoining the site of Jay's Mill was woods beyond a point two hundred yards or so from the mill.

Most of the open ground to the left of the road, riding from Jay's Mill to Alexander's, was timber, and a considerable part to the right of it.

The first division of Confederate troops to arrive on the battle field was Bushrod Johnson's. His column consisted of his own three brigades, and that of Robertson of Hood's Division temporarily serving with them, three batteries, Forrest and his cavalry escort, and eight pieces of the reserve artillery. Gen. Johnson left Ringgold early in the morning of the 18th, and encountered Minty's Cavalry Brigade at Pea Vine Creek three miles east of Reed's Bridge about noon. By the stubborn resistance of Minty, aided at last by a part of Wilder's Mounted Brigade of Infantry, Johnson was delayed in crossing until 3 P. M., and his line did not reach Jay's Mill until 4 o'clock. Here Gen. Hood arrived and took command. The column then moved toward Lee and Gordon's. Both Minty and Wilder retired from Alexander's before it to the crest next east of the Viniard field, where Wilder bivouacked in close contact with Hood's force.

Walthall's Brigade of Liddell's Division, in attempting to force a crossing at Alexander's Bridge on the afternoon of the 18th in the face of Wilder's Brigade, lost 105 men in capturing the bridge, only to find that Wilder's men had dismantled it under fire and rendered it useless. Liddell's troops then moved down the river a mile, crossed at Byram's Ford, and, following Hood's column, bivouacked about three-quarters of a mile west of Alexander's. During the night of the 18th, and the early morning of the 19th, the divisions of Stewart, Preston, Cheatham, and Walker, and the remainder of Hood's Division, crossed the river and were formed for battle about 7 o'clock.

The forests effectually concealed the movements of each army from the other. At the hour just named they were thus disposed upon the field. Buckner's Corps of Stewart's and Preston's Divisions was on the left of Bragg's line near Hall's Ford, at the present observation tower. Bushrod Johnson's Division was in the center, and Hood's (McLaw's) Division on its right. Cheatham's Division was the reserve, and Walker's Corps, of Liddell's and Walker's Divisions, was coming up from the rear to take its place on the right of the front line. The columns faced the La Fayette Road, a thousand yards distant, and were formed to attack Crittenden's Corps, whose three divisions lay along the west side of that road with the right of their line at Lee and Gordon's Mill. Forrest's Cavalry was near Jay's Mill. At that hour Crittenden was supposed by Bragg to be the left of Rosecrans' army.

But Thomas' and McCook's Corps, the former leading, had been marching the entire night from McLemore's Cove along the Crawfish Springs Road toward its junction with the La Fayette Road at Kelly's Farm. At 7 o'clock, Brannan's Division had passed this point as far as McDonald's, and, turning there to the right, had reached the vicinity of Jay's Mill in close proximity to Forrest's Cavalry, then in line at the latter point.

Baird's Division was formed between Kelly's and Poe's, facing east, ready to support Brannan. Steedman's Division of Granger's Corps, which had bivouacked near Jay's Mill,

Lee and Gordon's Mill—From La Fayette Road. (See page xi.)

and skirmished there with Forrest's picket line at daylight, was being withdrawn to Rossville. Reynolds' Division was following after Thomas' column on the Crawfish Springs Road, and McCook's Corps had reached the vicinity of Crawfish Springs. Negley's Division of Thomas' Corps was near Glass' Mill, confronting Breckinridge's Division on the opposite bank.

At 7:30 A. M., Croxton's Brigade, the right of Brannan's Division, struck Forrest close to Jay's Mill, and was at once sharply engaged. A half-hour later, Van Derveer's Brigade, on the left and rear of Croxton, moved rapidly forward, and the fighting became severe along the lines of both brigades. Connell's Brigade supported these on the front line. Thus opened the battle of Chickamauga, two miles and a half to the right and rear of the ground on which Bragg had expected to deliver it.

Nearly at the same hour, J. Beatty's and Stanley's Brigades of Negley's Division were engaged with Helm's Brigade of Breckinridge's Division at Glass' Mill, on the Confederate left, nine miles distant. This was mainly an artillery contest. It lasted till about 11 o'clock, when both sides were withdrawn, and started for the center of battle.

Forrest's troops fought dismounted, and with such regular lines that those opposed to them supposed they were engaged with infantry. The battle had opened with that desperation on both sides which characterized it throughout. Forrest soon went in person for support. Wilson's Infantry Brigade of Walker's Division was found near Alexander's and rushed forward. It came into action on Croxton's right flank, and his line was faced south to meet it. Forrest's right was soon struck by Van Derveer's advance, and Forrest went for more infantry. He found Ector's Brigade of Walker's Division west of Alexander's and hurried it to Van Derveer's front. Before infantry support arrived, the cavalry had lost over a quarter of those engaged. Croxton and Wilson fought fiercely, and with varying success. Van Derveer cleared his front. Baird's Division marched eastward from Kelly's, King's Brigade relieved Croxton, and Scribner, on its right, was on the flank of Wilson. Walthall and Govan were dispatched from the right rear of Bragg's morning line toward the increasing battle. Walthall, forming with his right at the old shop near Alexander's, with Govan on his left, swept to the east of the Winfrey House, over the left of Scribner. Govan struck the right of that brigade, captured its battery, and forced it to the rear. Walthall, pushing to the next ridge north, dispersed King's Brigade of Regulars, took its guns, and drove its shattered lines north and west over Van Derveer's Brigade, and was there checked and repulsed. The Ninth Ohio Infantry charged from Van Derveer's right and recaptured the regular battery. Govan, pushing on, was taken in flank by Croxton, who was again advancing, and both Govan and Walthall retired in haste to their right, and formed behind Cheatham's advancing line. Bragg's whole morning formation was dissolving, turning northward, and being fast drawn into the swirling vortex. Cheatham's Division had five brigades. It had been the main reserve of the early array. With three brigades on its first line and two on its second, it moved into action with the front of a mile. Its right was near Winfrey's. Its advance swept back Starkweather's Brigade of Baird, and struck Croxton, who was folowing Govan, from the field. Cheatham's center was in the Brock Field, its left west of it and within 400 yards of the La Fayette Road.

Upon the long, low ridge north of Cheatham's right, it encountered Johnson's Division of McCook's Corps, which had been ordered to Thomas. After two hours' bitter fighting, in which Cheatham's second line advanced and relieved the first, his right and right center were driven back until they rested on the high ground beyond Winfrey's. Palmer's Division, sent in haste, without orders, by Crittenden, from Lee and Gordon's Mill to Thomas, had marched up the La Fayette Road to the Poe House, hastily formed its brigades in echelons and moved south-east toward the Brock Field. A few minutes after noon, it was heavily engaged with Cheatham's advancing left. Hazen's, Palmer's left brigade, was in touch with Johnson's right, and fought in the Brock Field against Cheatham's line, which it pushed back into the woods east of it. Cruft's Brigade was on the west line of the field, and Grose's still further to the right. This whole great field and its vicinity was a seething arena of battle.

On the extreme left, Van Derveer was closing the fight in that quarter by rapid and desperate work. Connell's Brigade of Baird had first assisted Croxton, and, at the vital moment, came with two regiments and a full battery to Van Derveer. Forrest, moving under cover of the woods, had formed in four lines under the crest north of Van Derveer's left. But this watchful officer discovered these at the moment when the move had nearly achieved success. Changing direction on a run, and with his own and Connell's Battery (Church's First Michigan) on a gallop, the brigade whirled northward to the crest toward which Forrest's lines were charging. It was almost a hand-to-hand struggle. There were ten guns near the center of Van Derveer's line. He caused his left to fall back slowly, fighting heavily, until the batteries opened with double-shotted canister, at only forty paces, with almost an enfilading fire, through Forrest's lines. Even under this these staggered forward into the very flame of the rifles, and with this supreme effort of valor against lines which did not flinch, they abandoned the contest. It was one o'clock, and the battle on the left had ended. Forrest withdrew to the vicinity of Jay's Mill to reorganize, and Walker reformed behind Cheatham. About the middle of the afternoon, Walthall and Govan were again in action for a short time.

At 3 o'clock Johnson had established his lines as far forward as the Winfrey House, and was unmolested until dusk. Reynolds reached the Poe House with his division at 1 o'clock, and sent Turchin to Palmer's left, and Edward King to aid his right. The left of Cheatham had been pushed back of the Brock Field, and Stewart's Division in column of brigades, Clayton leading, Brown following, and Bate in the rear, had entered the field at its south-western corner soon after noon. Cheatham's left brigade had just been repulsed. Stewart turned Clayton toward Brotherton's. After hot and persistent fighting, Brown took his place, to become desperately engaged, and be in turn, relieved by Bate. Van Cleve, with two of his brigades, had arrived at Brotherton's from Lee and Gordon's just before Stewart's appearance, and had repulsed the left brigade of Cheatham, and captured its battery. Van Cleve, in turn, was first forced across the La Fayette Road at Brotherton's by Stewart's troops, and next through and beyond the Dyer Field, Clayton following to the Tan Yard. Bate had forced back the Union line at Poe's, and the Union center was thus broken to a point south of Brotherton's. Palmer, with Hazen's and Grose's Brigades, came back to the La Fayette Road. Turchin's Brigade charged through the Brock Field upon the right regiment (Forty-fourth Alabama) of Law's Brigade of Hood's Division and repulsed it. The other regiments of Law, under command of Col. W. C. Oates of the Fifteenth Alabama, became engaged farther south on the right of Bushrod Johnson's Division, and moved with it across the La Fayette Road.

After the fighting had ceased on the extreme left, Brannan and Baird had been withdrawn to the glade east of McDonald's. Brannan was now dispatched to the Dyer Field to assist in restoring the line. He entered the northern part of the field just as Negley, who had marched from Glass' Mill, appeared, moving toward it from Widow Glenn's. That portion of Stewart's forces in the Dyer Field at once withdrew with little fighting into the forest east of the La Fayette Road.

Bate was still advancing northward toward Poe's. On the northern crest in the Poe Field, Reynolds had hastily gathered twenty guns, and various infantry lines to support them. Palmer assisted with his forces. As Bate advanced into the open ground he soon came close into the face of this array of rifles and artillery. His persistent advance was finally repulsed, and the battle ended on the Union center.

On the Confederate left, about Viniard's, a fierce battle had been in progress throughout the afternoon, beginning soon after 1 o'clock. About 12 o'clock, Davis' Division of McCook's Corps, consisting of Carlin's and Heg's Brigades, Post's Brigade being with the trains, had reached Rosecrans' headquarters at the Widow Glenn's. He was turned eastward toward Viniard's with orders to develop the Confederate left. Forming south-west of Viniard's, he crossed the La Fayette Road and advanced to the edge of the descent in the open ground east of it. Barnes' Brigade of Van Cleve's Division, which had been left at Lee and Gordon's, had arrived in haste and formed on Davis' right. Wilder's Brigade, which had been observing the enemy's left since daylight, now moved up on Davis' left, and at once the whole line became bitterly engaged with Trigg's Brigade of Preston's Division and all of Bushrod Johnson's Division. After severe fighting the enemy gained the Viniard House, and the Union line was forced to the west side of the fields behind it. The enemy was next in turn driven back to its lines of first attack, whence they swept westward again. While actively rallying his brigade from one of these repulses Col. Heg was killed.

It was four o'clock, and Davis' forces were suffering severely and were well-nigh exhausted by the alternate ebb and flow of the dreadful tide. In one of the advances of the Confederates west of the road, Wilder rushed two guns from his left into the head of the low ground before his front and enfiladed the massed lines toward the Viniard House, causing general slaughter.

At 4 o'clock Buell's and Harker's Brigades of Woods' Division appeared, coming at double quick from Lee and Gordon's Mill. Buell restored the right of Davis' line, and Harker, pushing on to its left, sent part of his force northeastward, when the engagement again became desperate on his and Buell's fronts. Wilder had enfiladed the left of

Bushrod Johnson's Division when it crossed the La Fayette Road into the fields north of the Viniard Farm, and forced it to retire. With his two remaining regiments Harker moved rapidly northward along the La Fayette Road, crossed to the west of it, and before he was discovered fell upon the rear of Fulton's Brigade, the right of Bushrod Johnson's line, which was attacking Van Cleve's left in the Brotherton Field, and forced its hasty withdrawal into the forest east of the La Fayette Road. Lastly, Sheridan arrived, having marched from Crawfish Springs by Lee and Gordon's, and with Bradley's Brigade went into action on Buell's right, and forced the Confederates from its front. At sundown the latter withdrew and the battle ended which had raged here throughout the afternoon with an intensity not exceeded in any part of the field.

Then followed a short period of absolute quiet, when the silence became oppressive. Suddenly this was relieved by a tornado of furious battle swelling up in the gathering darkness on Johnson's and Baird's lines a mile east of the Brotherton House. Baird had been sent forward in the afternoon to strengthen Johnson's left, which rested near the Winfrey House. Cheatham's line was formed just behind the crest of the high ground south-east of it, and had contented itself after 3 o'clock with a plunging artillery fire upon Johnson's front.

When Walker's Divisions fell back before Brannan's and Baird's attacks, Cleburne's Division had been sent from east of the Chickamauga to attack from the direction of Jay's Mill. In his haste, Cleburne closed his columns and marched them across the river with the water up to the arm-pits of the men, hurried them on to the mill, reached there at 6 o'clock, immediately formed, and at once pressed forward. His line struck on the fronts of both Baird's and Johnson's Divisions, and a battle broke out in the darkness, in which each side was guided only by the flashes of the opposing guns. The two right brigades of Cheatham's line followed Cleburne in his advance. The Union divisions had just received orders to withdraw toward Kelly's when this attack opened. After an hour's confused fighting, in which the Confederates lost Preston Smith, and the Union forces Colonel Baldwin, each commanding brigades, Baird and Johnson withdrew from under fire, and marched to the Kelly Field to bivouac, while Cleburne's men and his wounded, soaked in the cold water of the river, lay down on the frosty ground without fires to wait for the morning.

As the result of the long day's fierce battle, Rosecrans had pounded his lines into position between Bragg and Chattanooga.

CHAPTER V.

THE SECOND DAY'S BATTLE AT CHICKAMAUGA, SUNDAY, SEPTEMBER 20, 1863.

There was busy re-arrangement of the lines on both sides during Saturday night, and the early morning of Sunday. With the exception of two brigades, Post's, with the trains, and Lytle's, which had remained at Lee and Gordon's Mill, Gen. Rosecrans had put every available man into Saturday's engagement. On the other side, Gen. Bragg had Breckinridge's, Hindman's, and Kershaw's Divisions, Gracie's and Kelly's Brigades of Preston's Division, and Gist's of Walker's, none of which had been engaged on Saturday. Gen. Longstreet in person arrived at 11 P. M. The army was then divided into right and left wings, Polk being assigned to the command of the right, and Longstreet to the left. Bragg's army had fought after a fair night's rest. The Union troops in greater part had marched all night before the battle and fought through the day without breakfast. To offset these disadvantages, the Union lines had the best position, being in the main on higher ground, and the circumstances compelling the Confederates to attack.

The La Fayette Road was again to be the prize of battle, and Bragg's plan of thrusting his columns beyond the Union left, and between it and Chattanooga, still controlled in arranging his lines. The troops from the Union right near Viniard's, and Lytle's Brigade from Lee and Gordon's, were brought back to the high ground near Widow Glenn's. The Union center was in rear of the Brotherton Field, and the left, crossing to the east side of the La Fayette Road between Poe's and Kelly's, ran around the south and east sides

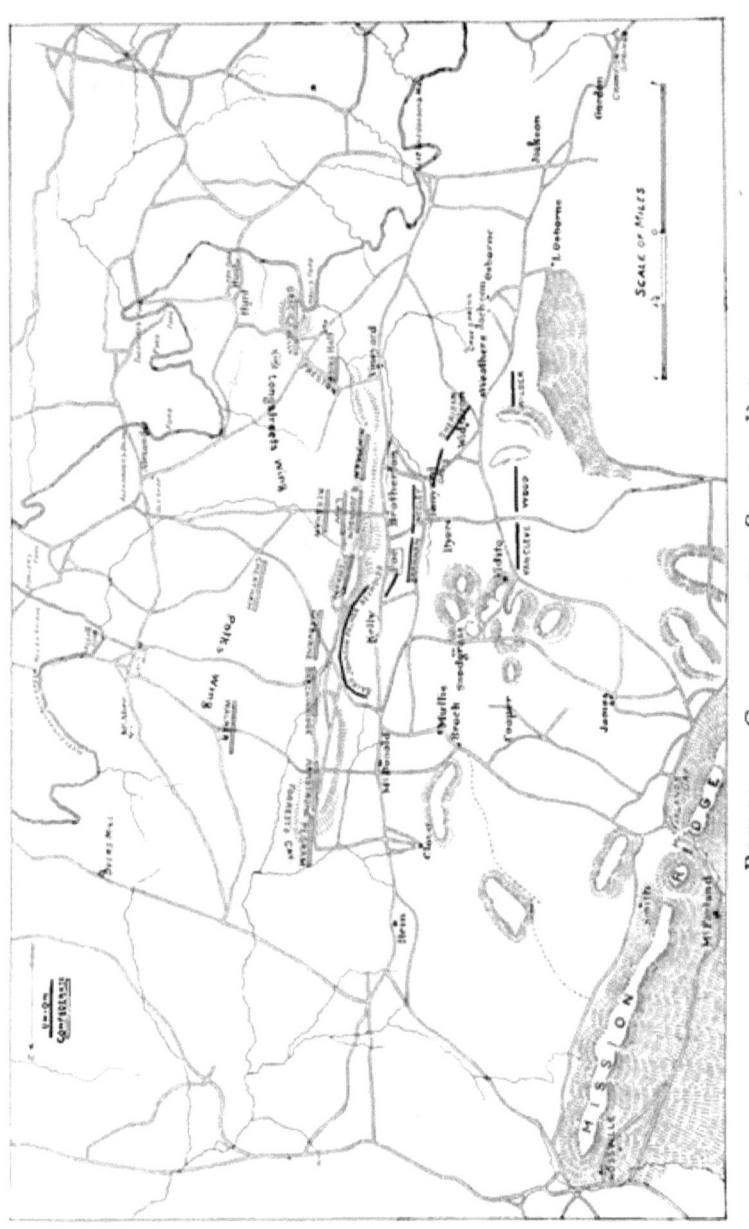

BATTLE OF CHICKAMAUGA—SECOND DAY.

of the Kelly Field, and half way back to the road along its northern border.

A glance at the map at the opening of this chapter will show the arrangement of divisions on Rosecrans' line. Beginning at the left, Baird's, Johnson's, Palmer's and Reynolds' were east of the La Fayette Road, Brannan's next west of it along the western side of the Poe Field, Negley west of Brotherton's, and Sheridan in front of Widow Glenn's. Wilder's Brigade of mounted infantry, with Harrison's Regiment, also mounted, were on the high ground to the right and rear of Sheridan. Van Cleve's, Woods', and Davis' Divisions were, at an early hour, in rear of the center waiting for the final adjustment of the front line. Bragg's line overlapped Rosecrans' by a full division on the Union right, and two brigades and a full division on its left, besides the mounted division of Forrest's Corps still to the right of Armstrong's, which latter was dismounted.

Bragg's line, beginning on his right, ran by divisions, as follows: Forrest, with two divisions of cavalry, Pegram's and Armstrong's, was east of Cloud's. Breckinridge, Cleburne, and Stewart covered the east and south lines of the Kelly Field, and the east line of the Poe Field, Walker's two divisions were in reserve in rear of Breckinridge, and Cheatham's five brigades in rear of Cleburne. Bushrod Johnson was posted with his center 700 yards east of Brotherton's, and, with Law's and Kershaw's Divisions directly in rear of his own, formed a central column of three divisions. Hindman was on the left of Johnson, and Preston on the extreme left, east and south of Viniard's. Stewart's Division was the right of Longstreet's wing, and Cleberne's the left of Polk's. Stewart's and Johnson's fronts were protected by rude defenses. The Union line throughout was covered by rough barricades of rails, logs, stones, and stumps. These barricades around the Kelly Field were of considerable strength, but elsewhere the protection of the Union lines was slight. No rifle-pits were dug on any part of them.

Before the battle opened, Dodge's Brigade of Johnson's Division was transferred to Baird's left, but this did not extend his flank more than half way to the La Fayette Road. Gen. Thomas was using most energetic means to obtain a division from the center to prolong Baird's left along the crest to the high ground on the La Fayette Road north of McDonald's, when the battle opened, about 9:30 o'clock, by the advance of Breckinridge's Division upon Baird's position. At the moment, John Beatty's Brigade was being stretched in thin line from Baird's left toward the McDonald house.

Bragg was bitterly disappointed by non-compliance with his orders for an attack at daylight by his right, to be taken up successively toward the left by divisions. This delay was of the greatest consequence to the Union forces.

Breckinridge's Division moved from a line about 700 yards east of the glade in front of Baird's position. His left brigade was Helm's; his center, Stovall's; and right, Adams'. Two regiments of Helm's left and three companies of the next one struck on the salient at Baird's left, and were shattered. At the same time, in advancing, they were enfiladed by the salient at Baird's right. Helm was mortally wounded while rallying his line in its recoil from this terrible blow. The whole brigade suffered greatly, but two regiments and seven companies of the third from the right passed by the Union front and into its rear as far as the La Fayette Road. Here this right of Helm met stubborn resistance from the thin line of John Beatty's Brigade, which just before had been still more attenuated by the attempt to stretch it out to the McDonald House and with it cover nearly a division space. Two of Beatty's guns were captured, and his brigade hopelessly confused. but he himself, with what he could gather, rode to Snodgrass Hill and rendered most valuable service till the close of the battle. But Helm's (now Lewis') Brigade had also been so badly broken as to necessitate its withdrawal. Its loss in this assault was one man in three.

Stovall and Adams, however, kept on. They reached the

La Fayette Road without opposition. They had passed the Union left, and were three hundred yards in its rear, and still beyond the position from which they had moved was a division of Forrest's Cavalry dismounted, and beyond that a mounted division—so largely overlapped on this flank was the Union line.

Breckinridge had only to swing his two brigades to the left when a short advance would take him into the Kelly Field. This move he made. Facing south with the road between his brigades, he moved forward. Stovall's left struck the left of Baird and was checked. Stanley's Brigade of Negley's Division had arrived in haste from the center, formed across Adams' pathway, and stopped him also by hard blows. At that moment, Stanley's Brigade was ordered to the left toward Snodgrass Hill. At the same instant Stovall had struggled by the hot fire on the left of Baird, and burst full into the Kelly Field from its northern border. Adams, too, found his way open along the line which Stanley had blocked, and he, too, advanced again. It seemed as if the Union left was fatally enveloped. It lines around the field could not stir, for Cleburne was assaulting from the east, and Stewart from the east and south. The balls which missed these fronts were falling fast all over the west side of the field. Suddenly, a brigade deployed in two lines, rushed out of the forest on the west side of the field just north of the Kelly House, whirled into the face of Stovall, and laid its lines down less than a hundred yards from his advance. The front line of this Union brigade fired a full volley, and Stovall was checked. The rear line sprang to its feet, charged over the front on a run, and Stovall broke. The first line followed the second in the charge, and the enemy was driven back around the Union left. Adams, with his flank exposed and enfiladed, had retired with Stovall. All this time the whole line of four divisions around the field was under furious and most courageous assault from Cleburne and Stewart. But these latter found themselves powerless to cross the

Kelly Field Looking North, where Breckinridge Gained the Union Rear. (See page vii.)

Union line of low works, for whenever successive Confederate assaults were delivered, all who could crowd up to the log-works fired, and all who could not lay down behind them, loaded rifles, and passed them up to those who could. The Confederate officers describe the fire they here encountered as an unbroken stream of lead. In one of these assaults, Gen. Deshler, who commanded one of Cleburne's Brigades, was killed, and Col. Roger Q. Mills succeeded him.

It was Van Derveer's Brigade of Brannan's Division that had saved the Union left almost as by a miracle. It was at a heavy cost of men, and the severity of the fire may be judged by the fact that every horse in the brigade but two was disabled in the short charge.

Thomas had sent for Brannan's Division, which, by agreement at the council the night before, was to be left as a movable reserve, but which, without Thomas' knowledge, had been moved before daylight into the front line at Poe's. At the moment the order to go to Thomas arrived, the attack of Stewart on Brannan's front was opening. Hastily consulting with Gen. Reynolds, near him, and both agreeing, he stood fast awaiting attack, and sent word to Rosecrans of the situation, asking if he should go in spite of the surroundings. Meantime, in partial compliance with the order, he dispatched his reserve brigade (Van Derveer's). The latter was proceeding under orders to report to Baird, when suddenly, with its lines in the underbrush, it received an enfilading fire from Adams and Stovall. Van Derveer rushed his line into the open, handled them as above described, and the position was saved.

But while Van Derveer was clearing the Union left with his brigade, Longstreet with his column of three divisions from the forest east of Brotherton's was moving through the Union center, and dire calamity there seemed unavoidable.

Negley's Division, which held the line west of the Brotherton Field, had been replaced by Wood shortly before the order reached Brannan to report to Thomas at the left, as

Brotherton's from the East—Scene of Longstreet's Piercing the Union Line. (See page xii.)

before related. Rosecrans, supposing Brannan would move at once under the order, sent directions to Wood on his right to close up rapidly on Reynolds and support him. Brannan, not having left the line, and Reynolds being to the left of Brannan, Wood moved rapidly into the rear of Brannan and toward Reynolds. At this moment, Longstreet's attack was delivered, and Bushrod Johnson's Division burst through the opening left by Wood. Buell's, Wood's right brigade, was caught while thus marching by the flank and broken up. Davis' Division, to the right and rear of Wood, was hurried toward the gap, and Rosecrans galloped to the Widow Glenn's to rush Sheridan also to the center. But the disaster could not be repaired. Laws' Division, following Johnson's, had turned toward the right against Brannan at Poe's, and the left of Stewart also bore down on Brannan's left. His division fought stubbornly, but Johnson was soon full on its flank, and it was forced to abandon its line.

Meantime, Wood, seeing Hood's forces moving north through the Dyer Fields, performed an act which ranks, as a vital move, with that of Van Derveer's in the Kelly Field. Harker's Brigade, which had proceeded well toward the left in rear of Brannan when Longstreet attacked, was hurried back into the Dyer Field in front of Hood's advance, taking position on the crest which crosses that field near its northern limits, and there awaited Hood. Laws' Division was in advance. Harker first checked it by fierce musketry, and then charged down into its face, forcing it back into the woods, and so disabling it that it was not again brought into action. One of its regiments, however, the Fifteenth Alabama, Col. W. C. Oates, subsequently joined Kershaw's advance.

This check enabled Brannan to form his line with some deliberation in rear of Harker on Snodgrass Hill. When Harker was at length pushed back by Kershaw's Division advancing over Law's, he took position on the low open crest to Brannan's left, and Snodgrass Hill became the Union right. Next on the right of Harker, Stanley's Brigade of

DYER'S FIELD—LOOKING NORTH. (See page xii.)

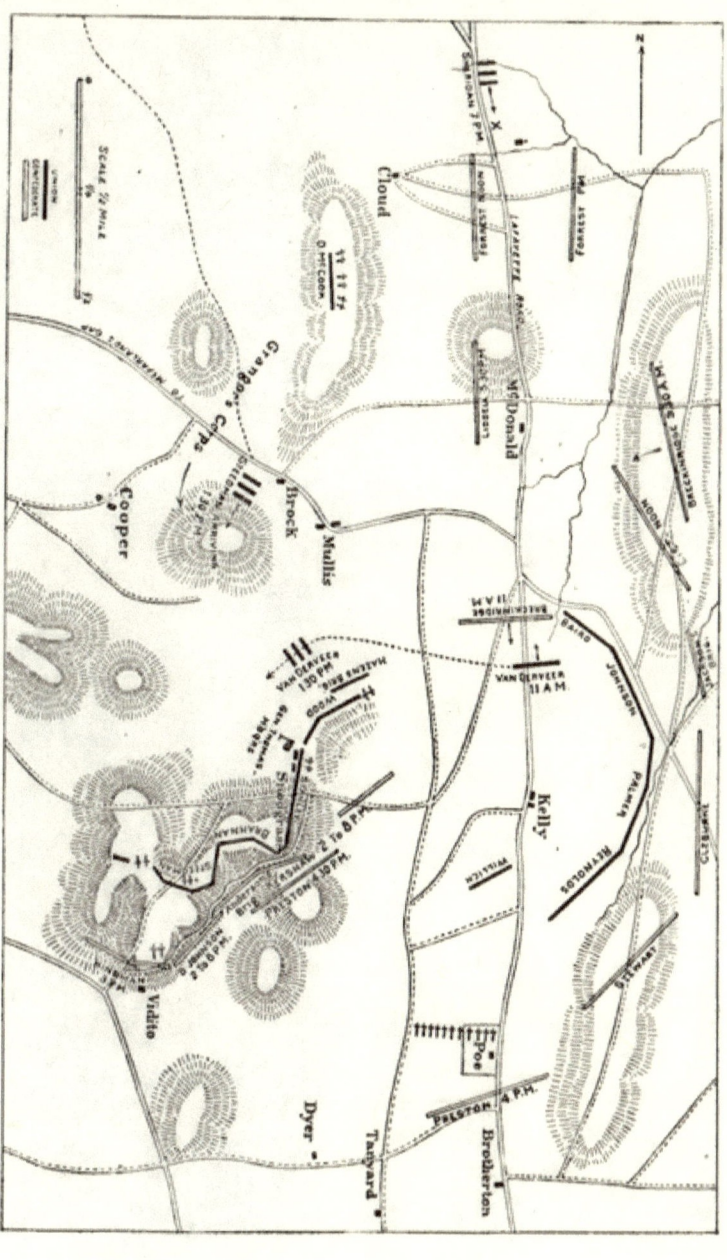

Kelly Field and Snodgrass Hill—Afternoon of Second Day.

Negley's Division formed, and to its right were Brannan's troops. On his extreme right Brannan formed the Twenty-first Ohio of nearly 800 men of Sirwell's Brigade, which Negley had sent to him before abandoning the field.

All to the right of Brannan on the original line had been swept off the field. Davis' and Sheridan's Divisions, while hastening to the left to close the gap caused by Wood's withdrawal, were attacked in front and on their right by Hindman's Division, and on their left by Bushrod Johnson's. Gen. Lytle was killed in a supreme effort to face these lines with his brigade. This right composed of five brigades was pushed off the field without fault of their own, and continued in much confusion to McFarland's Gap. From this point, Davis, hearing that Thomas was steadfast on the field, upon receiving a request from him through a staff officer, turned back to join him. Sheridan, declining to regard this request, moved on to Rossville, and thence by the La Fayette Road toward Thomas. He reached Cloud's at dusk. Two corps of the enemy then held the road between that point and Thomas, and Sheridan returned to Rossville.

Negley's Division, as has been seen, was early divided. John Beatty's Brigade had been sent at 8 o'clock to the left of Baird, Negley himself had followed later with Stanley's Brigade, and returned under orders to gather all artillery at hand in rear of the line, and post it on the high ground overlooking Baird's left. About fifty guns were collected, and conducted, instead, to the ridge occupied later by Gordon Granger's troops, and stationed on Gen. Brannan's right, with considerable infantry support. Very soon, and before they were directly attacked, the whole was ordered to the rear by Gen. Negley, and marched to Rossville.

Gens. Rosecrans, Crittenden, and McCook had been cut off by the break at the center, and borne off the field in the confused retreat of the right. Rosecrans proceeded to Chattanooga and Thomas came into command on the field.

Returning to the break in the center: While Hood's Divisions were sweeping northward toward the Snodgrass House through the eastern side of the Dyer Field and the adjoining woods, Bushrod Johnson turned to the right toward the ridge on the western side of the field. On its crest he captured fifteen guns which had been hastily gathered there, reaching them before they could do much execution. After reforming his line, he soon moved over this ridge, and arranged his forces to assault Snodgrass Hill. With his left at the Viditoe House, and Anderson's Brigade of Hindman's Division on his right, his line reached around the base of Horseshoe Ridge half way to the Snodgrass House, and joined the left of Kershaw's Brigade, which further extended the line to the road running up to that house. Humphrey's Brigade of Kershaw's Division formed the right of the assaulting lines, and faced the open crest beyond the house where Harker had taken final stand on the left of Brannan. The Union right rested above this array on the crest of the Horseshoe. It consisted of three brigades and one battery, with no reserve.

While two Confederate divisions are preparing to assault and envelop that short line, there will be time to again consider the Union left around the Kelly Field.

Forrest's Cavalry, in front of Cloud's, had moved forward before noon and captured the Union hospitals at the church and about the spring. Cleburne and Stewart had fought bitterly but unsuccessfully until 1 o'clock. Walker's two divisions (Gist's and Liddell's) had replaced Breckinridge, and at noon Gist's Division assaulted where Helm had been repulsed. Col. Peyton H. Colquitt, commanding a brigade, was killed, and the division repulsed. The troops of Liddell, in turn, advanced, and their leading brigade was also driven back. Then, from 1 o'clock till nearly sunset, there was no fighting of moment along the Kelly Field front. The eight divisions, four on each side, facing each other there, and the Confederate reserves, rested on their arms and listened hour after

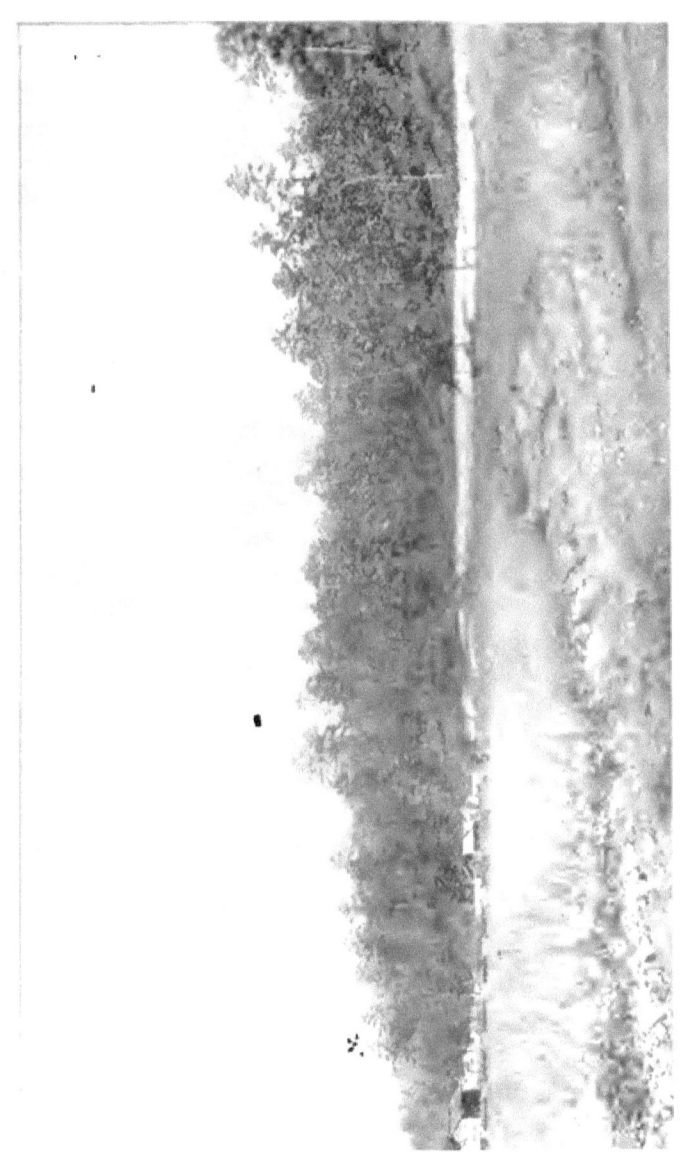

hour to the terrible pendulum swings of Longstreet's constantly repeated assaults on Snodgrass Hill. From 2 till 3 o'clock, Bushrod Johnson's and Kershaw's Divisions, with Anderson's Brigade of Hindman, struggled unremittingly against the short line on the crest. Before the hour ended, half of Brannan's troops were out of ammunition and standing behind their bayonets, and the left of Johnson had advanced and was crossing the crest which Negley had vacated on their right. Then help came to this line at bay as unexpectedly as if dropped from heaven. Gordon Granger with Steedman's Division, and Dan McCook's Brigade of J. D. Morgan's Division at McAfee's Church, over three miles away, had been impatiently listening to the terrific firing about the Horseshoe. At noon, he decided to march there without orders; and, just as the situation was full of gloom for Thomas, the head of Steedman's Division reached him. The column marched hastily into the ravine back of the Snodgrass House, attacked the line crossing the crest to Brannan's rear, drove it back by fighting which cost at least a third of those engaged, occupied the crest on Brannan's right, and extended Thomas' line to the crest overlooking the road to Rossville. Besides this welcome service, it divided its ammunition with Brannan's men. To make the relief still greater and sufficient, Van Derveer's Brigade, intact, arrived at the same moment from its charge upon Breckinridge in the Kelly Field. Like Granger's command, it had marched without orders toward the sound of the guns. It formed on Steedman's left, ascended the ridge, and made Brannan's thinned right a solid line again.

At 3 o'clock, Maingault's and Deas' Brigades of Hindman's Division had formed near Viditoe's, on the left of Johnson, and three full divisions began a fresh assault. Johnson gained the extremity of a spur above the Viditoe House with Fulton's and part of Maingault's Brigades, and established two batteries there. At all other points, this most desperate assault, or rather series of assaults, failed. At 3 o'clock, Preston's large division, two brigades of which had not yet been engaged either day of the battle, was hurried up to Brotherton's from Hall's Ford, and sent over at 4 o'clock to Snodgrass Hill. At 4:30, it relieved Kershaw's Brigade, and assaulted on Stanley's and Brannan's fronts, many of Kershaw's troops marching with it, and Johnson and Hindman advancing simultaneously. Gracie's Brigade carried the salient spur of Stanley's line, and held its outer point an hour, being at length driven down by a charge led by Lt.-Col. C. H. Grosvenor, of the Eighteenth Ohio, assisted by the Nineteenth Illinois, Lt.-Col. A. W. Raffner, on its right, and the Twenty-second Michigan, Lt.-Col. Melvin Mudge, on its left. Like the other assaults, at the end of an hour and a half, this last, the fiercest of all, was beaten back. It is doubtful whether the history of wars affords a severer test of soldierly courage and endurance than was shown by these continuing Confederate assaults, from 2 o'clock till sundown, over slopes which successive failures had thickly strewn with dead and wounded comrades. Of the single line which faced such soldiers, with scarce a semblance of works, and at times with empty barrels, till darkness gathered and the battle was done, it need only be said, for men and officers alike, that they were found equal to the tremendous requirements of the hour.

At the close of this final attack, Steedman's Division, which, with the rest of the line, had sustained persistent assaults, was out of ammunition, and was withdrawn at sunset to the ridge in its rear. An hour later, it marched to McFarland's Gap, and thence to Rossville. It was almost immediately followed over the crest to the foot of the slope where its lines had been, and there the Confederate left flank halted.

Three regiments, the Twenty-first and Eighty-ninth Ohio and Twenty-second Michigan, which were on the left of Whittaker's Brigade, did not receive notice to withdraw with him, and were almost bodily captured at dusk by Trigg's Brigade, the left of Preston's Division, crossing the ridge to their right and turning into their rear, while Kelly's Brigade of the same division advanced on their front. A similar attempt by the same Confederate brigades to capture Van Derveer's Brigade, next on the left of these and constituting the right of Brannan, was discovered and repulsed.

The fighting having ceased, Wood's and Brannan's lines were withdrawn from Snodgrass Hill, the movement beginning on the left of Harker at 7 o'clock, and ending at 8 o'clock on the right of Brannan, at the present observation tower, the whole passing through McFarland's Gap to Rossville.

The withdrawal of the line about the Kelly Field was ordered by Gen. Thomas at 5:30 o'clock. Reynolds' Division began the movement by marching north by the flank on the La Fayette Road to the northern limits of the Kelly Field, there filing to the left in the woods, facing north, and encountering Liddell's Division, as related on p. 200, thence turning westward to the first high ground, where Willich, following, also formed, the two together composing the covering force for the rest of the Kelly Field line as it left the position.

Palmer's Division followed Reynolds. It was half way across the Kelly Field before the Confederate skirmishers of a general advance appeared at the breastworks which Palmer had left. His line was there subjected to a heavy artillery fire from each flank, but it was soon in order after reaching the forest west of the La Fayette Road.

Johnson's and Baird's Divisions were sustaining a heavy attack just as the order went to them to withdraw. This general advance of Bragg's right had been ordered at 3 o'clock. It did not begin till nearly sundown. These remaining Union divisions, the last on the line, bore the whole brunt of this attack. But, though fired upon from in front and on both flanks, and thrown into much confusion, they reached the west side of the field in such condition as enabled them thereafter to move in order and follow the Union column to McFarland's Gap.

Arriving at Rossville, the whole army, with the exception of the remnants of Van Cleve's Division, which were sent to Chattanooga, was placed in position in Rossville Gap, and on Missionary Ridge to the right and left of it, and across the valley to Lookout. At daylight, the object of the withdrawal was revealed by the fact that the Union army again stood across Bragg's pathway to Chattanooga. It remained in position throughout the 21st. At midnight, it marched on to Chattanooga. On Tuesday, September 22d, its lines were solidly formed around the city, and the prize of the campaign was won.

A brief consideration of the relative strength and losses of each army properly closes this chapter.

Gen. Rosecrans had crossed the Tennessee with an effective force of all arms equipped for duty of a few hundred more than 60,000. Of this number Wagner's Brigade, with 2,061 effectives, held Chattanooga, leaving the Union force in front of Bragg slightly less than 58,000. It was several thousand less at the battle, Post's Brigade of Davis' Division and three regiments of infantry and one battery being engaged in guarding supply trains. This made eight regiments of infantry absent. A small part of the Union cavalry was severely engaged, while most of Forrest's cavalry fought as infantry and was desperately engaged the first day. A maximum figure for Gen. Rosecrans' force in action that day would be 55,000.

It is difficult to arrive at Gen. Bragg's force. He reported it a week after the battle as 38,846 effectives. At the same time he reported his losses at 18,000, which would make his strength at the battle 56,846.

In a letter from Gen. Lee to President Davis, dated September 14, 1863, the following figures of Bragg's actual and prospective strength are thus stated:

"If the report sent to me by Gen. Cooper since my return from Richmond is correct, Gen. Bragg had, on the 20th of August last, 51,101 effective men; Gen. Buckner, 16,118. He was to receive from Gen. Johnson 9,000. His total force will, therefore, be 76,219, as large a number as I presume he can operate with. This is independent of the local troops, which, you may recollect, he reported as exceeding his expectations."

Gen. Bragg, after the battle, reported Longstreet's force, which was not included by Lee, at 5,000. This, according to the figures furnished Gen. Lee, gave Bragg 81,219. According to Gen. Johnson's correspondence, after he had sent 9,000 to Bragg, he subsequently dispatched him two small brigades, and these latter reached him the day before the battle.

The absence of specific reports makes it impossible to reconcile these discrepencies.

Some of the figures of the remarkable losses on each side will be found on pages 227, 229.

The battle was desperate from the moment it opened till its close. For the most part the lines fought at close range and, in the countless assaults, often hand to hand. On the first day there were no field works of any kind. On the second, Thomas was protected on portions of his line by such rude barricades as could be hastily thrown together. Brannan and Steedman were without a semblance of works. The battle in the main, on both sides, was dogged, stand-up fighting, far within the limits of point-blank range. For the second day, on the Confederate side, the contest was one continued series of brave and magnificent assaults.

CHAPTER VI.

ORGANIZATION OF THE ARMY OF THE CUMBERLAND, COMMANDED BY MAJ.-GEN. WILLIAM S. ROSECRANS, AT THE BATTLE OF CHICKAMAUGA, GA., SEPTEMBER 19 AND 20, 1863.

[Roster compiled by Hon. J. W. KIRKLEY, Board of Publication of War Records.]

GENERAL HEADQUARTERS.

1st Battalion Ohio Sharpshooters.
10th Ohio Infantry, Lieut.-Col. William M. Ward.
15th Pennsylvania Cavalry, Col. Wm. J. Palmer.

FOURTEENTH ARMY CORPS.

Maj.-Gen. GEORGE H. THOMAS.

GENERAL HEADQUARTERS.

Provost-Guard.
9th Michigan Infantry,° Col. John G. Parkhurst.

Escort.
1st Ohio Cavalry, Company I., Capt. John D. Barker.

FIRST DIVISION (FOURTEENTH CORPS).

Brig.-Gen. ABSALOM BAIRD.

First Brigade.	*Second Brigade.*
Col. BENJAMIN F. SCRIBNER.	Brig.-Gen. JOHN C. STARKWEATHER.
38th Indiana, Lieut.-Col. Daniel F. Griffin.	24th Illinois;
2d Ohio:	Col. Geza Mihalotzy.
Lieut.-Col. Obadiah C. Maxwell.	Capt. August Mauff.
Maj. William T. Beatty.	79th Pennsylvania, Col. Henry A. Hambright.
Capt. James Warnock.	
33d Ohio, Col. Oscar F. Moore.	1st Wisconsin, Lieut.-Col. George B. Bingham.
94th Ohio, Maj. Rue P. Hutchins.	
10th Wisconsin:	21st Michigan:
Lieut.-Col. John H. Ely.	Lieut.-Col. Harrison C. Hobart.
Capt. Jacob W. Roby.	Capt. Charles H. Walker.
1st Michigan, Light Battery A:	Indiana Light, 4th Battery:
Lieut. George W. Van Pelt.	Lieut. David Flansburg.
Lieut. Almerick W. Wilbur.	Lieut. Henry J. Willits.

° Not engaged; on train and provost duty.

Third Brigade.

Brig.-Gen. JOHN H. KING.

15th United States, 1st Battalion, Capt. Albert B. Dod.
16th United States, 1st Battalion:
    Maj. Sidney Coolidge.
    Capt. Robt. E. A. Crofton.
18th United States, 1st Battalion, Capt. Geo. W. Smith.
18th United States, 2d Battalion, Capt. Henry Haymond.
19th United States, 1st Battalion:
    Maj. Samuel K. Dawson.
    Capt. Edmund L. Smith,
5th United States Artillery, Battery H.:
    Lieut. Howard M. Burnham.
    Lieut. Joshua A. Fessenden.

Moved from McLemore's Cove during the night of September 18th to Kelly's, marched east early on the 19th, and became engaged north of Winfrey House, and toward Jay's Mill. First and Second Brigades in action at night on the same ground. Engaged September 20th around the north-east corner of the Kelly Field.

SECOND DIVISION (FOURTEENTH CORPS).

Maj.-Gen. JAMES S. NEGLEY.

First Brigade.

Brig.-Gen. JOHN BEATTY.
104th Illinois, Lieut.-Col. Douglas Hapeman.
42d Indiana, Lieut.-Col. Wm. T. B. McIntire.
88th Indiana, Col. George Humphrey.
15th Kentucky, Col. Marion C. Taylor.
Illinois Light, Bridges' Battery, Capt. Lyman Bridges.

Second Brigade.

Col. TIMOTHY R. STANLEY.
Col. WILLIAM L. STOUGHTON.
19th Illinois, Lieut.-Col. Alexander W. Raffen.
11th Michigan:
    Col. William L. Stoughton.
    Lieut.-Col. Melvin Mudge.
18th Ohio, Lieut.-Col. Charles H. Grosvenor.
1st Ohio Light, Battery M, Capt. Frederick Schultz.

Third Brigade.

Col. WILLIAM SIRWELL.

37th Indiana, Lieut.-Col. William D. Ward.
21st Ohio:
    Lieut.-Col. Dwella M. Stoughton.
    Major Arnold McMahan.
    Capt. Charles H. Vantine.
74th Ohio, Capt. Joseph Fisher.
78th Pennsylvania, Lieut.-Col. Archibald Blakeley.
1st Ohio Light, Battery G, Capt. Alexander Marshall.

Morning of the 19th, at Glass' Mill; at 5 P. M., in Dyer Field at

Tan-yard, and Brotherton's. In the morning of the 20th, Beatty and Stanley were engaged at the north-west corner of the Kelly Field. In the afternoon, Stanley and portions of the rest were on Snodgrass Hill.

THIRD DIVISION (FOURTEENTH CORPS).
Brig.-Gen. JOHN M. BRANNAN.

First Brigade.
Col. JOHN M. CONNELL.
82d Indiana, Col. Morton C. Hunter.
17th Ohio, Lieut.-Col. Durbin Ward.
31st Ohio, Lieut.-Col. Frederick W. Lister.
38th Ohio,° Col. Edward H. Phelps.
1st Michigan Light, Battery D, Capt. Josiah W. Church.

Second Brigade.
Col. JOHN T. CROXTON.
Col. CHARLES W. CHAPMAN.
Col. WILLIAM H. HAYS.
10th Indiana:
  Col. William B. Carroll.
  Lieut.-Col. Marsh B. Taylor.
74th Indiana:
  Col. Charles W. Chapman.
  Lieut.-Col. Myron Baker.
4th Kentucky:
  Lieut.-Col. P. Burgess Hunt.
  Maj. Robert M. Kelly.
10th Kentucky:
  Col. William H. Hays.
  Maj. Gabriel C. Wharton.
14th Ohio, Lieut.-Col. Henry D. Kingsbury.
1st Ohio Light, Battery C, Lieut. Marco B. Gary.

Third Brigade.
Col. FERDINAND VAN DERVEER.
87th Indiana, Col. Newell Gleason.
2d Minnesota, Col. James George.
9th Ohio, Col. Gustave Kammerling.
35th Ohio, Lieut.-Col. Henry V. Boynton.
4th U. S. Artillery, Battery I, Lieut. Frank G. Smith.

Arrived at Kelly's from McLemore's Cove at sunrise of the 19th. Marched at once to McDonald's, and thence to the Ridge overlooking Jay's Mill and Reed's Bridge, and there opened the battle of Chickamauga. Fought the forenoon of the 20th along the west side of the Poe Field, Van Derveer's Brigade being engaged in the Kelly Field. In the afternoon, the division was on Snodgrass Hill.

° Not engaged; train guard.

ORGANIZATION OF THE ARMY OF THE CUMBERLAND.

FOURTH DIVISION (FOURTEENTH CORPS).

Maj.-Gen. JOSEPH J. REYNOLDS.

First Brigade.[*]
Col. JOHN T. WILDER.
92d Illinois, Col. Smith D. Atkins.
98th Illinois:
    Col. John J. Funkhouser.
    Lieut.-Col. Edward Kitchell.
123d Illinois, Col. James Monroe.
17th Indiana, Maj. William T. Jones.
72d Indiana, Col. Abram O. Miller.
Indiana Light, 18th Battery, Capt. Eli Lilly.

Second Brigade.
Col. EDWARD A. KING.
Col. MILTON S. ROBINSON.
68th Indiana, Capt. Harvey J. Espy.
75th Indiana:
    Col. Milton S. Robinson.
    Lieut.-Col. William O'Brien.
101st Indiana, Lieut.-Col. Thomas Doan.
105th Ohio, Maj. George T. Perkins.
Indiana Light, 19th Battery:
    Capt. Samuel J. Harris.
    Lieut. Robert S. Lackey.

Third Brigade.
Brig.-Gen. JOHN B. TURCHIN.
18th Kentucky:
    Lieut.-Col. Hubbard K. Milward.
    Capt. John B. Heltemes.
11th Ohio, Col. Philander P. Lane.
36th Ohio:
    Col. William G. Jones.
    Lieut.-Col. Hiram F. Devol.
92d Ohio:
    Col. Benjamin D. Fearing.
    Lieut.-Col. Douglas Putnam, Jr.
Indiana Light, 21st Battery, Capt. William W. Andrew.

Reached Poe's from McLemore's Cove, September 19th, at 10 o'clock. In action east of that point, and in the Poe Field until night. September 20th occupied the lines south of and around the south-east corner of Kelly Field.

TWENTIETH ARMY CORPS.

Maj.-Gen. ALEXANDER McD. McCOOK.

GENERAL HEADQUARTERS.

Provost Guard.
81st Indiana Infantry, Company H, Capt. William J. Richards.

Escort.
2d Kentucky Cavalry, Company I, Lieut. George W. L. Batman.

---

[*] Detached from the division; engaged as mounted infantry.

FIRST DIVISION (TWENTIETH CORPS).

Brig.-Gen. JEFFERSON C. DAVIS.

First Brigade.°
Col. P. SIDNEY POST.
59th Illinois, Lieut.-Col. Joshua C. Winters.
74th Illinois, Col. Jason Marsh.
75th Illinois, Col. John E. Bennett.
22d Indiana, Col. Michael Gooding.
Wisconsin Light Artillery, 5th Battery, Capt. George Q. Gardner.

Second Brigade.
Brig.-Gen. WILLIAM P. CARLIN.
21st Illinois:
  Col. John W. S. Alexander.
  Capt. Chester K. Knight.
38th Illinois:
  Lieut.-Col. Daniel H. Gilmer.
  Capt. Willis G. Whitehurst.
81st Indiana:
  Capt. Nevil B. Boone.
  Maj. James E. Calloway.
101st Ohio:
  Lieut.-Col. John Messer.
  Maj. Bedan B. McDanald.
  Capt. Leonard D. Smith.
Minnesota Light Artillery, 2d Battery:
  Lieut. Albert Woodbury.
  Lieut. Richard L. Dawley.

Third Brigade.
Col. HANS C. HEG.
Col. JOHN A. MARTIN.

25th Illinois:
  Maj. Samuel D. Wall.
  Capt. Wesford Taggart.
35th Illinois, Lieut.-Col. William P. Chandler.
8th Kansas:
  Col. John A. Martin.
  Lieut.-Col. James L. Abernathy.
15th Wisconsin, Lieut.-Col. Ole C. Johnson.
Wisconsin Light Artillery, 8th Battery, Lieut. John D. McLean.

Reached Widow Glenn's at noon. 19th, marched east to Viniard's and was engaged there till sunset. September 20th, at noon was forced back at the Tanyard and off the field by the break at the center. Turned back and reached the vicinity of Thomas' right again at sundown.

° Not engaged; guarding trains.

SECOND DIVISION (TWENTIETH CORPS).

Brig.-Gen. RICHARD W. JOHNSON.

First Brigade.

Brig.-Gen. AUGUST WILLICH.
89th Illinois:
    Lieut.-Col. Duncan J. Hall.
    Maj. William D. Williams.
32d Indiana, Lieut.-Col. Frank Erdelmeyer.
39th Indiana,* Col. Thomas J. Harrison.
15th Ohio, Lieut.-Col. Frank Askew.
49th Ohio:
    Maj. Samuel F. Gray.
    Capt. Luther M. Strong.
1st Ohio Light Artillery, Battery A.
    Capt. Wilbur F. Goodspeed.

Second Brigade.

Col. JOSEPH B. DODGE.
79th Illinois, Col. Allen Buckner.
29th Indiana, Lieut.-Col. David M. Dunn.
30th Indiana, Lieut.-Col. Orrin D. Hurd.
77th Pennsylvania:
    Col. Thomas E. Rose.
    Capt. Joseph J. Lawson.
Ohio Light Artillery, 20th Battery, Capt. Edward Grosskopff.

Third Brigade.

Col. PHILEMON P. BALDWIN.
Col. WILLIAM W. BERRY.
6th Indiana:
    Lieut.-Col. Hagerman Tripp.
    Maj. Calvin D. Campbell.
5th Kentucky:
    Col. William W. Berry.
    Capt. John M. Huston.
1st Ohio, Lieut.-Col. Bassett Langdon.
93d Ohio:
    Col. Hiram Strong.
    Lieut.-Col. William H. Martin.
Indiana Light Artillery, 5th Battery, Capt. Peter Simonson.

Reached Kelly's at noon 19th. Marched east and went into action north of Winfrey's, being engaged there until 3 P. M., and again at night. September 20th, occupied a portion of the east line of Kelly's Field until 5:30 o'clock.

---

* Detached from its brigade and serving as mounted infantry.

THIRD DIVISION (TWENTIETH CORPS).

Maj.-Gen. PHILIP H. SHERIDAN.

First Brigade.

Brig.-Gen. WILLIAM H. LYTLE.
Col. SILAS MILLER.
36th Illinois:
   Colonel Silas Miller.
   Lieut.-Col. Porter C. Olson.
88th Illinois, Lieut.-Col. Alexander S. Chadbourne.
21st Michigan:
   Col. William B. McCreery.
   Maj. Seymour Chase.
24th Wisconsin:
   Lieut.-Col. Theodore S. West.
   Maj. Carl von Baumbach.
Indiana Light Artillery, 11th Battery, Capt. Arnold Sutermeister.

Second Brigade.

Col. BERNARD LAIBOLDT.
44th Illinois, Col. Wallace W. Barrett.
73d Illinois, Col. James F. Jacquess.
2d Missouri, Maj. Arnold Beck.
15th Missouri, Col. Joseph Conrad.
1st Missouri Light Artillery, Battery G. Lieut. Gustavus Schueler.

Third Brigade.

Col. LUTHER P. BRADLEY.
Col. NATHAN H. WALWORTH.

22d Illinois, Lieut.-Col. Francis Swanwick.
27th Illinois, Col. Jonathan R. Miles.
42d Illinois:
   Col. Nathan H. Walworth.
   Lieut.-Col. John A. Hottenstein.
51st Illinois, Lieut.-Col. Samuel B. Raymond.
1st Illinois Light Artillery, Battery C, Capt. Mark H. Prescott.

Reached Viniard's from Lee and Gordon's at 4 P. M, and was heavily engaged until sunset. September 20th was enveloped between Widow Glenn's and the Tan-yard by Hindman's on the front and right, and Bushrod Johnson on the left, and forced off the field. Advanced again at 5 P. M. from Rossville, reaching Cloud's at dusk.

TWENTY-FIRST ARMY CORPS.

Maj.-Gen. THOMAS L. CRITTENDEN.

GENERAL HEADQUARTERS.

Escort.

15th Illinois Cavalry, Company K, Capt. Samuel B. Sherer.

FIRST DIVISION (TWENTY-FIRST CORPS).

Brig.-Gen. THOMAS J. WOOD.

First Brigade.
Col. GEORGE P. BUELL.
100th Illinois:
  Col. Frederick A. Bartleson.
  Maj. Charles M. Hammond.
58th Indiana, Lieut.-Col. James T. Embree.
13th Michigan:
  Col. Joshua B. Culver.
  Maj. Willard G. Eaton.
26th Ohio, Lieut.-Col. William H. Young.
Indiana Light, 8th Battery, Capt. George Estep.

Second Brigade.[*]
Brig.-Gen. GEORGE D. WAGNER.
15th Indiana, Col. Gustavus A. Wood.
40th Indiana, Col. John W. Blake.
57th Indiana, Lieut.-Col. George W. Lennard.
97th Ohio, Lieut.-Col. Milton Barnes.
Indiana Light, 10th Battery, Lieut. William A. Naylor.

Third Brigade.
Col. CHARLES G. HARKER.
3d Kentucky, Col. Henry C. Dunlap.
64th Ohio, Col. Alexander McIlvain.
65th Ohio:
  Lieut.-Col. Horatio N. Whitbeck.
  Maj. Samuel C. Brown.
  Capt. Thomas Powell.
125th Ohio, Col. Emerson Opdycke.
Ohio Light, 6th Battery, Capt. Cullen Bradley.

Marched from Lee and Gordon's and went into action at Viniard's at 4 o'clock, September 19th. Under orders, moved out of line at Brotherton's the morning of September 20th, and became involved in the break there. Harker's Brigade was moved back into the Dyer Field, checked the enemy's advance, retired to Snodgrass Hill, and held its line there till night. Gen. Wood being with the command.

---

[*] Not engaged. At Chattanooga.

SECOND DIVISION (TWENTY-FIRST CORPS).

Maj.-Gen. JOHN M. PALMER.

First Brigade.

Brig.-Gen. CHARLES CRUFT.
31st Indiana, Col. John T. Smith.
1st Kentucky,* Lieut.-Col. Alva R. Hadlock.
2d Kentucky, Col. Thos. D. Sedgewick.
90th Ohio, Col. Charles H. Rippey.
1st Ohio Light, Battery B, Lieut. Norman A. Baldwin.

Second Brigade.

Brig.-Gen. WILLIAM B. HAZEN.
9th Indiana, Col. Isaac C. B. Suman.
6th Kentucky:
   Col. Geo. T. Shackelford.
   Lieut.-Col. Richard Rockingham.
   Maj. Richard T. Whitaker.
41st Ohio, Col. Aquila Wiley.
124th Ohio:
   Col. Oliver H. Payne.
   Maj. James B. Hampson.
1st Ohio Light, Battery F, Lieut. Giles J. Cockerill.

Third Brigade.

Col. WILLIAM GROSE.

84th Illinois, Col. Louis H. Waters.
36th Indiana:
   Lieut.-Col. Oliver H. P. Carey.
   Maj. Gilbert Trusler.
23d Kentucky, Lieut.-Col. James C. Foy.
6th Ohio:
   Col. Nicholas L. Anderson.
   Maj. Samuel C. Erwin.
24th Ohio, Col. David J. Higgins.
4th United States Artillery, Battery H, Lieut. Harry C. Cushing.
4th United States Artillery, Battery M, Lieut. Francis L. D. Russell.

Reached Poe's from Lee and Gordon's at noon, and went at once into action east of that point and toward the Brock Field. At 5 o'clock assisted in the repulse of the enemy from Poe's and Brotherton's. Fought September 20th until 5:30 P. M., on east line of the Kelly Field. Hazen fought on Snodgrass Hill after 3 P. M.

---

* Five companies serving as wagon guard.

THIRD DIVISION (TWENTY-FIRST CORPS).
Brig.-Gen. HORATIO P. VAN CLEVE.

First Brigade.
Brig.-Gen. SAMUEL BEATTY.
79th Indiana, Col. Frederick Knefler.
9th Kentucky, Col. George H. Cram.
17th Kentucky, Col. Alexander M. Stout.
19th Ohio, Lieut.-Col. Henry G. Stratton.
Pennsylvania Light, 26th Battery:
  Capt. Alanson J. Stevens.
  Lieut. Samuel M. McDowell.

Second Brigade.
Col. GEORGE F. DICK.
44th Indiana, Lieut.-Col. Simon C. Aldrich.
86th Indiana, Maj. Jacob C. Dick.
13th Ohio:
  Lieut.-Col. Elhannon M. Mast.
  Capt. Horatio G. Cosgrove.
59th Ohio, Lieut.-Col. Granville A. Frambes.
Indiana Light, 7th Battery, Capt. George R. Swallow.

Third Brigade.
Col. SIDNEY M. BARNES.
35th Indiana, Maj. John P. Dufficy.
8th Kentucky:
  Lieut.-Col. James D. Mayhew.
  Maj. John S. Clark.
21st Kentucky,* Col. S. Woodson Price.
51st Ohio:
  Col. Richard W. McClain.
  Lieut.-Col. Charles H. Wood.
99th Ohio, Col. Peter T. Swaine.
Wisconsin Light, 3d Battery, Lieut. Cortland Livingston.

Reached Brotherton's from Lee and Gordon's with Dicks' and S. Beatty's Brigades about 2 P. M., and went into action south-east of that point. At 3:30, was forced back to the high ground south of Brotherton's, and at 4:30 was forced to the west side of the Dyer Field. September 19th, Barnes' Brigade fought at Viniard's and throughout the 20th with Baird, north of the Kelley Field. Portions of the other brigades rallied on Snodgrass Hill.

---
* Not engaged; at Whitesides.

RESERVE CORPS.

Maj.-Gen. GORDON GRANGER.

FIRST DIVISION (RESERVE CORPS).

Brig.-Gen. JAMES B. STEEDMAN.

First Brigade.

Brig.-Gen. WALTER C. WHITAKER.
96th Illinois, Col. Thomas E. Champion.
115th Illinois, Col. Jesse H. Moore.
84th Indiana, Col. Nelson Trusler.
22d Michigan :*
   Col. Heber Le Favour.
   Lieut.-Col. William Sanborn.
   Capt. Alonzo M. Keeler.
40th Ohio, Lieut.-Col. William Jones.
89th Ohio :
   Col. Caleb H. Carlton.
   Capt. Isaac C. Nelson.
Ohio Light Artillery, 18th Battery,
   Capt. Charles C. Aleshire.

Second Brigade.

Col. JOHN G. MITCHELL.
78th Illinois :
   Lieut.-Col. Carter Van Vleck
   Lieut. George Green.
98th Ohio :
   Capt. Moses J. Urquhart.
   Capt. Armstrong J. Thomas.
113th Ohio, Lieut.-Col Darius B. Warner.
121st Ohio, Lieut.-Col. Henry B. Banning.
1st Illinois Light Artillery, Battery M,
   Lieut. Thomas Burton.

SECOND DIVISION (RESERVE CORPS).

Brig.-Gen. JAMES D. MORGAN.†

Second Brigade.

Col. DANIEL MCCOOK.

85th Illinois, Col. Caleb J. Dilworth.
86th Illinois, Lieut.-Col. David W. Magee.
125th Illinois, Col. Oscar F. Harmon.
52d Ohio, Maj. James T. Holmes.
69th Ohio,‡ Lieut.-Col. Joseph H. Brigham.
2d Illinois Light Artillery, Battery I, Charles M. Barnett.

Early on September 19th, Mitchell's Brigade supported D. McCook's near Reed's Bridge in slight skirmishing with Forrest's Cavalry. These brigades were withdrawn to Rossville Gap at 7 o'clock, and were not engaged on Saturday. Early September 20th, the corps was concentrated at McAfee's Church, and at noon marched to the relief of Gen. Thomas at Snodgrass Hill, McCook's Brigade being left on the high ground next south of Cloud's, Steedman's

---

* Temporarily attached.
† With other part of his division, guarding communications.
‡ Temporarily attached.

Division carrying the ridge to the right of Brannan, and extending Gen. Thomas' line to the ravine leading down to Viditoe's.

CAVALRY CORPS.
Brig.-Gen. ROBERT B. MITCHELL.

The cavalry operated at the upper fords of the Chickamauga during the 19th, and about Glass' Mill and Crawfish Springs, September 20th. In the afternoon of the 20th, Long's Brigade was severely engaged between these points, and finally driven back to Crawfish Springs.

FIRST DIVISION (CAVALRY CORPS).
Col. EDWARD M. McCOOK.

First Brigade.
ARCHIBALD P. CAMPBELL.
2d Michigan, Maj. Leonidas S. Scranton.
9th Pennsylvania, Lieut.-Col. Roswell M. Russell.
1st Tennessee, Lieut.-Col. James P. Brownlow.

Second Brigade.
COL. DANIEL M. RAY.
2d Indiana, Maj. Joseph B. Presdee.
4th Indiana, Lieut.-Col. John T. Deweese.
2d Tennessee, Lieut.-Col. William R. Cook.
1st Wisconsin, Col. Oscar H. LaGrange.
1st Ohio Light Artillery, Battery D (section), Lieut. Nathaniel M. Newell.

Third Brigade,
COL. LOUIS D. WATKINS.
4th Kentucky, Col. Wickliffe Cooper.
5th Kentucky, Lieut.-Col. William T. Hoblitzell.
6th Kentucky, Maj. Louis A. Gratz.

SECOND DIVISION (CAVALRY CORPS).

Brig.-Gen. GEORGE CROOK.

First Brigade.
Col. ROBERT H. G. MINTY.
3d Indiana (battalion), Lieut.-Col. Robert Klein.
4th Michigan, Maj. Horace Gray.
7th Pennsylvania, Lieut.-Col. James J Seibert.
4th United States, Capt. James B. McIntyre.
Chicago Board of Trade Battery (one section), Capt. James H. Stokes.

Second Brigade.
COL. ELI LONG.
2d Kentucky, Col. Thomas P. Nicholas.
1st Ohio;
  Lieut.-Col. Valentine Cupp.
  Maj. Thomas. J. Patton.
2d Ohio, Lieut.-Col. Charles B. Seidel.
4th Ohio, Lieut.-Col. Oliver P. Robie.
Chicago Board of Trade Battery (one section), Capt. James H. Stokes.

ORGANIZATION OF THE ARMY OF TENNESSEE, GEN. BRAXTON BRAGG, C. S. ARMY, COMMANDING, AT THE BATTLE OF CHICKAMAUGA.

Escort.

Capt. GUY DREUX.

Dreux's Company Louisiana Cavalry, Lieut. O. De Buis.
Holloway's Company Alabama Cavalry, Capt E. M. Holloway.

RIGHT WING.

Lieut.-Gen. LEONIDAS POLK.

Escort.

Greenleaf's Company Louisiana Cavalry, Capt. Leeds Greenleaf.

POLK'S CORPS.

Lieut.-Gen. LEONIDAS POLK.

ORGANIZATION OF THE ARMY OF TENNESSEE.

CHEATHAM'S DIVISION (POLK'S CORPS).
Maj.-Gen. BENJAMIN FRANKLIN CHEATHAM.
Escort.
Company G, 2d Georgia Cavalry, Capt. Thomas M. Merritt.

Jackson's Brigade.
Brig.-Gen. JOHN K. JACKSON.
1st Georgia (Confederate), 2d Battalion Maj. James Clarke Gordon.
5th Georgia, Col. Charles P. Daniel.
2d Georgia Battalion (Sharpshooters), Maj. Richard H. Whiteley.
5th Mississippi:
  Lieut.-Col. W. L. Sykes.
  Maj. John B. Herring.
8th Mississippi, Col. John C. Wilkinson.
Scogin's (Georgia) Battery, Capt. John Scogin.

Maney's Brigade.
Brig.-Gen. GEORGE MANEY.
1st Tennessee, } Col. Hume R. Field.
27th Tennessee, }
4th Tennessee (Provisional Army):
  Col. James A. McMurry.
  Lieut.-Col. Robert N. Lewis.
  Major Oliver A. Bradshaw.
  Capt. Joseph Bostick.
6th Tennessee, } Col. George C. Porter.
9th Tennessee, }
24th Tennessee Battalion (Sharpshooters), Maj. Frank Maney.
Smith's (Mississippi) Battery, Lieut. William B. Turner.

Smith's Brigade.
Brig.-Gen. PRESTON SMITH.
Col. ALFRED JEFFERSON VAUGHAN, JR.
11th Tennessee, Col. George W. Gordon.
12th Tennessee, } Col. William M. Watkins.
47th Tennessee, }
13th Tennessee, { Col. Alfred Jefferson Vaughan, Jr.
154th Tennessee, { Lieut.-Col. R. W. Pitman.
29th Tennessee, Col. Horace Rice.
Dawson's Battalion Sharpshooters:
  Maj. J. W. Dawson.
  Maj. William Green.
  Maj. James Purl.
Scott's (Tennessee) Battery:
  Lieut. John H. Marsh.
  Lieut. A. T. Watson.
  Capt. William L. Scott.

Wright's Brigade.
Brig.-Gen. MARCUS J. WRIGHT.
8th Tennessee, Col. John H. Anderson.
16th Tennessee, Col. D. M. Donnell.
28th Tennessee, Col. Sidney S. Stanton.
38th Tennessee and Maj. Thomas B. Murray's (Tennessee) Battalion, Col. John C. Carter.
51st Tennessee, } Lieut.-Col. John G. Hall.
52d Tennessee, }
Carnes' (Tennessee) Battery, Capt. William W. Carnes.

Strahl's Brigade.
Brig.-Gen. OTHO F. STRAHL.
4th Tennessee, } Col. Jonathan J. Lamb.
5th Tennessee, }
19th Tennessee, Col. Francis M. Walker.
24th Tennessee, Col. John A. Wilson.
31st Tennessee, Col. Egbert E. Tansil.
33d Tennessee, Col. Warner P. Jones.
Standford's (Mississippi) Battery, Capt. Thomas J. Stanford.

Marched from the vicinity of Hunt's, September 19th, at 11

o'clock, directly north, and went into action on a line running through the Brock Field from west of its south-west corner to the crossing of the Alexander Bridge and Brotherton Roads. It advanced to the north of the Brock Field, and finally was forced back to the high ground south of Winfrey's. It took part in the night attack at that point. September 20th, it was in reserve until the final advance.

HINDMAN'S DIVISION (POLK'S CORPS).

Maj.-Gen. THOMAS CARMICHAEL HINDMAN.
Brig.-Gen. PATTON ANDERSON.

Escort.

Lenoir's Company Alabama Cavalry, Capt. T. M. Lenoir.

Anderson's Brigade.

Brig.-Gen. PATTON ANDERSON.
Col. J. H. SHARP.
7th Mississippi, Col. W. H. Bishop.
9th Mississippi, Maj. T. H. Lynam.
10th Mississippi, Lieut.-Col. James Barr.
41st Mississippi, Col. W. F. Tucker.
44th Mississippi:
    Col. J. H. Sharp.
    Lieut.-Col. R. G. Kelsey.
9th Mississippi Battalion Sharpshooters, Maj. W. C. Richards.
Garrity's (Alabama) Battery, Capt. James Garrity.

Deas' Brigade.

Brig.-Gen. ZACH. C. DEAS.
19th Alabama, Col. Samuel K. McSpadden.
22d Alabama:
    Lieut. Col. John Weedon.
    Capt. Harry T. Toulmin.
25th Alabama, Col. George D. Johnston.
39th Alabama, Col. Whitfield Clark.
50th Alabama, Col. J. G. Coltart.
17th Alabama Battalion Sharpshooters, Capt. James F. Nabers.
Dent's (Alabama) Battery (formerly Robertson's), Capt. S. H. Dent.

Manigault's Brigade.

Brig.-Gen. A. M. MANIGAULT.
24th Alabama Col. N. N. Davis.
28th Alabama, Col. John C. Reid.
34th Alabama, Maj. John N. Slaughter.
10th South Carolina, } Col. James F. Pressley.
19th South Carolina, }
Waters' (Alabama) Battery, Lieut. Charles W. Watkins.

Was not engaged September 19th. September 20th, forced the right of the Union line off the field. At 3 o'clock, took part in the assault on Snodgrass Hill from the Viditoe place, and was engaged until sundown, being the left of the Confederate line.

HILL'S CORPS.

Lieut.-Gen. DANIEL H. HILL.

CLEBURNE'S DIVISION (HILL'S CORPS).

Maj.-Gen. PATRICK R. CLEBURNE.

Escort.

Sanders' Company Tennessee Cavalry, Capt. C. F. Sanders.

Wood's Brigade.

Brig.-Gen. S. A. M. WOOD.

16th Alabama:
    Maj. John H. McGaughy.
    Capt. Frederick A. Ashford.
33d Alabama, Col. Samuel Adams.
45th Alabama, Col. E. B. Breedlove.
18th Alabama Battalion:
    Maj. John H. Gibson.
    Col. Samuel Adams (33d Alabama).
33d Mississippi, }
45th Mississippi, } Col. M. P. Lowrey.
15th Mississippi Battalion Sharpshooters:
    Maj. A. T. Hawkins.
    Capt. Daniel Coleman.
Semple's Alabama Battery:
    Capt. Henry C. Semple.
    Lieut. R. W. Goldthwaite.

Polk's Brigade.

Brig.-Gen. LUCIUS E. POLK.

1st Arkansas, Col. John W. Colquit.
3d Confederate, } Col. J. A. Smith.
5th Confederate, }
2d Tennessee, Col. Wm. D. Robison.
35th Tennessee, Col. Benj. J. Hill.
48th Tennessee, Col. George H. Nixon.
Calvert's (Arkansas) Battery, Lieut. Thomas J. Key.

Deshler's Brigade.

Brig.-Gen. JAMES DESHLER.
Col. ROGER Q. MILLS.

19th Arkansas, } Lieut.-Col. A. S. Hutchinson.
24th Arkansas, }
6th Texas Infantry, } Col. Roger Q. Mills.
10th Texas Infantry, } Lieut.-Col. T. Scott Anderson.
15th Texas Cavalry,* }
17th Texas Cavalry,* } Col. F. C. Wilkes.
18th Texas Cavalry, } Lieut.-Col. John T. Coit.
24th Texas Cavalry, } Maj. Wm. A. Taylor.
25th Texas Cavalry, }
Douglas' (Texas) Battery, Capt. James P. Douglas.

Crossed the Chickamauga at 4 P. M., September 19th, and pro-

---

* Dismounted.

ceeded in haste to Jay's Mill, where it formed in rear of Walker's troops, with its right at the mill, and its line extending nearly a mile along the road to Alexander's. At 6 o'clock, it advanced and engaged Baird's and Johnson's Divisions, the battle lasting an hour after dark. September 20th, the division repeatedly assaulted the Union lines east of the Kelly Field. It took part there in the final advance at 5:30 P. M.

BRECKINRIDGE'S DIVISION (HILL'S CORPS).
Maj.-Gen. John C. BRECKINRIDGE.
Escort.
Foules' Company Mississippi Cavalry, Capt. H. L. Foules.

Helm's Brigade.
Brig.-Gen. BEN. HARDIN HELM.
Col. JOSEPH H. LEWIS.
41st Alabama, Col. Martin L. Stansel.
2d Kentucky :
    Lieut.-Col. James W. Hewitt.
    Lieut.-Col. James W. Moss.
4th Kentucky :
    Col. Joseph P. Nuckols.
    Maj. Thomas W. Thompson.
6th Kentucky :
    Col. Joseph H. Lewis.
    Lieut.-Col. Martin H. Cofer.
9th Kentucky:
    Col. John W. Caldwell.
    Lieut.-Col. John C. Wickliffe.
Cobb's (Kentucky) Battery, Capt. Robert Cobb.

Adams' Brigade.
Brig.-Gen. DANIEL W. ADAMS.
Col. RANDALL LEE GIBSON.
32d Alabama, Maj. John C. Kimball.
13th Louisiana, } Col. Randall Lee Gibson.
20th Louisiana, } Col. Leon von Zinken.
              } Capt. E. M. Dubroca.
16th Louisiana, } Col. Daniel Gober.
25th Louisiana, }
19th Louisiana :
    Lieut.-Col. Richard W. Turner.
    Maj. Loudon Butler.
    Capt. H. A. Kennedy.
14th Louisiana Battalion, Maj. J. E. Austin.
Slocomb's (Louisiana) Battery, Capt. C. H. Slocomb.
Graves (Kentucky) Battery, Lieut. S. M. Spencer.

Stovall's Brigade.
Brig.-Gen. MARCELLUS A. STOVALL.
1st Florida, } Col. William S. Dilworth.
3d Florida, }
4th Florida, Col. W. L. L. Bowen.
47th Georgia :
    Capt. William S. Phillips.
    Capt. Joseph S. Cone.
60th North Carolina :
    Lieut.-Col. James M. Ray.
    Capt. James Thomas Weaver.
Mebane's (Tennessee) Battery, Capt. John W. Mebane.

The artillery of Helm's Brigade was engaged early September 19th at long range with John Beatty's and Stanley's Brigades of

Negley's Division, at Glass' Mill. The division was withdrawn and ordered to the Confederate right north-east of the Kelly Field, which point it reached before daylight, September 20th. It opened the battle, attacking at 9:30 A. M., and entered this field in the Union rear. From this point it was forced back to its first position. It took part in the general advance about sundown, and bivouacked in the Kelly Field.

RESERVE CORPS.

Maj.-Gen. W. H. T. WALKER.

WALKER'S DIVISION (WALKER'S CORPS).

Brig.-Gen. STATES RIGHTS GIST.

Gist's Brigade.

Brig.-Gen. STATE RIGHTS GIST.
Col. PEYTON H. COLQUITT.
Lieut.-Col. LEROY NAPIER.
4th Georgia.
    Col. Peyton H. Colquitt.
    Maj. A. M. Speer.
8th Georgia Battalion:
    Lieut.-Col. Leroy Napier.
    Maj. Z. L. Watters.
16th South Carolina,º Col. James McCullough.
24th South Carolina:
    Col. Clement H. Stevens.
    Lieut.-Col. Ellison Capers.

Ector's Brigade.

Brig.-Gen. MATTHEW DUNCAN ECTOR.
Stone's Alabama Battalion Sharpshooters, Maj. T. O. Stone.
Pound's Mississippi Battalion Sharpshooters, Capt. M. Pound.
29th North Carolina, Col. William B. Creasman.
9th Texas, Col. William H. Young.
10th Texas Cavalry,† Lieut.-Col. C. R. Earp.
14th Texas Cavalry,† Col. J. L. Camp.
32d Texas Cavalry,† Col. Julius A. Andrews.

Wilson's Brigade.

Col. CLAUDIUS C. WILSON.
25th Georgia, Lieut.-Col. A. J. Williams.
29th Georgia, Lieut. George R. McRea.
30th Georgia, Lieut.-Col. James S. Boynton.
1st Georgia Battalion Sharpshooters, Maj. Arthur Shaaff.
4th Louisiana Battalion, Lieut.-Col. John McEnery.

Artillery.

Ferguson's (South Carolina) Battery,º Lieut. R. T. Beauregard.
Howell's (Georgia) Battery (formerly Martin's), Capt. Evan P. Howell.

Sent early September 19th from the vicinity of Alexander's

º Not engaged; at Rome.
† Serving as infantry.

to the assistance of Forrest at Jay's Mill. Was severely engaged during the forenoon. September 20th it relieved Breckinridge at noon, and unsuccessfully assaulted the Union left. At 5:30 P. M. it reached the La Fayette Road south of McDonald's, and bivouacked east of it.

LIDDELL'S DIVISION (WALKER'S CORPS).

Brig.-Gen. ST. JOHN R. LIDDELL.

Liddell's Brigade.

Col. DANIEL C. GOVAN.

2d Arkansas, } Lieut.-Col. Reuben F. Harvey.
15th Arkansas, } Capt. A. T. Meek.

5th Arkansas, } Col. L. Featherston.
13th Arkansas, } Lieut.-Col. John E. Murray.

6th Arkansas, } Col. D. A. Gillespie.
7th Arkansas, } Lieut.-Col. Peter Snyder.

8th Arkansas:
Lieut.-Col. George F. Baucum.
Maj. A. Watkins.
1st Louisiana (Regulars,):
Lieut.-Col. George F. Baucum.
Maj. A. Watkins (8th Arkansas).
Warren Light Artillery (Mississippi Battery), Lieut. H. Shannon.

Walthall's Brigade.

Brig.-Gen. EDWARD CARY WALTHALL.

24th Mississippi:
Lieut.-Col. R. P. McKelvaine.
Maj. W. C. Staples.
Capt. B. F. Toomer.
Capt. J. D. Smith.
27th Mississippi, Col. James A. Campbell.
29th Mississippi, Col. William F. Brantly.
30th Mississippi:
Col. Junius I. Scales.
Lieut.-Col. Hugh A. Reynolds.
Maj. James M. Johnson.
34th Mississippi:
Maj. William G. Pegram.
Capt. H. J. Bowen.
Lieut.-Col. Hugh A. Reynolds (30th Mississippi).
Fowler's (Alabama) Battery, Capt. William H. Fowler.

Followed Walker's Division into action, September 19th, becoming engaged just north of the Winfrey House, taking Baird's Division in the right flank, Govan's Brigade capturing Scribner's guns, and Walthall's, those of King's Brigade, the left of Baird's line, on the next ridge north. The division was then forced to retire. It was less severely engaged in the afternoon. September 20th, it was in reserve until noon, when Walthall's Brigade assaulted, and was withdrawn. At 5:30 the division crossed the La Fayette Road at McDonald's, but was obliged to retire to the east of the road, where it bivouacked.

LEFT WING.

Lieut.-Gen. James Longstreet.

BUCKNER'S CORPS.

Maj.-Gen. Simon Bolivar Buckner.

Escort.

Clark's Company Tennessee Cavalry, Capt. J. W. Clark.

STEWART'S DIVISION (BUCKNER'S CORPS)

Maj.-Gen. Alexander P. Stewart.

Bate's Brigade.

Brig.-Gen. William Brimage Bate.
58th Alabama, Col. Bushrod Jones.
37th Georgia:
  Col. A. F. Rudler.
  Lieut.-Col. Joseph T. Smith.
4th Georgia Battalion Sharpshooters:
  Maj. T. D. Caswell.
  Capt. B. M. Turner.
  Lieut. Joel Towers.
15th Tennessee,
37th Tennessee,
  { Col. R. C. Tyler.
    Lieut.-Col. R. Dudley Frayser.
    Capt. R. M. Tankesley. }
20th Tennessee:
  Col. Thomas B. Smith.
  Maj. W. M. Shy.
Eufaula Artillery (Alabama Battery),
  Capt. McDonald Oliver.

Clayton's Brigade.

Brig.-Gen. Henry D. Clayton.
18th Alabama:
  Col. J. T. Holtzclaw.
  Lieut.-Col. R. F. Inge.
  Maj. P. F. Hunley.
36th Alabama, Col. Lewis T. Woodruff.
38th Alabama, Lieut.-Col. A. R. Lankford.
1st Arkansas Battery, Capt. John T. Humphreys.

Brown's Brigade.

Brig.-Gen. John C. Brown.
Col. Edmund C. Cook.
18th Tennessee:
  Col. Joseph B. Palmer.
  Lieut.-Col. William R. Butler.
  Capt. Gideon H. Lowe.

26th Tennessee :
  Col. John M. Lillard.
  Maj. Richard M. Saffell.
32d Tennessee :
  Col. Edmund C. Cook.
  Capt. Calaway G. Tucker.
45th Tennessee, Col. Anderson Searcy.
23d Tennessee Battalion :
  Maj. Tazewell W. Newman.
  Capt. W. P. Simpson.
T. H. Dawson's (Georgia) Battery, Lieut. R. W. Anderson.

Soon after noon, September 19th, Stewart moved north from the Park House to assist Cheatham, and became severely engaged between the Brock Field and Brotherton's, Clayton's Brigade penetrating the Union line at the latter point to the Tan-yard, and Bates' Brigade breaking it at Poe's. The division withdrew soon after 5 o'clock, upon the advance of Union re-inforcements. September 20th, at 11 A. M., the division assaulted the Union lines at the Poe House and on the south side of the Kelly Field, and withdrew about 1 o'clock to its first position. It took part in the general advance at 5:30 P. M., and bivoucked about the Kelly House.

PRESTON'S DIVISION (BUCKNER'S CORPS).

Brig.-Gen. WILLIAM PRESTON.

Gracie's Brigade.

Brig.-Gen. ARCHIBALD GRACIE, JR.
43d Alabama, Col. Young M. Moody.
1st Alabama Battalion : *
  Lieut.-Col. John H. Holt.
  Capt. George W. Huguley.
2d Alabama Battalion : *
  Lieut.-Col. Bolling Hall, Jr.
  Capt. W. D. Walden.
3d Alabama Battalion,* Maj. John W. A. Sanford.
4th Alabama Battalion,† Maj. John D. McLennan.
63d Tennessee :
  Lieut.-Col. Abraham Fulkerson.
  Maj. John A. Aiken.

Trigg's Brigade.

Col. ROBERT C. TRIGG.
1st Florida Cavalry (dismounted), Col. G. Troup Maxwell.
6th Florida, Col. J. J. Finley.
7th Florida, Col. Robert Bullock.
54th Virginia, Lieut.-Col. John J. Wade.

---

* Hilliard's Legion.
† Artillery Battalion, Hilliard's Legion, serving as infantry.

Third Brigade.
Col. JOHN H. KELLY.
65th Georgia, Col. R. H. Moore.
5th Kentucky, Col. H. Hawkins.
58th North Carolina, Col. John B. Palmer.
63d Virginia, Maj. James M. French.

Artillery Battalion.
Maj. A. LEYDEN.
Jeffress' (Virginia) Battery, Capt. William C. Jeffress.
Peeples' (Georgia) Battery, Capt. Tyler M. Peeples.
Wolihin's (Georgia) Battery, Capt. Andrew M. Wolihin.

September 19th, at 3 P. M., Trigg's Brigade took part in the battle at Viniard's. The division was not further engaged, until 4:20, September 20th, when it joined in the assault on Snodgrass Hill and fought until sundown. At dusk it crossed the ridge to the right of Brannan and captured the greater part of three Union regiments, which were isolated there.

RESERVE CORPS ARTILLERY.
Maj. SAMUEL C. WILLIAMS.

Baxter's (Tennessee) Battery, Capt. Edmund D. Baxter.
Darden's (Mississippi) Battery, Capt. Putnam Darden.
Kolb's (Alabama) Battery, Capt. R. F. Kolb.
McCants' (Florida) Battery, Capt. Robert P. McCants.

These four batteries, under command of Maj. Williams, crossed the river at Alexander's Bridge early on the 19th, and were posted as a reserve to Buckner's Corps. Baxter's Battery was then sent to Gracie's Brigade, and McCants' to Trigg's. The remaining batteries moved with Preston's Division, Sunday afternoon, to Brotherton's, and about 5 P. M., advanced to the vicinity of Poe's, and opened fire, first with eight and then with eleven guns, upon the Union lines south of the Kelly Field.

DETACHMENT FROM THE ARMY OF NORTHERN VIRGINIA.

LONGSTREET'S CORPS* (HOOD'S).

Maj.-Gen. JOHN B. HOOD.

McLAW'S DIVISION (HOOD'S CORPS).

Brig.-Gen. JOSEPH BREVARD KERSHAW.
Maj.-Gen. LAFAYETTE McLAWS.

Kershaw's Brigade.
Brig.-Gen. JOSEPH BREVARD KERSHAW.
2d South Carolina, Lieut.-Col. Franklin Gaillard.
3d South Carolina, Col. James D. Nance.
7th South Carolina:
   Lieut.-Col. Elbert Bland.
   Maj. John S. Hard.
   Capt. E. J. Goggans.
8th South Carolina, Col. John W. Henagan.
15th South Carolina, Col. Joseph F. Gist.
3d South Carolina Battalion, Capt. Joshua M. Townsend.

Wofford's Brigade.†
Brig.-Gen. WILLIAM T. WOFFORD.
16th Georgia.
18th Georgia.
24th Georgia.
3d Georgia Battalion Sharpshooters.
Cobb's (Georgia) Legion.
Phillips' (Georgia) Legion.

Humphreys' Brigade.
Brig.-Gen. BENJAMIN G. HUMPHREYS.
13th Mississippi, Lieut.-Col. Kennon McElroy.
17th Mississippi, Lieut.-Col. John C. Fiser.
18th Mississippi, Capt. W. F. Hubbard.
21st Mississippi, Lieut.-Col. D. N. Moody.

Bryan's Brigade.†
Brig.-Gen. GOODE BRYAN.
10th Georgia.
50th Georgia.
51st Georgia.
53d Georgia.

Was not present September 19th. September 20th, formed the second line east of Brotherton's. It followed Johnson's Division through the Union line, turned north through the Dyer Field,

---

* Army of Northern Virginia. Organization taken from return of that army for August 31, 1863. Pickett's Division was left in Virginia.
† Did not arrive in time for the battle.

passed over Law's Division, which had been checked by Wood's troops, forced the latter back, and assaulted Snodgrass Hill. It was relieved by Preston at 4:30 P. M.

HOOD'S DIVISION (HOOD'S CORPS).

Maj. Gen. JOHN B. HOOD.
Brig.-Gen. EVANDER MCIVER LAW.

Jenkins' Brigade.°

Brig.-Gen. MICAH JENKINS.
1st South Carolina.
2d South Carolina Rifles.
5th South Carolina.
6th South Carolina.
Hampton Legion.
Palmetto Sharpshooters

Law's Brigade.

Brig.-Gen. EVANDER MCIVER LAW.
Col. JAMES L. SHEFFIELD.
Col. W. C. OATES.
4th Alabama, Col. Pinckney D. Bowles.
15th Alabama, Col. W. C. Oates.
44th Alabama, Col. William F. Perry.
47th Alabama, Maj. James M. Campbell.
48th Alabama, Lieut.-Col. William M. Hardwick.

Robertson's Brigade.†

Brig.-Gen. JEROME B. ROBERTSON.
Col. VAN H. MANNING.
3d Arkansas, Col. Van. H. Manning.
1st Texas, Capt. R. J. Harding.
4th Texas:
  Col. John P. Bane.
  Capt. R. H. Bassett.
5th Texas:
  Maj. J. C. Rogers.
  Capt. J. S. Cleveland.
  Capt. T. T. Clay.

Anderson's Brigade.°

Brig.-Gen. GEORGE T. ANDERSON.
7th Georgia.
8th Georgia.
9th Georgia.
11th Georgia.
59th Georgia.

Benning's Brigade.

Brig.-Gen. HENRY L. BENNING.

2d Georgia:
  Lieut.-Col. William S. Shepherd.
  Maj. W. W. Charlton.
15th Georgia:
  Col. Dudley M. DuBose.
  Maj. P. J. Shannon.
17th Georgia, Lieut.-Col. Charles W. Matthews.
20th Georgia, Col. J. D. Waddell.

September 19th, it was engaged about Viniard's from 2 P. M. until sunset. September 20th, it formed the third line east of Brother-

---

° Did not arrive in time to take part in the battle.
† Served first day in Johnson's Provisional Division.

ton's. It advanced through the Union line, but was repulsed by Harker's Brigade of Wood's Division toward the north end of the Dyer Field, and was not afterward engaged.

JOHNSON'S DIVISION° (HOOD'S CORPS).
Brig.-Gen. BUSHROD R. JOHNSON.

Gregg's Brigade.
Brig.-Gen. JOHN GREGG.
Col. CYRUS A. SUGG.
3d Tennessee, Col. Calvin H. Walker.
10th Tennessee, Col. William Grace.
30th Tennessee:
    Lieut.-Col. James J. Turner.
    Capt. Charles S. Douglass.
41st Tennessee, Lieut.-Col. James D. Tillman.
50th Tennessee:
    Col. Cyrus A. Sugg.
    Lieut.-Col. Thomas W. Beaumont.
    Maj. Christopher W. Robertson.
    Col. Calvin H. Walker (3d Tennessee).
1st Tennessee Battalion:
    Maj. Stephen H. Colms.
    Maj. Christopher W. Robertson (50th Tennessee).
7th Texas:
    Col. H. B. Granbury.
    Maj. K. M. Vanzandt.
Bledsoe's Missouri Battery, Lieut. R. L. Wood.

McNair's Brigade.
Brig.-Gen. EVANDER MCNAIR.
Col. DAVID COLEMAN.
1st Arkansas Mounted Rifles, Col. Robert W. Harper.
2d Arkansas Mounted Rifles, Col. James A. Williamson.
25th Arkansas, Lieut.-Col. Eli Hufstedler.
4th and 31st Arkansas and 4th Arkansas Battalion (consolidated) Maj. J. A. Ross.
39th North Carolina, Col. David Coleman.
Culpeper's (South Carolina) Battery, Capt. James F. Culpeper.

Johnson's Brigade.
Brig.-Gen. BUSHROD R. JOHNSON.
Col. JOHN S. FULTON.
17th Tennessee, Lieut.-Col. Watt W. Floyd.
23d Tennessee, Col. R. H. Keeble.
25th Tennessee, Lieut.-Col. R. B. Snowden.
44th Tennessee:
    Lieut.-Col. John S. McEwen, Jr.
    Maj. G. M. Crawford.
Company E, 9th Georgia Artillery Battalion (Billington W. York's Battery), Lieut. William S. Everett.

Forced a crossing of the Chickamauga at Reed's Bridge, September 18th, and advanced nearly to Viniard's. Took part in the battle at that point during the afternoon of the 19th. Occupied the

---

° A provisional organization, embracing Johnson's and part of the time Robertson's Brigades, as well as Gregg's and McNair's. September 19th, attached to Longstreet's Corps, under Maj.-Gen. Hood.

front line east of Brotherton's, September 20th; penetrated the Union line, advanced over the ridge at the west side of the Dyer Field and assaulted Snodgrass Hill at and west of Viditoe's until night.

CORPS ARTILLERY⁰ (LONGSTREET'S).
Col. E. Porter Alexander.

Fickling's (South Carolina) Battery.
Jordan's (Virginia) Battery.
Moody's (Louisiana) Battery.
Parker's (Virginia) Battery.
Taylor's (Virginia) Battery.
Woolfolk's (Virginia) Battery.

RESERVE ARTILLERY.
Maj. Felix H. Robertson.

Barret's (Missouri) Battery, Capt. Overton W. Barret.
Havis' (Georgia) Battery, Capt. M. W. Havis.
Lumsden's (Alabama) Battery, Capt. Charles L. Lumsden.
Massenburg's (Georgia) Battery, Capt. T. L. Massenburg.

FORREST'S CORPS (CAVALRY).
Brig.-Gen. Nathan Bedford Forrest.
Escort.
Jackson's Company Tennessee Cavalry, Capt. J. C. Jackson.

ARMSTRONG'S DIVISION (FORREST'S CORPS).
Brig.-Gen. Frank C. Armstrong.

Armstrong's Brigade.
Col. James T. Wheeler.
3d Arkansas, Col. A. W. Hobson.
2d Kentucky, Lieut.-Col. Thomas G. Woodward.
6th Tennessee, Lieut.-Col. James H. Lewis.
18th Tennessee Battalion, Maj. Charles McDonald.

Forrest's Brigade.
Col. George G. Dibrell.
4th Tennessee, Col. Wm. S. McLemore.
8th Tennessee, Capt. Hamilton McGinnis.
9th Tennessee, Col. Jacob B. Biffle.
10th Tennessee, Col. Nicholas N. Cox.
11th Tennessee, Col. Daniel Wilson Holman.
Shaw's Battalion, O. P. Hamilton's Battalion, and R. D. Allison's Squadron (consolidated), Maj. Joseph Shaw.
Huggins' (Tennnessee) Battery (formerly Freeman's), Capt. A. L. Huggins.
Morton's (Tennessee) Battery, Capt. John W. Morton, Jr.

⁰ Did not arrive in time for the battle.

PEGRAM'S DIVISION * (FORREST'S CORPS).

Brig.-Gen. JOHN PEGRAM.

Davidson's Brigade.
Brig.-Gen. H. B. DAVIDSON.
1st Georgia, Col. J. J. Morrison.
6th Georgia, Col. John R. Hart.
6th North Carolina, Col. Geo. N. Folk.
Rucker's 1st Tennessee Legion, Col. E. W. Rucker (12th Tennessee Battalion, Maj. G. W. Day, and 16th Tennessee Battalion, Capt. John Q. Arnold).
Huwald's (Tennessee) Battery, Capt. Gustave A. Huwald.

Scott's Brigade.
Col. JOHN S. SCOTT.
10th Confederate, Col. C. T. Goode.
Detachment of John H. Morgan's command, Lieut.-Col. R. M. Martin.
1st Louisiana, Lieut.-Col. Jas. O. Nixon.
2d Tennesssee, Col. H. M. Ashby.
5th Tennessee, Col. Geo. W. McKenzie.
N. T. N. Robinson's (Louisiana) Battery (one section), Lieut. Winslow Robinson.

September 19th, Dibbrell's, Davidson's, and part of Scott's Brigades became engaged with Brannan's troops near Jay's Mill at 7:30 A. M., opening the battle of Chickamauga. Their engagement continued until 1 P. M. September 20th, the corps formed the Confederate right east of Cloud's. At 11 A. M., it captured the Union hospitals at that point, but was driven from there at noon by Whitaker's Brigade of Granger's troops, which were advancing from McAfee's Church to Snodgrass Hill.

WHEELER'S CORPS (CAVALRY).

Maj.-Gen. JOSEPH WHEELER.

WHARTON'S DIVISION (WHEELER'S CORPS).

Brig.-Gen. JOHN A. WHARTON.

First Brigade.
Col. C. C. CREWS.
Malone's (Alabama) Regiment, Col. J. C. Malone, Jr.
2d Georgia, Lieut.-Col. F. M. Ison.
3d Georgia, Col. R. Thompson.
4th Georgia, Col. Isaac W. Avery.

Second Brigade.
Col. THOMAS HARRISON.
3d Confederate, Col. W. N. Estes.
1st Kentucky, Lieut.-Col. J. W. Griffith.
4th Tennessee, Lieut.-Col. Paul F. Anderson.
8th Texas, Lieut.-Col. Gustave Cook.
11th Texas, Col. G. R. Reeves.
White's (Tennessee) Battery, Capt. B. F. White, Jr.

---

* Taken from Pegram's and Scott's reports and assignments.

MARTIN'S DIVISION, WHEELER'S CORPS.
Brig.-Gen. WILLIAM T. MARTIN.

First Brigade.	*Second Brigade.*
Col. JOHN T. MORGAN.	Col. A. A. RUSSELL.
1st Alabama, Lieut.-Col. D. T. Blakey.	4th Alabama (Russell's Regiment), Lieut.-Col. J. M. Hambrick.
3d Alabama, Lieut.-Col. T. H. Mauldin.	1st Confederate, Capt. C. H. Conner.
51st Alabama, Lieut.-Col. N. L. Kirkpatrick.	J. H. Wiggins' (Arkansas) Battery, Lieut. J. P. Bryant.
8th Confederate, Lieut.-Col. John S. Prather.	

These divisions operated along the upper fords of the Chickamauga during the 19th. September 20th, they crossed at Glass Mill, and forced Long's Brigade back to Crawfish Springs. They then recrossed the river, proceeded to Lee and Gordon's, and advanced from that point to Crawfish Springs, capturing the Union hospitals there about sundown.

CHATTANOOGA—LOOKOUT MOUNTAIN—MISSIONARY RIDGE.

CHAPTER VII.

ROSECRANS AT CHATTANOOGA—BRAGG'S INEVESTMENT.*

At midnight of September 20th, the Union army had reached Rossville, where it bivouacked under direction of Gen. Thomas, covering Rossville and McFarland's Gaps. During the night rations and ammunition were sent from Chattanooga by Gen. Rosecrans. Early in the morning the various divisions and corps were assembled and placed in position.

Crittenden's Corps occupied Missionary Ridge north of Rossville Gap, Thomas' Corps, the gap and the road to McFarland's Gap, and McCook's Corps, the mounted infantry and the cavalry, the Chattanooga Valley to Lookout.

Palmer's Division of Crittenden's Corps held the point of Missionary Ridge next to Rossville Gap with Wood's Division to its left on the ridge, and Steedman's Division of Granger's Corps still to the left as a reserve. Van Cleve's Division was sent to Chattanooga during the night of the 20th, and Dick's Brigade of that division with the 39th Indiana Mounted Infantry, Col. Harrison, was sent at 1 P. M. to hold the gaps in Missionary Ridge east of the city, and the bridge on the Harrison Road over the Chickamauga.

Baird's Division of Thomas' Corps held Rossville Gap with Negley's Division thrown forward to the spurs overlooking the roads to Ringgold and the battle field. John Beatty's and D. McCook's Brigades held the point of the ridge next south of Rossville Gap. Brannan's and Reynolds' Divisions were placed across the road to McFarland's Gap, and Johnson's, Sheridan's, and Davis' Divisions of McCook's

---

* See map, page 110.

Corps continued the line westward across Chattanooga Valley.

Mitchell's Cavalry occupied McFarland's Gap, and resisted the advance of Wheeler's Cavalry on that flank. Minty's Cavalry was thrown forward on the Ringgold Road to the vicinity of McAfee's Church.

Except an advance of Forrest's command toward Rossville Gap on the La Fayette and Ringgold Roads, and of a part of Wheeler's command toward McFarland's Gap, and slight skirmishing with the Union lines, the latter were not disturbed during the day.

During the night of the 21st, the Union army was withdrawn to Chattanooga. Crittenden's two divisions moved to their left along Missionary Ridge, followed at midnight by Steedman's Division. Thomas' Corps marched on the direct road from Rossville; Brannan's Division occupied a line at dusk half way to the city, and held it until the other three divisions of the corps had passed, and followed them soon after midnight. McCook's Corps then withdrew by divisions from left to right. Each brigade of the army left its pickets with a regiment to support them, and Baird's Division remained as a reserve of all the pickets. In front of the infantry pickets was the cavalry. At daylight these covering lines of infantry withdrew and their places were taken by the cavalry. At an early hour Forrest advanced upon the latter at Rossville Gap, and Wheeler pressed Mitchell in Chattanooga Valley. McLaw's Infantry Division of Hood's Corps was sent forward to assist Forrest, and thus supported, the latter pushed forward to within two miles of Chattanooga to the vicinity of the Watkin's House. Gen. Wheeler formed a junction with him at that point.

Meantime, the Union lines had been formed in front of Chattanooga with McCook's Corps on the right, Thomas' in the center, and Crittenden's on the left. By noon of Septemter 22d, this line was fairly covered by rifle pits.

Chattanooga in 1863. (See page xiii.)

Gen. Bragg's infantry began its march from the battle field on the afternoon of the 21st, Polk's wing beginning the movement, followed the next day by Longstreet's wing. Cheatham's Division led the column with orders for Hindman's Division of the same corps (Polk's) to join it on the march. It was followed by Walker's Corps, and that by Hill's. The line of march was by Ringgold Bridge and Mission Mills toward Chickamauga Station. Cheatham's Division reached Shallow Ford the morning of the 22d, and moved thence on the direct road toward Chattanooga. At 9 o'clock, he encountered the skirmishers of Dick's Brigade of Van Cleve's Division deployed east of Missionary Ridge, and at 2 P. M. occupied the ridge at the crossing of the Shallow Ford Road (now McCallie Avenue).

A general movement upon Chattanooga was ordered for 7 A. M., September 23d, the right wing by the Shallow Ford and Mission Mills Roads, and the left wing by the Rossville Road. Gen. Cheatham's Division formed in line of battle at the foot of the ridge west of the point where the Shallow Ford Road crosses it, with Hindman's (Anderson's) Division on its left, both divisions being sufficiently advanced from the ridge to allow Walker's Division to form in their rear as a general reserve to the right wing. Hill's Corps crossed the ridge on the Mission Mills Road.

Gen. Longstreet's wing (left) moved on the direct road from Rossville, and reached the Watkin's House, two miles from Chattanooga, at 11 A. M., and occupied the day in forming its lines from near the foot of Lookout Mountain to the left of Hill's Corps, which had advanced from the foot of Missionary Ridge on the Mission Mills Road.

September 24th, a reconnaissance in force from the Union lines found the Confederates encamped beyond Chattanooga Creek, from the base of Lookout eastward through the Watkin's place to Missionary Ridge, and northward along the base of the ridge to a point beyond the Shallow Ford Road.

September 25th, skirmishers were advanced along Bragg's entire front, to ascertain if the Union army was evacuating.

Upon the Confederates appearing in force on Lookout Mountain, Gen. Rosecrans had retired McCook's Corps on the right to a position in the outskirts of the city, and occupied Moccasin Point, opposite Lookout. The Confederate right established a strong line through Orchard Knob, with its pickets thrown well forward toward Fort Wood, the eastern salient of the Union line.

The Confederate cavalry under Gen. Wheeler was sent north of the Tennessee to operate against the Union lines of supply. These latter were soon confined to the mountain roads over Walden's Ridge and the Cumberlands by the occupation of the heights on the south side of the river by Gen. Longstreet's forces, at a point where they commanded the road along the north bank.

During October, the Union army became very short of rations, and the question of holding the city resolved itself into one of obtaining supplies. It was regarded as impossible for Bragg to carry the Union works.

Early in the month, the Twentieth and Twenty-first Corps were consolidated into the Fourth, Gens. McCook and Crittenden being relieved, and Gen. Gordon Granger being placed in command of the new corps. October 16th, Gen. Grant was assigned to the command of the Union forces in and to be concentrated in the Departments of the Ohio and the Cumberland. He reached Chattanooga on the 23d. On the 19th, Gen. Thomas had succeeded Gen. Rosecrans.

September 30th, the head of Gen. Hooker's command from the Army of the Potomac reached Bridgeport. This was composed of the Eleventh and Twelfth Corps, of two divisions each.

September 23d, the movement of four divisions of Grant's army on the Mississippi toward Chattanooga began at Vicksburg. The head of Gen. Sherman's column reached Lookout Valley, November 18th.

Both the Union and the Confederate armies were reorganized during October, and on the 26th of that month, active operations began on the Union side for re-opening the Tennessee River to Bridgeport.

CHAPTER VIII.

THE CHICKAMAUGA CAMPAIGN SKELETONIZED.

The map which accompanies this chapter affords a rapid, comprehensive, and easy study of the Chickamauga campaign.

It does not take notice of the details of maneuvering or concentration, but represents the respective armies as concentrated and in hand for each of their successive movements.

It shows (1) why Bragg was compelled to retire from Chattanooga to save his communications and await reinforcements; and (2) the attempt of each army thereafter to thrust itself between the other and Chattanooga, in the struggle for the final possession of that city—the objective of Rosecrans' campaign.

September 7, 1863, Gen. Bragg held Chattanooga.

September 7th, Gen. Rosecrans having crossed the Cumberland Mountains, the Tennessee River, and the Raccoon Range south of it, began to cross Lookout Mountain into the rear of Chattanooga. This movement is fully set forth on the map of the theater of campaign. See Chapter II.

The center of the army September 8th was twenty-six miles south of the city, near Stevens' Gap, and the right forty-two miles south of it.

The night of September 7th Bragg withdrew to La Fayette behind Pigeon Mountains, opposite Rosecrans' center, and established his army there September 8th.

Rosecrans, until September 12th, was operating against Bragg in the direction of La Fayette, upon the theory that he was in retreat upon Rome, when, at that date, he was

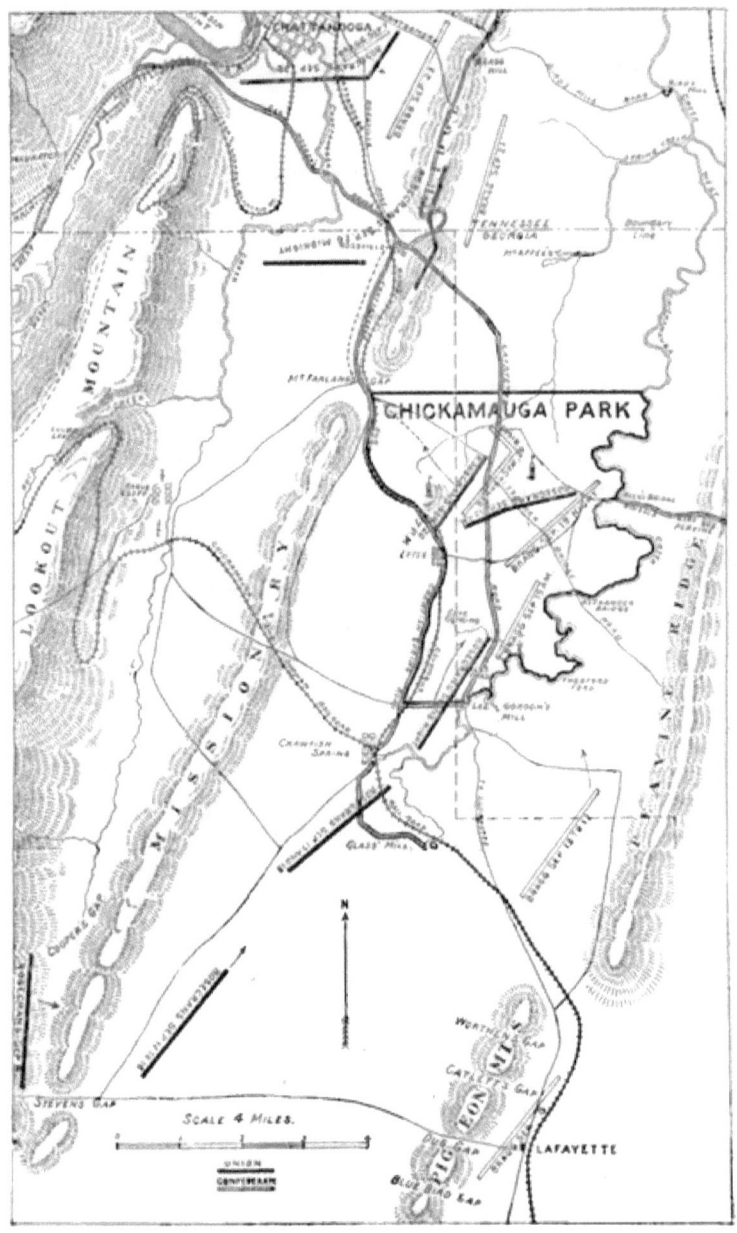

CHICKAMAUGA CAMPAIGN, SKELETONIZED.

found to have been reinforced, and concentrating toward Lee and Gordon's Mill for battle. Rosecrans was obliged to wait several days for McCook's Corps to arrive on his right. On the 17th he moved to Crawfish Springs.

September 17th Bragg had moved northward and was found on Rosecrans' left flank south of Lee and Gordon's Mill.

September 18th, at night, the left of Rosecrans was along the La Fayette Road, a mile north of Lee and Gordon's toward Chattanooga.

September 18th, during the afternoon and night, Bragg crossed the Chickamauga, and formed, facing the La Fayette Road, beyond Rosecrans' left flank, with the purpose of attacking that flank in the morning of the 19th, driving it back on the Union right, and the whole away from Chattanooga, and back into the mountains.

But the same night, September 18th, Rosecrans had moved his right and center several miles to the left of Bragg's new position, and formed at daylight across the La Fayette, or Chattanooga Road, and eastward to the Chickamauga. At 7:30 A. M. his left attacked Forrest's Cavalry Corps, which was near Reed's Bridge, guarding Bragg's right and rear.

September 19th, Bragg's plan of battle being destroyed, he moved to his right, and the first day's battle of Chickamauga followed. At its close Rosecrans was fully between Bragg and Chattanooga.

September 20th the second day's battle of Chickamauga took place, Bragg's plan still being to gain the La Fayette Road beyond Rosecrans'. left flank. At the close of the battle he had succeeded in this, as the map shows.

September 20th, at night, Gen. Thomas moved the army through McFarland's Gap to Rossville, and at midnight formed it across the La Fayette Road again in the gap and on Missionary Ridge to the right and left of it, and across the plain toward Lookout Mountain. A considerable portion of the Union army had been forced off the field early in the day, but nearly all of this was assembled at Rossville.

Throughout the 21st the Army of the Cumberland remained in position there, across Bragg's direct road to Chattanooga, offering battle.

September 21st Bragg moved to his right parallel to Missionary Ridge and beyond Rosecrans' left.

The night of September 21st the Union army marched to Chattanooga. At sunrise of the 22d its lines were established around the city, and Rosecrans was in full possession.

September 22d Bragg crossed Missionary Ridge, and an attack upon Chattanooga was ordered for September 23d. This, however, was not delivered, and an investment of the city was undertaken.

CHAPTER IX.

RE-OPENING OF THE TENNESSEE RIVER—THE BROWN'S FERRY AFFAIR.

In four weeks, Chattanooga had been so strongly fortified as to defy attack. October 13th, the army was receiving three-fourths rations, and upon that day 300,000 full rations arrived. Ten days before, Gen. Wheeler, in his noted raid north of the river, had destroyed nearly 300 wagons, and the fall rains had so softened the roads that the trains could haul but little more than forage enough to last the animals during the trip of sixty miles over the mountains from Bridgeport. The re-opening of the river to the latter point therefore became imperative.

Gen. Rosecrans had been ready to undertake the movement upon Gen. Hooker's arrival at Bridgeport. The latter reached that point October 1st, and the same day was ordered by Gen. Rosecrans to lay his bridges and make immediate preparations to cross the river and move toward Chattanooga. But Gen. Hooker's wagon trains had been turned in at Alexandria when his troops started for the west, under the belief that he could be at once refitted at Nashville. Being without means of supplying his troops, he could not move forward. Gen. Rosecrans repeated his order, October 12th, directing Gen. Hooker to move up to Wauhatchie to assist in opening the river, but, for the same reason, he was still unable to do so.

October 19th, the order was again given by Gen. Rosecrans for the troops at Bridgeport to be ready to move. That day he rode as far as Brown's Ferry with Gen. W. F. Smith, his chief engineer, and Gen. J. J. Reynolds, his chief

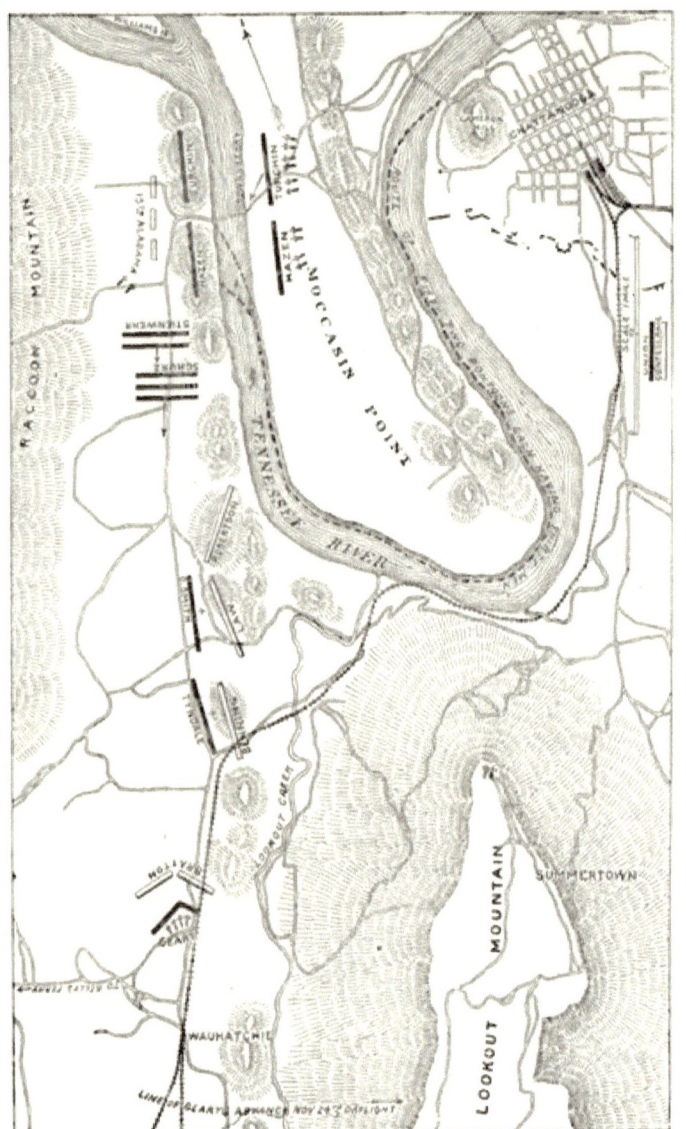

Brown's Ferry Movement—Battle of Wauhatchie.

of staff, making a general examination of the river with respect to selecting a point below Lookout Mountain for throwing the bridges, and a special examination of Brown's Ferry where the bridge was finally thrown. The plan was that of Gen. Rosecrans. The details were left to Gen. Smith.

A glance at the map will show the features of the project. It is but a few miles from Chattanooga across the narrow neck of Moccasin Point to Brown's Ferry. The latter point was on the old stage road to Nashville, and beyond the reach of the Confederate batteries on Lookout. If Gen. Hooker could march from Bridgeport along the south side of the river to that point, boats could ascend to it, or near it, and the wagon haul into the city would then be but six or eight miles. The movement would also open two wagon roads to Bridgeport, one on each side of the river.

Upon reaching his headquarters after his return from reconnoitering Brown's Ferry, Gen. Rosecrans found an order relieving him and putting Gen. Thomas in command, and at daylight he left for the north. The same night, Gen. Thomas directed Gen. Hooker to be ready to obey the order given him in the morning by Gen. Rosecrans. But Gen. Hooker's trains did not reach him till October 25th and 26th. At daylight of the 27th, he crossed to the south side of the river and moved toward Chattanooga in execution of his part of the plan for opening the river.

Gen. Grant had arrived, October 23d. The plans for the movement were explained to him by Gen. Thomas, and approved, and Gen. Smith was directed to execute them and given command of the movement from Chattanooga.

Gen. Rosecrans had selected Brown's Ferry as the point for throwing his bridge. At this place a low ridge ran on the south bank parallel to the river, and the road from the ferry penetrated it through a gorge. This was held by the enemy, and the Confederate pickets along the river bank extended seven miles up stream to the mouth of Chattanooga Creek, and down stream to the bluffs of Raccoon Mountain.

Brown's Ferry, Moccasin Point, Craven House, and Chattanooga from Lookout Mountain. (See page xiii.)

The plan involved simultaneous movements from Chattanooga and Bridgeport. Gen. Thomas' troops were to seize Brown's Ferry; and Gen. Hooker was to cross the river at Bridgeport, march by Whitesides to Wauhatchie and Brown's Ferry, and occupy Lookout Valley.

For the seizure of Brown's Ferry, fifty pontoons with oars were prepared at Chattanooga, each having room for the crew and twenty-five infantry men, and two flat-boats to carry forty and seventy-five men, respectively.

The troops assigned to the expedition were the brigades of Gen. Turchin, of Baird's Division of the Fourteenth Corps, and Gen. Hazen, of Wood's Division of the Fourth Corps. The boat and bridge construction was in charge of Capt. P. V. Fox, of the Michigan Mechanics and Engineers.

Fifteen hundred men were put into the boats at the Chattanooga Landing the night of October 26th, and at 3 A. M. of the 27th, the flotilla of fifty-two boats, with 1,600 men, including the crews, all under the command of Gen. Hazen, and accompanied by Gen. Smith, rowed to the north shore and started down the river. By previous observations of logs floating from the city to Brown's Ferry, the starting was so timed as to reach the latter point at daybreak. The column of boats proceeded without discovery under the shadows of the willows on the north bank along the whole seven miles of the enemy's pickets on the south shore, and, guided by range lights, landed, surprised the pickets at the ferry, and hastily occupied the position and points above it. The boats were then rowed across the river, to which point the remainder of the force, that had not come in the pontoons, had been marched under command of Gen. Turchin. These crossed rapidly and occupied the ridge below the ferry. By daylight, the position was strongly protected by felled timber. The losses in the skirmishing incident to seizing the position were 6 killed, 23 wounded, and 9 missing. The picketing of the river next below Lookout, and the station at Brown's Ferry, was in charge of the Fourth and Fifteenth Alabama

Regiments, of Law's Brigade, Hood's Division, Longstreet's Corps. After October 23d, this brigade was the only Confederate force west of Lookout Mountain. Withdrawing their pickets, these regiments retired to Lookout Creek, where they were joined by the rest of the brigade. In the affair at the ferry, Col. W. C. Oates, of the Fifteenth Alabama, was severely wounded. Gen. Hooker left Bridgeport at daylight of the 27th of October, and encamped at Whitesides. The next afternoon, at 3 o'clock, his head of column reached Wauhatchie, where Geary's Division of the Twelfth Corps went into camp, at the junction of the Kelly's Ferry Road; while the Eleventh Corps marched on, reaching Brown's Ferry at 5 o'clock.

The Union forces having fully occupied Lookout Valley, thus commanding the river to Brown's Ferry and the wagon roads to Chattanooga on both banks of the river, had opened safe and speedy lines of supplies. The question of holding these communications was decided in their favor by the battle of Wauhatchie, which occurred the succeeding night.

CHAPTER X.

RE-OPENING OF THE TENNESSEE RIVER—BATTLE OF WAUHATCHIE.*

At 3 P. M. on the 28th of October, the head of Gen. Hooker's column arrived from Bridgeport at Wauhatchie Station, in Lookout Valley. Gen. Steinwehr's Division of the Eleventh Corps led, followed by Gen. Schurz's Division, with Gen. O. O. Howard in command of the corps. This force continued to Brown's Ferry, where, at 5 P. M., it united with the troops from Chattanooga, which had occupied that point the day before. Upon reaching the junction of the road over the point of Lookout to Chattanooga with the road to Brown's Ferry, the head of the column was fired upon from the right near the railroad bridge by troops of Law's Brigade, which had retired from Brown's Ferry the preceding day. This attack was repulsed, and the Confederate troops withdrew across Lookout Creek to the foot of Lookout Mountain.

Two brigades of Gen. Geary's Division of the Twelfth Corps reached Wauhatchie at 4:30 P. M., and took position at the Kelly's Ford Road. This was three miles from Gen. Schurz's camp, near Brown's Ferry. Gen. Geary directed his troops to bivouac on their arms, with their cartridge boxes on. Shortly after midnight, his lines were suddenly and heavily assaulted by Jenkins' Brigade of Hood's Division.

Gen. Longstreet was in command of the left of the Confederate line in Chattanooga Valley east of the mountain, with Law's Brigade of Hood's Division in Lookout Valley west of it. The chief duty of this brigade was to picket the river to its passage through the Raccoon Range, six miles

---

* See map, page 100.

below Brown's Ferry. From this lower point, it had been able to prevent the Union army from using the river road to Bridgeport, on the north bank, and thus forced it to bring its supplies by mountain roads.

The advance of Gen. Hooker's forces from Shellmound was reported to Gen. Longstreet in the afternoon of the 27th, but not credited by Gen. Bragg. While the latter was with Longstreet on the mountain, during the afternoon of the 28th, for the purpose of examining the position of the Union forces at Brown's Ferry, with a view to a movement by Gen. Longstreet to dislodge them, the head of Gen. Hooker's column came in view beyond Wauhatchie, and marched in plain sight of these generals to a junction with the forces at Brown's Ferry. In an hour, they saw Gen. Geary's troops arrive at Wauhatchie, and halt there three miles in rear of the rest of the column. It was immediately decided to make a night attack on them, and, if this succeeded, to turn the attacking force toward Brown's Ferry, attempt to carrry that position, and force those holding it over the river. It was necessary that the entire movement should be completed during the night, since the Union batteries at Moccasin Point so swept the north slopes of the mountain as to make it impossible for a column to cross it during daylight.

Gen. Jenkins, commanding Hood's Division, was sent for by Gen. Longstreet, and reached the summit in time to closely observe the Union positions before dark. He was ordered to concentrate at the foot of the mountain three brigades of his division which were east of it, and be ready to cross the moment it was dark enough to conceal his troops from the Moccasin Point batteries. Gen. Law's Brigade was ordered to move forward as soon as it was dusk, from the lower bridge over Lookout Creek near its mouth, and occupy the ridge near the junction of the road from the creek with the road to Brown's Ferry. This ridge commanded the latter.

Upon the arrival of the three brigades from the east side

of the mountain, Gen. Jenkins sent Robertson's Brigade to the support of Law's Brigade that had reached the ridge to which it was ordered. Gen. Robertson's regiments were disposed on the right and left of Law's, and also guarded the bridge and picketed a line to the mouth of Lookout Creek.

Jenkins' Brigade of six regiments, under command of Col. Bratton, was ordered to advance on the force at Wauhatchie, while Benning's Brigade was held on the left of Law's position, ready to reinforce Bratton.

Col. Bratton attacked Gen. Geary's lines shortly after midnight, finding them fully formed, although he had advanced without skirmishers. Gen. Geary's outposts had given timely warning, and the troops had bivouacked in line with their accouterments on. The fighting continued at close quarters for three hours, when the Confederates withdrew.

Eight regiments of Gen. Geary's command had not come up, leaving six and a battery available for action. Two held an important position, but were engaged only for a few minutes. Gen. Geary's loss was 34 killed, 174 wounded, 8 missing; total, 216. The loss in Col. Bratton's attacking brigade of six regiments was 31 killed, 286 wounded, 39 missing; total, 356.

When the firing opened on Geary's line, Gen. Howard ordered Gen. Schurz's Division forward, with directions to push its leading brigade as rapidly as possible to Geary. Smith's Brigade of Steinwehr's Division, when passing the position occupied in the afternoon by Law's Brigade, was fired upon from its wooded crest, which was parallel to the road. Smith at once assaulted it, under a heavy fire from the summit, and carried it. Tyndale's Brigade of Schurz's Division soon after came under a sharp fire from a more southern crest overlooking the road on which it was proceeding toward Geary, and, after a sharp engagement, carried the hill by a charge. The enemy withdrew across Lookout Creek, and Gen. Jenkins regained his camps on the east side of the mountain before daylight. As a result of these operations, the Confederates abandoned Lookout Valley west of the creek, and thenceforth the Union army at Chattanooga had uninterrupted communication, by way of Brown's Ferry, with Bridgeport and Stevenson, both by the river and the wagon roads on each bank.

A season of great activity followed on the part of Gen. Grant's forces, to prepare for offensive operations. Supplies of all kinds, clothing, ammunition, and heavy guns were rapidly brought forward, and the day of attack finally depended upon the arrival of Gen. Sherman's reinforcements.

CHAPTER XI.

BATTLE OF CHATTANOOGA—ORCHARD KNOB—LOOKOUT MOUN-
TAIN—MISSIONARY RIDGE.

Gen. Grant's orders for attacking Bragg's position on Missionary Ridge were sent to Gen. Thomas, Wednesday, November 18, directing the movement to begin Saturday, the 21st, at daylight. On account of the impossibility of Gen. Sherman's troops arriving in time, the attack was first postponed until Sunday, then until Tuesday morning, when, the same conditions still existing, it was delayed until the next day. The battle opened on Wednesday afternoon, November 23d, by a movement of Gen. Thomas against Orchard Knob, not contemplated in the original order.

Gen. Grant's order of battle was as follows:

HEADQUARTERS MILITARY DIVISION OF THE MISSISSIPPI,
CHATTANOOGA, TENN., *November* 18, 1863.

Major-General Geo. H. Thomas,
Commanding Department and Army of the Cumberland.

GENERAL.—All preparations should be made for attacking the enemy's position on Missionary Ridge by Saturday morning at daylight. Not being provided with a map giving names of roads, spurs of the mountain, and other places, such definite instructions can not be given as might be desirable. However, the general plan, you understand, is for Sherman, with his force brought with him, strengthened by a division from your command, to effect a crossing of the Tennessee River just below the mouth of the Chickamauga; his crossing to be protected by artillery from the heights on the north bank of the river (to be located by your chief of

CHATTANOOGA—LOOKOUT MOUNTAIN—MISSIONARY RIDGE.

artillery), and to carry the heights from the northern extremity to about the railroad tunnel, before the enemy can concentrate a force against him.

You will co-operate with Sherman. The troops in Chattanooga Valley should be well concentrated on your left flank, leaving only the necessary force to defend fortifications on the right and center, and a movable column of one division in readiness to move wherever ordered. This division should show itself as threateningly as possible, on the most practicable line for making an attack up the valley. Your effort will then be to form a junction with Sherman, making your advance well toward the north end of Missionary Ridge, and moving as near simultaneously with him as possible. The junction once formed and the ridge carried, communications will be at once established between the two armies, by roads on the south bank of the river. Further movements will then depend on those of the enemy.

Lookout Valley, I think, will be easily held by Geary's Division and what troops you may still have there belonging to the old Army of the Cumberland. Howard's Corps can then be held in readiness to act either with you at Chattanooga, or with Sherman. It should be marched on Friday night to a position on the north side of the river, not lower down than the first pontoon bridge, and there held in readiness for such orders as may become necessary.

All the troops will be provided with two days' cooked rations in their haversacks, and one hundred rounds of ammunition on the person of each infantry soldier.

Special care should be taken by all officers to see that ammunition is not wasted, or unnecessarily fired away. You will call on the engineering department for such preparations as you may deem necessary for crossing your infantry and artillery over Citico Creek.

I am, General, very respectfully, your obedient servant,

U. S. GRANT,
Major-General U. S. Volunteers, Commanding.

While General Thomas immediately made all preparations in accordance with this plan, it was materially changed in its execution at each succeeding stage of the battle.

At the opening of the engagement which continued through the 23d, 24th, and 25th of November, the Union forces were disposed as follows:

The divisions of Wood, Baird, Sheridan, and Johnson, of the Army of the Cumberland, held the fortifications of Chattanooga, while Jeff. C. Davis' Division, of the same army, had been sent over the river to cover the point of crossing for Sherman's army three miles above.

The Eleventh Corps of Hooker's command had been brought into the city on the 22d, and camped on the right of Fort Wood.

During the 23d, three divisions of Gen. Sherman's troops, namely, Morgan L. Smith's, Ewing's, and John E. Smith's, which had marched from Bridgeport and Shellmound and crossed the river at Brown's Ferry, reached their destination near the mouth of North Chickamauga ready for crossing during the night to a point below the north end of Missionary Ridge.

Gen. Hooker, on the night of the 23d, had with him, in Lookout Valley, Geary's Division of the Twelfth Corps, Cruft's Division of the Fourth Corps, and Osterhaus' Division of Sherman's army. The latter had not been able to join Gen. Sherman, owing to the breaking of the bridge at Brown's Ferry.

Forty guns had been placed in position on the north bank by Gen. Brannan, Gen. Thomas' Chief of Artillery, to assist in covering Gen. Sherman's crossing, and the only cavalry with the Army of the Cumberland (Long's Brigade) was sent to protect Sherman's left flank during the crossing, and to co-operate with him after he should reach the south side.

The Confederate forces, on the morning of November 23d, were thus disposed:

Three divisions of Hardee's Corps held Lookout Mountain and the line of works from its eastern base to Chattanooga Creek. The top of the mountain was occupied by Stevenson's Division, the northern and western slopes by Cheatham's Division, and the line eastward to Chattanooga Creek by Walker's Division.

Three divisions of Breckinridge's Corps held the line of earthworks from Chattanooga Creek to a point near the western foot of Missionary Ridge, in the vicinity of the Shallow Ford Road (now McCallie Avenue). The left of Stewart's Division rested on Chattanooga Creek, Bate's Division was on Stewart's right, and Hindman's (Patton Anderson), on the right of Bate, formed the right of the Confederate line. Missionary Ridge was not occupied in force, the Confederate camps being at the base of it, and stretching across the plain to Lookout.

Longstreet's Corps, consisting of McLaw's and Hood's Divisions, had been sent to Knoxville, November 4th. Buckner's Division of Breckinridge's Corps, and Cleburne's of Hardee's Corps, had started for Knoxville on the 22d.

The Confederates had no cavalry in the battle.

First Day's Operations—Advance on Orchard Knob.

Gens. Grant and Thomas, during the delays attending Gen. Sherman's movements, had been much concerned lest their purposes should become known to Gen. Bragg. On the night of the 22d, a deserter came in, who declared that the Confederates were withdrawing. On the 23d, Gen. Thomas was directed to test this statement by driving in the enemy's pickets, and ascertaining whether he still held his camps in the valley. A reconnoissance in force was at once organized, and five divisions were posted to participate if developments made it necessary. The divisions of Wood and Sheridan of the Fourth Corps (Granger's) were deployed soon after noon on the slope east of Fort Wood. Schurz's and Steinwehr's Divisions of the Eleventh Corps (Howard's) were placed to the left and rear of this line, and Baird's

Division of the Fourteenth Corps (Palmer's) to its right and rear.

Wood's Division, upon the order to advance being given, went forward with great rapidity, and soon reached and, after sharp fighting, occupied Orchard Knob. Sheridan's Division pushed forward to the low elevations to the right and rear of the knob. The Eleventh Corps advanced to Citico Creek. The movement developed the fact that the Confederates still occupied their lines in force. The important position thus gained was strengthened and held.

Orchard Knob and the low ranges south of it were formidable outposts of the Confederate line in front of Missionary Ridge, and were the strong points of their position in the plain. The troops defending them were mainly from Anderson's Division. They continued fighting till overwhelmed.

The advance of the Union forces, and the results of the day's operations, led to several changes in the disposition of the Confederate forces. Gen. Cleburne, who was at Chickamauga station attending to the transportation to Knoxville of his own and Buckner's (Bushrod Johnson's) Divisions, was ordered to return in haste to Missionary Ridge, and to order back Johnson's Division, which had started, but halted at Charleston. Cleburne returned with his division and Reynolds' Brigade of Johnson's Division. The latter was sent into the trenches at the western foot of Missionary Ridge, and remained there until the general assault upon the ridge by the Army of the Cumberland on the afternoon of November 25th.

Cleburne's Division at daybreak of the 24th began the construction of earthworks along the crest of the ridge from Bragg's Headquarters to the crossing of the Shallow Ford Road (McCallie Avenue).

On the 23d, Marcus J. Wright's Brigade of Cheatham's Division, stationed at Charleston, was also ordered to return by the first train, guard the Shallow Ford and railroad bridges over the Chickamauga, and proceed to the mouth of that

Orchard Knob—Headquarters of Grant and Thomas, November 25. (See page xiv.)

stream to resist any attempted crossing of the Tennessee. Gen. Wright reached the lower railroad bridge over the Chickamauga, and was there attacked from the opposite side of the creek by forces from Gen. Sherman's command, which had crossed the Tennessee before Wright's arrival.

On the evening of the 23d, Walker's Division was withdrawn from the line between the eastern base of Lookout Mountain and Chattanooga Creek, and sent to the extreme right of Bragg's line, where it was posted on Missionary Ridge with its right resting about a mile and a quarter from the north end of the ridge. The position vacated by Walker's Division was occupied by Jackson's Brigade of Cheatham's Division and Cumming's Brigade of Stevenson's Division, which were brought down from Lookout. Walker's was the first Confederate division to occupy the ridge in the movements attending the battle.

Second Day's Operations—Battle of Lookout Mountain.

On the 22d, Gen. Thomas urged Gen. Grant to allow Gen. Hooker to make a demonstration against Lookout Mountain with his own troops, and the two divisions of Gen. Sherman's which had been prevented from crossing the river by the breaking of the bridge at Brown's Ferry. Gen. Grant consented, so far as to agree that Hooker might make a demonstration with his own, and such troops as might be on his side of the river at the time Gen. Sherman should reach the position assigned him. The evening of the 23d, Gen. Sherman was ready to cross the river at North Chickamauga with three of his divisions, the fourth, Osterhaus', being still detained in Lookout Valley by the broken bridge.

At 3:15 o'clock A. M. of the 24th, it was decided that there was no chance for Osterhaus to cross in time to join Gen. Sherman's movement, and Gen. Hooker's orders for the attack on the mountain were issued.

His force for the demonstration consisted of Geary's Division of the Twelfth Corps, Cruft's (two brigades) of the

Fourth, which had marched from Shellmound and Whitesides during the 23d, Osterhaus' (two brigades) of the Fifteenth, Battery K, First Ohio, and I, First New York of the Eleventh Corps, part of the Second Kentucky Cavalry, and Company K, Fifteenth Illinois Cavalry. Three regiments from each of Cruft's Brigades of nine regiments each were left at Shellmound and Whitesides, and Geary's picket force from Lookout Creek to Raccoon Mountain was left in position. Gen. Hooker's aggregate force for the attack was 9,681.

The Confederate force, available to oppose him, consisted of Walthall's, Jackson's, and Moore's Brigades of Cheatham's Division, and Pettus', Brown's, and Cummings' of Stevenson's Division.

Walthall's Brigade was posted in a line of rough works on the west slope of the mountain at the same elevation as the Craven House plateau, overlooking Lookout Valley. The left of his line was protected by slashed timber, and rested about 1,500 feet south of the north point of the palisades. Nearly one-third of the brigade was on picket duty in Lookout Valley along a line about a mile in extent, and most of this force was captured.

Moore's Brigade was on the eastern slope of the mountain east of and below the Craven House.

Pettus' and Brown's Brigades were on the top of the mountain, the latter guarding various trails on the western edge of the summit from the north point to Nickajack trace ten miles south of it. Jackson's and Cummings' Brigades were at the foot of the eastern slope.

Gen. Hooker's movement began at daylight, November 24th. Gen. Geary's Division, followed by Whitaker's Brigade of Cruft's Division, taking the road which turns down toward Lookout Creek just south of Wauhatchie Station, crossed that stream at Light's Mill without opposition. Cobham's Brigade, followed by Ireland's, marched by the flank directly up the mountain till the head of the column reached

HOOKER'S BATTLE FIELD, ON THE WEST SLOPE OF LOOKOUT MOUNTAIN. (See page xiv.)

the palisades. The line then faced toward the north point of the mountain. Candy's Brigade formed on its left slightly echeloned to the rear, and Whitaker, at starting, formed the reserve. After marching nearly a mile and a half, Geary struck the left flank of Walthall's works. Meantime, Osterhaus' Division, followed by Grose's Brigade of Cruft's Division, had crossed Lookout Creek about a half mile above the railroad bridge, and advanced with Williamson's Brigade on the right and Woods' on its left. Four regiments of Grose's troops were on the right of Williamson, and two on the left of Woods'. The left of this line followed the road to Chattanooga, along the crest of the river bluffs, while the right reached to the vicinity of the Craven House. Geary's lines conforming to the slope, moved upon the flank of Walthall's works, passed along their entire length, and swung around upon the Craven House plateau, there uniting with Osterhaus' line. Walthall's Brigade, which fought stubbornly, and unassisted, except by sharpshooters and some artillery firing from the summit, which, on account of the fog, was of little consequence, was forced about four hundred yards east of the Craven House. His line had at no time reached below Craven's and at his final stand extended from the road leading east from Craven's to the foot of the palisades. Here, after the Union advance had been checked, it was relieved by Pettus' Brigade, and retired to procure ammunition. It returned at once to Pettus' line, which was extended 150 yards down the mountain, to connect with the left of Moore's Brigade. This line was then held covering the Summertown Road, by which, during the night, the entire Confederate force was withdrawn from the mountain.

During the action, the Union batteries upon Moccasin Point were in active play upon the mountain. A portion of Gen. Brown's Brigade upon the summit was busy during the day as sharpshooters and in rolling rocks upon the plateau below. Two Napoleon guns upon the extreme point shelled the Union forces after they reached the Craven House. The day was foggy and misty throughout, and the firing from the summit was of necessity inaccurate.

Just before night Carlin's Brigade of Johnson's Division crossed Chattanooga Creek near its mouth, pushed up the mountain to the Craven House, carrying supplies of ammunition, and relieved the right of Geary's line next to the palisades. Picket firing continued throughout the night. In the morning it was found that the enemy had abandoned the mountain, the object of the resistance during the night having been to cover the Summertown Road as the line of retreat.

Sherman's Crossing.

While Gen. Hooker was organizing to attack Lookout Mountain, at daylight of the 24th, Gen. Sherman's forces were crossing the Tennessee from the mouth of North Chickamauga, six miles above Chattanooga

One hundred and sixteen boats with oarsmen, and twenty-five additional boats ready to follow, were prepared at North Chickamauga. The landing place selected was two miles and a half below, about the mouth of the South Chickamauga. At midnight of the 23d the boats were filled by Giles A. Smith's Brigade of Morgan L. Smith's Division and floated down and across to a point above the mouth of the latter stream. A landing was effected, and all the enemy's pickets but one captured. The boats then returned for the rest of this division, which was landed below the mouth of the South Chickamauga. The division of John E. Smith followed, and at daylight 8,000 men were over the river and in line near it, west of and facing Tunnel Hill. Ewing's Division and the artillery and horses for the generals and staff were next ferried over in the steamer Dunbar, under the direction of Gen. James H. Wilson, the assistant of Gen. W. F. Smith, Chief Engineer, who had charge of all preparations for the crossing, and the execution of the movement. At 12:30 P. M. the bridge was completed. Gen. Sherman was the first to cross. He was met on the south shore by Gen.

Howard of the Eleventh Corps, who had ridden unmolested from Chattanooga with his escort accompanied by three regiments of infantry. Gen. Jeff. C. Davis' Division of the Army of the Cumberland, which, with forty pieces of artillery posted by Gen. Brannan, Chief of Artillery to Gen. Thomas, had covered the construction of the bridge and the crossing, came over last.

At 1 o'clock the advance toward Missionary Ridge began. This had been designed to carry the north end of the Ridge to the tunnel before the enemy could concentrate for its defense. Morgan L. Smith's Division held the left of the line, John E. Smith's the center, and Ewing's the right rear. Davis' Division followed as a reserve to the whole.

At the time this movement began the north end of Missionary Ridge was not occupied by the Confederates. The nearest force of the enemy was the right of Walker's Division then resting on the crest of the ridge, a mile and a quarter south of its northern extremity.

Because of the want of sufficient reconnoisance, and the misty atmosphere, the march, instead of being directed against the north end of Missionary Ridge, was toward the detached range of hills next north and west of its real extremity. These detached hills were occupied without resistance at 4 P. M. Just as their summits were reached, Smith's Brigade of Cleburne's Division appeared at their foot, but, after brief skirmishing, withdrew to the main ridge. Gen. Sherman fortified the crests which he had gained, and arranged his lines in position for the night. Lightburn's Brigade of Morgan L. Smith's Division held the left of the line on the crest; Alexander's, of John E. Smith's Division, the center; and Cockerill's, of Ewing's Division, the right. Giles A. Smith's Brigade of Morgan L. Smith's Division, closed the gap on the left of Lightburn to the Chickamauga. Ewing's remaining brigades extended Cockerill's line into the valley, and two brigades of John E. Smith's Division were placed at the foot of the ridge back of the center of the line. Jeff. C. Davis' Division was posted in column of brigades, one in contact with Sherman's reserve, one at the river landing, and one half way between the other two.

The movement on the Confederate side to resist Sherman's advance began at 2 P. M. of the 24th. During the forenoon, Polk's Brigade of Cleburne's Division, with Semple's Battery, had been sent to guard the East Tennessee Railroad Bridge over the Chickamauga. Gen. Cleburne was then engaged in erecting defenses along the ridge from the crossing of the Shallow Ford Road (McCallie Avenue) to Bragg's Headquarters. At 2 o'clock, he was ordered to proceed with his remaining three brigades to Tunnel Hill, which point he reached at 2:30 P. M. He occupied the north end of Missionary Ridge, and sent Smith's Brigade to take position on the detached range beyond. This was found to be in possession of Sherman's advance, and, in accordance with orders, Smith returned to the main ridge and took position from the north point (Moon House) to Tunnel Hill (Trueblood House).

Confederate Movements on the Night of the 24th.

As a result of the capture of Lookout Mountain by Gen. Hooker's forces, and Gen. Sherman's lodgment on the heights near Missionary Ridge, Gen. Bragg, during the night of the 24th, abandoned Lookout and his lines in the valley in front of Chattanooga, and retired to Missionary Ridge. Stevenson's Division proceeded from Lookout to Tunnel Hill, reaching the left of Cleburne's position there about 9 o'clock of the 25th.

Cheatham's Division followed, and took position on the left of Walker's Division, which had been established on the ridge during the night of the 23d with its right about three-quarters of a mile south of the tunnel.

Stewart's Division fell back to the crest and occupied it with an attenuated line from Rossville Gap to near Bragg's

Headquarters. Bate's Division took position next north of Stewart's, and Patton Anderson joined Cheatham's left, leaving quite a gap on Bate's right. There were no changes in the positions of the Union forces during the night of the 24th.

Operations of November 25th—Battle of Missionary Ridge.
The closing day's battle was opened November 25th by Gen. Sherman on the Union left, about Tunnel Hill. Lightburn's Brigade on the left, Alexander's in the center, and Cockerill's on the right, were kept in position on the crests of the detached hills next north and west of the point of Missionary Ridge which Gen. Sherman had occupied the day before. Four guns of Callender's Battery were with Cockerill, two of Dillon's with Alexander, and Wood's Battery with Lightburn. These guns played on Cleburne's position at Tunnel Hill throughout the action.

Soon after sunrise, Corse's Brigade of Loomis' Division moved down from the heights, under fire from Cleburne's lines, into the ravine under the north point of Missionary Ridge, and assaulted that position. Corse was supported by Giles A. Smith's Brigade of Morgan L. Smith's Division on the left, operating along the eastern base of the ridge, and by Loomis' Brigade of Ewing's Division on the right, along the western slope. The brigades of Matthies and Raum of John E. Smith's Division were placed in support of Loomis. Gen. Lightburn also assisted Giles A. Smith with about half of his brigade.

Corse, supported by the Thirtieth Ohio from Lightburn, carried the point of the Ridge (now the Moon Place), and from this ground assaulted Cleburne's central position to the south of and commanding it. The effort to carry this position, which was held by Smith's Brigade of Cleburne's Division, was persistent until about 3 P. M., but failed. Gen. Corse was wounded about 10 o'clock near Smith's lines, his troops having charged to within fifty paces of Swett's Bat-

tery, on the Trueblood Knoll.   Col. C. C. Walcutt succeeded Corse.   About 12:30, Loomis' Brigade advanced toward the railroad, placing its left on the Tunnel Hill Road, in the vicinity of the Glass House.   The enemy was driven from the latter by Loomis' skirmishers, but returned later and burned it.   The enemy threatening Loomis' left by descending on the Tunnel Hill Road, two regiments of Bushbeck's Brigade of the Eleventh Corps, the Twenty-seventh and Seventy-third Pennsylvania, were ordered forward upon Loomis' left, the Seventy-third holding position at Glass' House, and the Twenty-seventh assaulting Tunnel Hill to the left of that position.   Bushbeck's Brigade had been left with Gen. Sherman the day before by Gen. Howard, and placed on the right of Gen. Sherman's line.

Early on the morning of the 25th Gen. Howard's remaining troops were ordered to Gen. Sherman.   Orland Smith's Brigade of Steinwehr's Division first took position to the right of Bushbeck's Brigade facing the Ridge, and, later, moved with Schurz's Division to the valley of the Chickamauga where the entire force was posted upon Sherman's extreme left and rear.   With the exception of Bushbeck's Brigade the troops of the Eleventh Corps were not engaged during the day.   Early in the forenoon Gen. Baird's Division of the Fourteenth Corps was ordered to proceed to Gen. Sherman.   Upon reaching Tunnel Hill he was informed that there was no room for him, and he returned to the center.

The enemy appearing in force, coming down the Tunnel Hill road upon the left and front of Loomis' Brigade, Matthies' Brigade was ordered forward and repulsed this attack. Matthies then assaulted Tunnel Hill to the right of Corse's Brigade, and, in conjunction with it, about 1 P. M. gained the crest just north of the present Trueblood House and within a short distance of the battery stationed at that point.   In this position it was supported by Raum's Brigade, but both were soon compelled to retire in haste by the attack from the crest, and the sudden appearance of the enemy in force on their right flank, issuing from the gorge of the tunnel and impetuously attacking with both artillery and infantry. Both Matthies and Raum were wounded. The assault was desperate for over two hours. A similar attack followed on the right flank and the front of Corse's Brigade, now commanded by Col. C. C. Walcutt, which still occupied the north point of the Ridge, and, later, it also retired. Giles A. Smith's Brigade held position during the day at Corse's right on the eastern slope of the Ridge, the Thirtieth and Thirty-seventh Ohio Regiments from Lightburn's Brigade gaining position in front of this force and toward the crest of the Ridge, and holding it till late in the afternoon. Gen. Jeff. C. Davis' Division of the Fourteenth Corps, which covered Gen. Sherman's crossing, followed his column and was held as a reserve force throughout the action, no portion of it being engaged except Battery I, Second Illinois Artillery, which moved with Gen. Ewing's troops. Between 4 and 5 o'clock Gen. Sherman's forces were withdrawn from their advanced positions.

The Confederate Defense of Tunnel Hill.

The forces confronting Gen. Sherman were Smith's, Govan's, and Lowrey's Brigades of Cleburne's Division, Brown's and Cummings' Brigades of Stevenson's Division, and Maney's Brigade of Walker's Division.

Polk's Brigade of Cleburne's Division, Lewis' of Bate's Division, and Wright's of Cheatham's Division, were posted to guard the railroad bridges over the Chickamauga upon Cleburne's right. The Confederate right wing was commanded by Lieut.-Gen. Hardee.

Gen. Cleburne's forces arrived at Tunnel Hill at 2:30 o'clock November 24th. Smith's Brigade was sent forward to occupy the detached hills to the north and west of Missionary Ridge, but found them in possession of Gen. Sherman's advance, and withdrew to Tunnel Hill, Gen. Cleburne's forces taking position on the Ridge from the Tunnel to its extreme north point, throwing up entrenchments about the latter. Govan's

Brigade was placed on the spur jutting out eastward from the Tunnel. There was no engagement during the afternoon.

At dark, Gen. Cleburne, hearing that Hooker had broken the Confederate lines on Lookout, and supposing that would decide Gen. Bragg to fall back from Missionary Ridge, since both flanks of the Confederate army were then exposed, sent his artillery and ordnance stores across the Chickamauga. At midnight he was informed that Missionary Ridge was to be held. He therefore ordered his artillery to return at daylight, brought up intrenching tools, and at that hour disposed his forces for battle. He drew back the right of Smith's Brigade from the rifle-pits at the extreme north point of the Ridge to the high knoll a few hundred yards south, now the grounds of the Trueblood House, leaving skirmishers in the pits. The Fifth, Tenth, and Fifteenth Texas, consolidated, under the command of Col. Roger Q. Mills, formed under the crest facing west, with their left extended toward the Tunnel and their right just north of the Trueblood House. Swett's Battery of four Napoleons was placed on the knoll so as to sweep the crest to its north point. The rest of Smith's Brigade, consisting of the Seventh Texas, Col. H. B. Granbury, and the Seventeenth, Eighteenth, Twenty-fourth, and Twenty-fifth dismounted Texas Cavalry, consolidated, Maj. W. A. Taylor commanding, was turned around the Trueblood Knoll to the right, and extended down the hill to the east. The right of Govan's Brigade was about two hundred yards in rear of Smith's right and nearly at right angles to his north front. Douglas' Battery was placed on this line. Lowrey's Brigade was on the advanced spur east of the north point of the Ridge with its left about two hundred yards in front of Govan's right. Calvert's Battery (Key's) was placed directly over the Tunnel. As soon as the rising mist revealed the Confederate position, Sherman's batteries on the detached hills opened fire, and the working parties which were throwing up earthworks around the knoll at Tunnel Hill were obliged to abandon their undertaking. Before the first assault on the position by Gen. Sherman, Gen. Cleburne was put in command of the forces from the Tunnel northward.

Brown's Brigade of Stevenson's Division arrived at the Tunnel from Lookout Mountain soon after sunrise, and was placed in position between the Tunnel and the left of Smith's Brigade. Cumming's Brigade of the same division followed, and formed on the left of Brown about 9:30 A. M., its right resting at the Tunnel. Maney's Brigade of Walker's Division moved up about 2 o'clock from its position three-quarters of a mile south of the Tunnel, and was placed in rear of Smith's Brigade at Tunnel Hill, and with Cumming's Brigade took part at that point in the repulse of the final Union attack. Pettus' Brigade was also engaged.

The brunt of the day's battle was borne by Smith's (Texas) Brigade, commanded, after the wounding of Smith, by Col. Roger Q. Mills; the Second, Fifteenth, and Twenty-fourth Arkansas consolidated of Govan's Brigade, and Swett's and Calvert's (Key's) Batteries. Gen. Cleburne denominated the engagement of the rest of his division as "heavy skirmishing." Brown's Brigade was engaged throughout the day in hot skirmishing between Smith's left and the tunnel. Portions of Cummings' Brigade participated in the fighting at the foot of the ridge about the Glass House, and took part with Maney's Brigade in the final charge from Tunnel Hill upon the forces which had gained the crest from the northern and western bases of the Ridge.

An hour before sunset, Brown's Brigade, followed soon after by Cummings' and Maney's, was sent in haste to report to Gen. Cheatham, some miles south of the Tunnel, at which point the troops of his division were engaged with the northward advance of Baird's Division of the Army of the Cumberland upon the crest of the Ridge. Brown reached Cheatham and formed on the left of Walthall's Brigade, which was then across the Ridge. The movement of Baird was checked at dusk mainly by Walthall's Brigade of Cheatham's

Division. The Confederate right wing, consisting of Cheatham's, Walker's, Stevenson's, and Cleburne's Divisions, withdrew in order with their material across the Chickamauga.

Confederate Withdrawal from Lookout—Hooker's Advance through Rossville Gap.

The Confederates held the slope of Lookout Mountain about four hundred yards east of the Craven House until 2 A. M., covering the Summertown Road, while the troops on the summit, with such stores as could be moved, were withdrawn. The Eighteenth and Twenty-sixth Tennessee consolidated withdrew by the McCullough Road. Walthall's and Pettus' Brigades held the line on which they had fought until 11 P. M., when they were relieved by Clayton's Brigade of Stewart's Division, commanded by Col. J. T. Holtzclaw. This brigade, with Moore's extending down the mountain to its right and rear, held their lines until 2 A. M., when they withdrew and followed the remainder of the troops which had held Lookout to Missionary Ridge.

The Confederate abandonment of the mountain was discovered at daylight. Shortly before that hour, Gen. Geary had ordered small reconnoitering parties to try to scale the cliffs and ascertain if the enemy was still on the mountain. Volunteers for this work being called for by Gen. Whitaker from the Eighth Kentucky, Col. Sidney M. Barnes, the following responded, scaled the palisades a short distance back from the point, and at sunrise unfurled their regimental colors on the point in the sight of both armies: Capt. John Wilson, Company C, Sergt. H. H. Davis and Private William Witt Company A, Sergts. Joseph Wagers and James G. Wood, of Company B, and Private Joel Bradley, of Company I. The Eighth Kentucky and Ninety-sixth Illinois, Col. Champion, followed to the summit, and, advancing along the top to Summertown, ascertained that the enemy had evacuated the mountain. Gen. Hooker reported a loss in the battle of

CRAVEN HOUSE, LOOKOUT MOUNTAIN—WALTHALL'S HEADQUARTERS. (See page xviii.)

65 killed and 377 wounded, 230 prisoners, two flags captured, and 130 Confederate dead left on the field.

At 10 A. M. of the 25th, Gen. Hooker's column started from the mountain and was directed against the Confederate left at Rossville. Osterhaus' Division led, followed by Cruft and Geary in the order named. The column was delayed about three hours a mile west of Rossville by the destruction of the bridge over Chattanooga Creek.. As soon as stringers were laid, the Twenty-seventh Missouri, Col. Thomas Curly, crossed, pressed forward as skirmishers into Rossville Gap, and developed the enemy's position, which was held by a portion of Clayton's Brigade of Stewart's Division with a section of artillery. Wood's Brigade of Osterhaus' Division formed on the right of the road through the gap, and Williamson's Brigade on the left with two regiments observing the west slope of Missionary Ridge. As soon as the bridge was completed so that the column could close up, Osterhaus pressed through the gap to a road running parallel to the Ridge, and about 1,000 yards from its eastern base, upon which he turned his column northward. After proceeding a short distance, he directed his two brigades in echelon toward the crest of Missionary Ridge, reaching the summit about a mile north of Rossville Gap.

Cruft followed Osterhaus into the gap until his center was opposite the south point of Missionary Ridge, where, facing to the left, he assaulted and carried it, moved northward along the crest and joined Osterhaus' Division, which had reached it from the eastern face. Geary's Division turned northward at Rossville along the western base of the Ridge, accompanied by five batteries. It had not been considered prudent to send artillery through the Gap. The skirmishers and batteries engaged the enemy on the crest. After an advance of about half a mile, Creighton's and Cobham's Brigades, moving along the base in columns of regiments with Ireland's in support of the artillery, were formed for assault with Creighton's Brigade in the first line and Cobham's in the second. The movement was oblique to the Ridge, in order to effect a junction with the right of Johnson's Division of the Army of the Cumberland, which had then gained the summit of the Ridge a half a mile to the north. Gen. Geary's line reached the crest at 6 P. M. Gen. Osterhaus' Division bivouacked on the eastern slope of the Ridge, in close proximity to Bragg's Headquarters.

Carlin's Brigade, upon descending the mountain, as soon as it could cross Chattanooga Creek, had rejoined its division (Johnson's) and formed on the right of it just in time to take part in the movement of the center against Missionary Ridge.

The Storming of Missionary Ridge.

The advance on Orchard Knob, the attack on Lookout Mountain, and Hooker's movement on Rossville Gap, were not contemplated in Gen. Grant's order for battle. The key movement of that plan was the occupation of the north end of Missionary Ridge to the Tunnel by Gen. Sherman before the enemy could concentrate there. At 3 o'clock, the attack at that point had failed, and Gen. Grant, then on Orchard Knob, his headquarters during the day, ordered a demonstration at the center against the enemy's works at the foot of the Ridge, to relieve the pressure upon Gen. Sherman. General Thomas, commanding the Army of the Cumberland, and Gen. Gordon Granger, commanding the Fourth Corps, also had their headquarters on Orchard Knob. The movement against the Confederate center was quickly arranged. Four divisions of the Army of the Cumberland were ready to advance as soon as orders could reach them. Of the six divisions which composed that army, Cruft was with Hooker, and Jeff. C. Davis with Sherman. Baird, who had been ordered to Sherman and had joined him at the Tunnel, was just returning to the center when the order for the demonstration against the Ridge was given, and quickly formed as the left of the advance.

The Union line ran through the plain, with Orchard Knob

and the low range to the south of it as the directing points. The storming line, by divisions from right to left, was composed of Johnson's, Sheridan's, Wood's, and Baird's. By brigades, it ran as follows: Carlin's and Stoughton's, of Johnson—Starkweather's, of this division, holding the earthworks about the city; Sherman's, Harker's, and Wagner's, of Sheridan; Hazen's, Willich's, and S. Beatty's, of Wood; Turchin's, Van Derveer's, and Phelps', of Baird. There were eighty-eight infantry regiments in the storming lines, and four field batteries, which, however, could render little service, operated with them. The center divisions of Sheridan and Wood belonged to the Fourth Corps, Gen. Gordon Granger commanding. The right, Johnson, and the left, Baird, belonged to the Fourteenth Corps, Gen. John M. Palmer commanding.

The Confederate line, counting from left to right, confronting this advance was composed of the divisions of Stewart, Breckinridge (Bate), Hindman (Patton Anderson), and Cheatham. The brigades composing the line, their order in battle not being fully shown by the reports, were: Clayton's, Stovall's, Strahl's, and Adams' of Stewart's Division; Tyler's (Bate's) and Finley's of Breckinridge's; and Anderson's, Manigault's, Deas', and Vaughn's of Hindman's; Jackson's, Moore's, and Walthall's of Cheatham's. Reynolds' Brigade of Buckner's Division was, with the greater part of Finley's Brigade, in the trenches at the foot of the Ridge. Lewis' Brigade of Bate's Division had been sent the night before to the bridges over the Chickamauga. Cheatham's artillery and the infantry on his left had an oblique fire on Baird's left. As near as can be ascertained from the reports, there were fifteen batteries along the ridge, and two siege pieces at Bragg's Headquarters, to oppose the Union advance. Gen. Stewart's Division was a very thin line on its left, the greater part of Clayton's Brigade having been hurried by Gen. Breckinridge to Rossville Gap, and the rest of the line being stretched along the Ridge to Gen. Bragg's Headquarters, thus covering three miles.

The average distance of the Union line from the top of the Ridge was over a mile, the average width of the slope of the Ridge about 600 yards, and the average height 400 feet. There were good trenches at its foot, light intermediate defenses upon its slope, and light rifle-pits and rude defenses along its crest. The slope was for the most part steep, rough, and tangled, and exceedingly difficult of ascent.

The orders given before the advance to the troops in Baird's Division on the left, and Johnson's on the right, contemplated their going to the top of the Ridge. Those received by the center divisions were construed to involve only a demonstration against the position at the foot of the Ridge, although Gen. Willich of Wood's Division did not so understand it, and, upon carrying the earthworks at the base, he at once ordered an advance upon the summit.

The signal for the movement was to be six guns fired in rapid succession from Orchard Knob. This was given at 3:15 P. M. The whole line started on a run, and there was no check at any part of it until the earthworks were reached and captured. Baird's Division on the left, with Beatty's and Willich's Brigades of Wood's Division next on its right, hastily rectified their lines at the earthworks, and started at once for the crest. Johnson's Division, on the extreme right, also moved continuously for the summit. Sheridan's Division and the right of Wood's halted at the earthworks under their orders, which at first contemplated only the carrying of the earthworks as a demonstration to relieve the pressure on Sherman. They were almost immediately ordered forward, and the whole line apparently reached the summit about the same time. As seen from Orchard Knob, six points on the Ridge were simultaneously occupied. The first troops on the crest appear to have been those in Thomas J. Wood's Division.

Upon reaching the summit, Gen. Sheridan's Division descended the eastern slope and began an active pursuit. It

Missionary Ridge, from Orchard Knob. (See page xv.)

was soon engaged with Bate's Division, which had taken a strong position a short distance east of Missionary Ridge and held it until after dark, when fighting ceased and it withdrew.

Gen. Baird's troops, on the left, turned northward along the crest in mass, with little regard for organization, and pushed Jackson's and Moore's Brigades of Cheatham's Division eastward and northward to the top of the third knoll. Here, Gen. Walthall's Brigade of Cheatham's Division, which had been thrown across the Ridge, made a firm stand. Brown's Brigade of Stevenson's Division, which had been hurried from Sherman's front at the Tunnel, formed on the left of it, and at dusk fighting ceased. From this point to Tunnel Hill, the Confederate lines withdrew in order to and across the Chickamauga.

The Union Artillery in Chattanooga.

During the three days' battle, the heavy guns in the works about the city were an important element. Gen. John M. Brannan, Chief of Artillery of the Army of the Cumberland, had mounted sixteen pieces of heavy ordnance in the forts of the outer works. Four 4½-inch Rodman guns were placed in Fort Wood, in addition to two 30-pounder Parrots already there; four 20-pounder Parrots were mounted in Fort Cheatham (Negley); four 4½-inch Rodmans in Battery Rousseau; and four 20-pounder Parrots in Fort Sheridan. The battery on Moccasin Point received two 20-pounder Parrots, and, with the guns of the Eighteenth Ohio and Tenth Indiana Batteries, commanded the face of Lookout about the Craven House, and played a very important part during Hooker's assault. During its progress, two 10-pounder Parrots of the Seventh Indiana Battery, and two howitzers from the Third Wisconsin, went into action near the mouth of Chattanooga Creek. Owing to the scarcity or emaciated condition of artillery horses, only four field batteries were brought into action during the engagements.

These heavy guns commanded the enemy's camps and intrenchments at the foot of Missionary Ridge and the east base of Lookout. On each of the three days, this heavy artillery was used with great effect, some of it being able to reach the crest of Missionary Ridge, and most of it proving effective against its slope during the advance of the assaulting lines toward the earthworks at the foot of the Ridge.

During the advance on Orchard Knob on the 23d, Gen. Howard, of the Eleventh Corps, sent Battery G, Fourth United States, and the First Ohio Battery, to support Gen. Sheridan, and Gen. Baird sent Battery I, Fourth United States, and Battery H, Fifth United States. These were all stationed on Bushy Knob, now the National Cemetery, and were actively engaged.

UNION LOSSES.

Movement on Orchard Knob.

	Killed.	Wounded.	Total.
Wood's Division,	32	165	197
Steinwehr's "	3	20	23
Schurz's "	1	12	13
	36	197	233

Hooker's Operations at Lookout, Missionary Ridge, and Ringgold.

	Killed.	Wounded.	Total.
Geary's Division,	56	285	341
Osterhaus' "	57	335	392
Cruft's "	21	123	144
Carlin's Brigade at Lookout,	12	24	36
	146	767	913
Loss at Ringgold,	65	377	442
	81	390	471

Leaving a total loss of 471 for Lookout and Missionary Ridge.

Storming of Missionary Ridge.

			Killed.	Wounded.
Carlin's	Brigade,	Johnson,	12	110
Stoughton's	"		25	137
Sherman's	"	Sheridan,	31	275
Wagner's	"		70	660
Harker's	"		29	278
Hazen's	"	Wood.	88	427
S. Beatty's	"		14	160
Willich's	"		46	288
Turchin's	"	Baird,	50	231
Van Derveer's	"		20	141
Phelps'	"		18	100
	Total,		403	2,807

Troops Operating with Gen. Sherman.

			Killed.	Wounded.
Giles A. Smith's	Brigade,	M. L. Smith,		14
Lightburn's	"		10	77
Loomis'	"	Ewing,	37	331
Corse's	"		34	210
Cockerill's	"			5
Alexander's	"	J. E. Smith,		4
Raum's	"		40	140
Matthies'	"		49	145
Bushbeck's	"	Steinwehr,	28	148
Orland Smith's	"		4	20
Tyndale's	"	Schurz,	1	4
Krzyzanowski's	"			3
Hecker's	"		1	10
Morgan's	"	Jeff. C. Davis,		9
John Beatty's	"		3	17
McCook's	"		2	4
	Total,		209	1,141

Confederate Losses at Lookout.

	Killed.	Wounded.
Walthall's Brigade,	8	91
Moore's "	4	48
Pettus' "	9	38
Total,	21	177

In addition, Walthall lost 845 captured, largely from his picket line at the base of the mountain. This was posted along Lookout Creek, and was nearly one-third of his total strength, 1,500.

The missing from Moore's Brigade were 199, and from Pettus', 9. Moore's strength was 1,200. Pettus had only three regiments.

The Confederate reports of losses at Missionary Ridge were very incomplete.

The three brigades of Cleburne's Division, which were engaged at Tunnel Hill, lost 42 killed, 178 wounded, and 2 missing.

Brown's Brigade lost at the same point, 2 killed, 35 wounded, and 13 missing. Cumming's Brigade lost 17 killed, 156 wounded, and 30 missing.

CHAPTER XII.

ORGANIZATION OF THE FORCES UNDER COMMAND OF MAJ.-GEN.
ULYSSES S. GRANT, U. S. ARMY, ENGAGED IN THE BATTLES
ABOUT CHATTANOOGA. NOVEMBER 23-25, 1863.

[Roster compiled by Hon. J. W. KIRKLEY, Board of Publication of War Records.]

ARMY OF THE CUMBERLAND.
Maj.-Gen. GEORGE H. THOMAS.

GENERAL HEADQUARTERS.
1st Ohio Sharpshooters, Capt. Gershom M. Barber.
10th Ohio Infantry, Lieut.-Col. William M. Ward.

FOURTH ARMY CORPS.
Maj.-Gen. GORDON GRANGER.

FIRST DIVISION (FOURTH CORPS).[a]
Brig.-Gen. CHARLES CRUFT.

Escort.
92d Illinois, Company E, Capt. Matthew Van Buskirk.

Second Brigade.
Brig.-Gen. WALTER C. WHITAKER,
96th Illinois :
  Col. Thomas E. Champion.
  Maj. George Hicks.
35th Indiana, Col. Bernard F. Mullen.
8th Kentucky, Col. Sidney M. Barnes.
40th Ohio, Col. Jacob E. Taylor.
51st Ohio, Lieut.-Col. Charles H. Wood.
99th Ohio, Lieut.-Col. John E. Cummins.

Third Brigade.
Col. WILLIAM GROSE.
59th Illinois, Maj. Clayton Hale.
75th Illinois, Col. John E. Bennett.
84th Illinois, Col. Louis H. Waters.
9th Indiana, Col. Isaac C. B. Suman.
36th Indiana, Maj. Gilbert Trusler.
24th Ohio, Capt. George M. Bacon.

Engaged, November 24th, at Lookout Mountain. November 25th, carried the south end of Missionary Ridge from Rossville Gap.

---

[a] The First Brigade and Battery M, Fourth U. S. Artillery, Col. D. A. Enyart, commanding, at Bridgeport, Ala.; the One Hundred and Fifteenth Illinois and Eighty-fourth Indiana, of the Second Brigade, and Fifth Indiana Battery, at Shellmound, Tenn., and the Thirtieth Indiana and Seventy-seventh Pennsylvania, of the Third Brigade, and Battery H, Fourth U. S. Artillery, at Whitesides, Tenn.

SECOND DIVISION (FOURTH CORPS).
Maj.-Gen. PHILIP H. SHERIDAN.

First Brigade.
Col. FRANCIS T. SHERMAN.
36th Illinois:
  Col. Silas Miller °
  Lieut.-Col. Porter C. Olson.
44th Illinois, Col. Wallace W. Barrett.
73d Illinois, Col. James F. Jacquess.
74th Illinois, Col. Jason Marsh.
88th Illinois, Lieut.-Col. George W. Chandler.
22d Indiana, Col. Michael Gooding.
2d Missouri:
  Col. Bernard Laiboldt.°
  Lieut.-Col. Arnold Beck.
15th Missouri:
  Col. Joseph Conrad.
  Capt. Samuel Rexinger.
24th Wisconsin, Maj. Carl von Baumbach.

Second Brigade.
Brig.-Gen. GEORGE D. WAGNER.
100th Illinois, Maj. Charles M. Hammond.
15th Indiana:
  Col. Gustavus A. Wood.°
  Maj. Frank White.
  Capt. Benjamin F. Hegler.
40th Indiana, Lieut.-Col. Elias Neff.
51st Indiana,† Lieut.-Col. John M. Comparet.
57th Indiana, Lieut.-Col. George W. Lennard.
58th Indiana, Lieut.-Col. Joseph Moore.
26th Ohio, Lieut.-Col. William H. Young.
97th Ohio, Lieut.-Col. Milton Barnes.

Third Brigade.
Col. CHARLES G. HARKER.
22d Illinois, Lieut.-Col. Francis Swanwick.
27th Illinois, Col. Jonathan R. Miles.
42d Illinois:
  Col. Nathan H. Walworth.*
  Capt. Edgar D. Swain.
51st Illinois:
  Maj. Charles W. Davis.
  Capt. Albert M. Tilton.
79th Illinois, Col. Allen Buckner.
3d Kentucky, Col. Henry C. Dunlap.
64th Ohio, Col. Alexander McIlvain.
65th Ohio, Lieut.-Col. William A. Bullitt.
125th Ohio:
  Col. Emerson Opdycke.°
  Capt. Edward P. Bates.

Artillery.
Capt. WARREN P. EDGARTON.
1st Illinois Light, Battery M, Capt. George W. Spencer.
10th Indiana Battery, Capt. William A. Naylor.
1st Missouri Light, Battery G, Lieut. Gustavus Schueler.
1st Ohio Light, Battery I,‡ Capt. Hubert Dilger.
4th United States, Battery G,‡ Lieut. Christopher F. Merkle.
5th United States, Battery H,‡ Capt. Francis L. Guenther.

November 23d, took part in the capture of Orchard Knob. November 25, engaged in the assault on Missionary Ridge, the center of the division reaching the crest at Bragg's Headquarters.

° Temporarily in command of a demi-brigade.
† Between Nashville and Chattanooga en route to join brigade.
‡ Temporarily attached.

THIRD DIVISION (FOURTH CORPS).

Brig.-Gen. THOMAS J. WOOD.

First Brigade.

Brig.-Gen. AUGUST WILLICH.
25th Illinois, Col. Richard H. Nodine.
35th Illinois, Lieut.-Col. William P. Chandler.
89th Illinois, Lieut.-Col. William D. Williams.
32d Indiana, Lieut.-Col. Frank Erdelmeyer.
68th Indiana:
   Lieut.-Col. Harvey J. Espy.
   Capt. Richard L. Leeson.
8th Kansas, Col. John A. Martin.
15th Ohio, Lieut.-Col. Frank Askew.
49th Ohio, Maj. Samuel F. Gray.
15th Wisconsin, Capt. John A. Gordon.

Second Brigade.

Brig.-Gen. WILLIAM B. HAZEN.
6th Indiana, Maj. Calvin D. Campbell.
5th Kentucky:
   Col. William W. Berry.
   Lieut.-Col. John L. Treanor.
6th Kentucky, Maj. Richard T. Whitaker.
23d Kentucky, Lieut.-Col. James C. Foy.
1st Ohio:
   Lieut.-Col. Bassett Langdon.
   Maj. Joab A. Stafford.
6th Ohio, Lieut.-Col. Alexander C. Christopher.
41st Ohio:
   Col. Aquila Wiley.
   Lieut.-Col. Robert L. Kimberly.
93d Ohio:
   Maj. William Birch.
   Capt. Daniel Bowman.
   Capt. Samuel B. Smith.
124th Ohio, Lieut.-Col. James Pickands.

Third Brigade.

Brig. Gen. SAMUEL BEATTY.
79th Indiana, Col. Frederick Knefler.
86th Indiana, Col. Geo. F. Dick.
9th Kentucky, Col. George H. Cram.
17th Kentucky, Col. Alexander M. Stout.
13th Ohio, Col. Dwight Jarvis, Jr.
19th Ohio, Col. Charles F. Manderson.
59th Ohio, Maj. Robert J. Vanosdoll.

Artillery.

Capt. CULLEN BRADLEY.
Illinois Light, Bridges' Battery, Capt. Lyman Bridges.
6th Ohio Battery, Lieut. Oliver H. P. Ayres.
20th Ohio Battery,* Capt. Edward Grosskopff.
Pennsylvania Light, Battery B, Lieut. Samuel M. McDowell.

November 23d, captured Orchard Knob. November 24th, took part in the assault on Missionary Ridge, the center of the division gaining the summit to the right of McCallie Avenue extended

---

* Temporarily attached from Artillery Reserve.

FOURTEENTH ARMY CORPS.

Maj.-Gen. JOHN M. PALMER.

Escort.

1st Ohio Cavalry, Company I., Capt. John D. Barker.

FIRST DIVISION (FOURTEENTH CORPS).

Brig.-Gen. RICHARD W. JOHNSON.

First Brigade.

Brig.-Gen. WILLIAM P. CARLIN.

104th Illinois, Lieut.-Col. Douglas Hapeman.
38th Indiana, Lieut.-Col. Daniel F. Griffin.
42d Indiana, Lieut.-Col. William T. B. McIntire.
88th Indiana, Col. Cyrus E. Briant.
2d Ohio, Col. Anson G. McCook.
33d Ohio, Capt. James H. M. Montgomery.
94th Ohio, Maj. Rue P. Hutchins.
10th Wisconsin, Capt. Jacob W. Roby.

Second Brigade.

Col. WILLIAM L. STOUGHTON.

19th Illinois, Lieut.-Col. Alexander W. Raffen.
11th Michigan, Capt. Patrick H. Keegan.
69th Ohio, Maj. James J. Hanna.
15th United States, 1st Battalion, Capt. Henry Keteltas.
15th United States, 2d Battalion, Capt. William S. McManus.
16th United States, 1st Battalion, Maj. Robert E. A. Crofton.
18th United States, 1st Battalion, Capt. George W. Smith.
18th United States, 2d Battalion, Capt. Henry Haymond.
19th United States, 1st Battalion, Capt. Henry S. Welton.

Third Brigade.[*]

Brig.-Gen. JOHN C. STARKWEATHER.

24th Illinois, Col. Geza Mihalotzy.
37th Indiana, Col. James S. Hull.
21st Ohio, Capt. Charles H. Vantine.
74th Ohio, Maj. Joseph Fisher.
78th Pennsylvania, Col. Archibald Blakeley.
79th Pennsylvania, Maj. Michael H. Locher.
1st Wisconsin, Lieut.-Col. George B. Bingham.
21st Wisconsin, Capt. Charles H. Walker.

Artillery.

1st Illinois Light, Battery C, Capt. Mark H. Prescott.
1st Michigan Light, Battery A, Captain Francis E. Hale.
5th United States, Battery H,[†] Capt. Francis L. Guenther.

November 23d and 24th, held the works at Chattanooga. Toward

---

[*] During the engagements of the 23d, 24th, and 25th, was in line of battle holding fort and breastworks at Chattanooga.

[†] Temporarily attached to Second Division, Fourth Army Corps.

evening of the 24th Carlin's Brigade ascended Lookout to the Craven House, and relieved the right of Hooker's line under the palisades.

November 25th. Stoughton's Brigade formed on the right of Sheridan's Division, where Carlin's Brigade joined it from Lookout Mountain. The division took part in the assault on Missionary Ridge, reaching the crest opposite East Lake.

SECOND DIVISION (FOURTEENTH CORPS).

Brig.-Gen. JEFFERSON C. DAVIS.

First Brigade.
Brig.-Gen. JAMES D. MORGAN.
10th Illinois, Col. John Tillson.
16th Illinois, Lieut.-Col. James B. Cahill.
60th Illinois, Col. William B. Anderson.
21st Kentucky, Col. Samuel W. Price.
10th Michigan, Lieut.-Col. Christopher J. Dickerson.
14th Michigan,° Col. Henry R. Mizner.

Second Brigade.
Brig.-Gen. JOHN BEATTY.
34th Illinois, Lieut.-Col. Oscar Van Tassell.
78th Illinois, Lieut.-Col. Carter Van Vleck.
3d Ohio,† Capt. Leroy S. Bell.
98th Ohio, Maj. James M. Shane.
108th Ohio, Lieut.-Col. Carlo Piepho.
113th Ohio, Maj. Lynn S. Sullivant.
121st Ohio, Maj. John Yager.

Third Brigade.
Col. DANIEL MCCOOK.
85th Illinois, Col. Caleb J. Dilworth.
86th Illinois, Lieut.-Col. David W. Magee.
110th Illinois, Lieut.-Col. E. Hibbard Topping.
125th Illinois, Col. Oscar F. Harmon.
52d Ohio, Maj. James T. Holmes.

Artillery.
Capt. WILLIAM A. HOTCHKISS.
2d Illinois Light, Battery I, Lieut. Henry B. Plant.
Minnesota Light, 2d Battery, Lieut. Richard L. Dawley.
Wisconsin Light, 5th Battery, Capt. George Q. Gardner.

November 19th, ordered to the north side of the Tennessee to prepare for and cover Sherman's crossing. Followed the rear of Sherman's column over the river at noon of November 24th. Remained unengaged during the battle as a reserve of Gen. Sherman's left.

° Detached at Columbia, Tenn.
† Detached at Kelley's Ferry, Tennessee River.

THIRD DIVISION (FOURTEENTH CORPS).

Brig.-Gen. ABSALOM BAIRD.

First Brigade.

Brig.-Gen. JOHN B. TURCHIN.
82d Indiana, Col. Morton C. Hunter.
11th Ohio, Lieut.-Col. Ogden Street.
17th Ohio:
   Maj. Benjamin F. Butterfield.
   Capt. Benjamin H. Showers.
31st Ohio, Lieut.-Col. Frederick W. Lister.
36th Ohio, Lieut.-Col. Hiram F. Devol.
89th Ohio, Capt. John H. Jolly.
92d Ohio:
   Lieut.-Col. Douglas Putnam., Jr.
   Capt. Edward Grosvenor.

Second Brigade.

Col. FERDINAND VAN DERVEER.
75th Indiana, Col. Milton S. Robinson.
87th Indiana, Col. Newell Gleason.
101st Indiana, Lieut.-Col. Thos. Doan.
2d Minnesota, Lieut.-Col. Judson W. Bishop.
9th Ohio, Col. Gustave Kammerling.
35th Ohio:
   Lieut.-Col. Henry V. Boynton.
   Maj. Joseph L. Budd.
105th Ohio, Lieut.-Col. William R. Tolles.

Third Brigade.

Col. EDWARD H. PHELPS.
Col. WILLIAM H. HAYS.
10th Indiana, Lieut.-Col. Marsh B. Taylor.
74th Indiana, Lieut.-Col. Myron Baker.
4th Kentucky, Maj. Robert M. Kelly.
10th Kentucky:
   Col. William H. Hays.
   Lieut.-Col. Gabriel C. Wharton.
18th Kentucky,[*] Lieut.-Col. Hubbard K. Milward.
14th Ohio, Lieut.Col. Henry D. Kingsbury.
38th Ohio, Maj. Charles Greenwood.

Artillery.

Capt. GEORGE R. SWALLOW.
Indiana Light, 7th Battery, Lieut. Otho H. Morgan.
Indiana Light, 19th Battery, Lieut. Robert G. Lackey.
4th United States Battery I, Lieut. Frank G. Smith.

November 23d, supported the right of the advance on Orchard Knob. Early November 25th joined the right of Sherman's line at Tunnel Hill. Rejoined Thomas' line at 3 P. M., and took part in the storming of Missionary Ridge, being the left of the Army of the Cumberland in that movement. The center of the division reached the crest at the De Long Tower, and advanced northward to the top of the second knoll beyond.

---

[*] Detached at Brown's Ferry.

CAVALRY.[*]

Second Brigade (Second Division).

Col. ELI LONG.

98th Illinois (mounted infantry), Lieut.-Col. Edward Kitchell.
17th Indiana (mounted infantry), Lieut.-Col. Henry Jordan.
2d Kentucky, Col. Thomas P. Nicholas.
4th Michigan, Maj. Horace Gray.
1st Ohio, Maj. Thomas J. Patten.
3d Ohio, Lieut.-Col. Charles B. Seidel.
4th Ohio (battalion), Maj. George W. Dobb.
10th Ohio, Col. Charles C. Smith.

Long's Brigade operated on the left of Sherman's forces during the battle. There was no other Union cavalry present.

ENGINEER TROOPS.

Brig.-Gen. WILLIAM F. SMITH.

Engineers.

1st Michigan Engineers (detachment), Capt. Perrin V. Fox.
13th Michigan Infantry, Maj. Willard G. Eaton.
21st Michigan Infantry, Capt. Loomis K. Bishop.
22d Michigan Infantry, Maj. Henry S. Dean.
18th Ohio Infantry, Col. Timothy R. Stanley.

Pioneer Brigade.

Col. GEORGE P. BUELL.
1st Battalion, Capt. Charles J. Stewart.
2d Battalion, Capt. Correll Smith.
3d Battalion, Capt. William Clark.

These troops prepared boats and bridges for the Brown's Ferry movement to re-open the Tennessee River and for Sherman's crossing. It was active in the construction of fortifications, and Gen. Smith carried out all the details of the Brown's Ferry expedition, commanding it in person.

---

[*] Corps headquarters and the First and Second Brigades and Eighteenth Indiana Battery, of the First Division, at and about Alexandria, Tenn.; the Third Brigade at Caperton's Ferry, Tennessee River. The First and Third Brigades, and the Chicago Board of Trade Battery, of the Second Division, at Maysville, Ala.

ARTILLERY RESERVE.

Brig.-Gen. JOHN M. BRANNAN.

FIRST DIVISION.

Col. JAMES BARNETT.

First Brigade.

Maj. CHARLES S. COTTER.
1st Ohio Light, Battery B, Lieut. Norman A. Baldwin.
1st Ohio Light, Battery C, Capt. Marco B. Gary.
1st Ohio Light, Battery E, Lieut. Albert G. Ransom.
1st Ohio Light, Battery F, Lieut. Giles J. Cockerill.

Second Brigade.

1st Ohio Light, Battery G, Capt. Alexander Marshall.
1st Ohio Light, Battery M, Capt. Frederick Schultz.
Ohio Light, 18th Battery, Lieut. Joseph McCafferty.
Ohio Light, 20th Battery,* Capt. Edward Grosskopff.

SECOND DIVISION.

First Brigade.

Capt. JOSIAH W. CHURCH.

1st Michigan Light, Battery D, Capt. Josiah W. Church.
1st Tennessee Light, Battery A, Lieut. Albert F. Beach.
Wisconsin Light, 3d Battery, Lieut. Hiram F. Hubbard.
Wisconsin Light, 8th Battery, Lieut. Obadiah German.
Wisconsin Light, 10th Battery, Capt. Yates V. Beebe.

Second Brigade.

Capt. ARNOLD SUTERMEISTER.

Indiana Light, 4th Battery, Lieut. Henry J. Willits.
Indiana Light, 8th Battery, Lieut. George Estep.
Indiana Light, 11th Battery, Capt. Arnold Sutermeister.
Indiana Light, 21st Battery, Lieut. William E. Chess.
1st Wisconsin Heavy, Company C, Capt. John R. Davies.

Besides the direction of the field artillery, Gen. Brannan constructed the batteries at Moccasin Point, and after the re-opening of the river, he armed the works of the city with heavy guns, which were used to cover the infantry advances against Lookout Mountain and Missionary Ridge.

POST OF CHATTANOOGA.

Col. JOHN G. PARKHURST.

44th Indiana, Lieut.-Col. Simeon C. Aldrich.
15th Kentucky, Maj. William C. Halpin.
9th Michigan, Lieut.-Col. William Wilkinson.

---

* Temporarily attached to Third Division, Fourth Army Corps.

DETACHMENT FROM THE ARMY OF THE POTOMAC.

ELEVENTH AND TWELFTH ARMY CORPS.

Maj.-Gen. JOSEPH HOOKER *

Provost Guard.

10th Maine, 1st Battalion, Capt. John D. Beardsley.

Escort.

15th Illinois Cavalry, Company K, Capt. Samuel B. Sherer.

ELEVENTH ARMY CORPS.

Maj.-Gen. OLIVER O. HOWARD.

GENERAL HEADQUARTERS.

Independent Company, 8th New York Infantry, Capt. Anton Bruhn.

SECOND DIVISION (ELEVENTH CORPS).

Brig.-Gen. ADOLPH VON STEINWEHR.

First Brigade.	*Second Brigade.*
Col. ADOLPHUS BUSHBECK.	Col. ORLAND SMITH.
33d New Jersey, Col. George W. Mindil.	33d Massachusetts, Lieut.-Col. Godfrey Rider, Jr.
134th New York, Lieut.-Col. Allen H. Jackson.	136th New York, Col. James Wood, Jr.
154th New York, Col. Patrick H. Jones.	55th Ohio, Col. Charles B. Gambee.
27th Pennsylvania:	73d Ohio, Maj. Samuel H. Hurst.
Maj. Peter A. McAloon.	
Capt. August Riedt.	
73d Pennsylvania:	
Lieut.-Col. Joseph B. Taft.	
Capt. Daniel F. Kelley.	
Lieut. Samuel D. Miller.	

Took part in the battle of Wauhatchie, October 28th, and the advance on Orchard Knob, November 23d. November 25th, Bushbeck formed the right of Sherman's line at the Tunnel and assaulted there.

---

* Maj.-Gen. Joseph Hooker, commanding Eleventh and Twelfth Army Corps, had under his immediate command for the battle at Chattanooga the First Division, Fourth Corps; the Second Division, Twelfth Corps; portions of the Fourteenth Corps, and the First Division, Fifteenth Corps.

THIRD DIVISION (ELEVENTH CORPS).

Maj.-Gen. CARL SCHURZ.

First Brigade.

Brig.-Gen. HECTOR TYNDALE.
101st Illinois, Col. Charles H. Fox.
45th New York, Maj. Charles Koch.
143d New York, Col. Horace Boughton.
61st Ohio, Col. Stephen J. McGroarty.
82d Ohio, Lieut.-Col. David Thompson.

Second Brigade.

Col. WLADIMIR KRZYZANOWSKI.
58th New York, Capt. Michael Esembaux.
119th New York, Col. John T. Lockman.
141st New York, Col. Wlilliam K. Logie.
26th Wisconsin, Capt. Frederick C. Winkler.

Third Brigade.

Col. FREDERICK HECKER.
80th Illinois, Capt James Neville.
82d Illinois, Lieut.-Col. Edward S. Salomon.
68th New York, Lieut.-Col. Albert von Steinhausen.
75th Pennsylvania, Maj. August Ledig.

Artillery.

Maj. THOMAS W. OSBORN.
1st New York Light, Battery I, Capt. Michael Wiedrich.
New York Light, 13th Battery, Capt. William Wheeler.
1st Ohio Light, Battery I,° Capt. Hubert Dilger.
1st Ohio Light, Battery K, Lieut. Nicholas Sahm.
4th United States, Battery G,° Lieut. Christopher F. Merkle.

Took part in the battle of Wauhatchie, October 28th. November 23d, supported the left of the attack on Orchard Knob. November 25th, marched to the support of Sherman's forces, and remained unengaged on their left and rear during the battle of Missionary Ridge.

TWELFTH ARMY CORPS.†

Maj.-Gen. HENRY W. SLOCUM.

° Temporarily attached to Second Division, Fourth Army Corps.
† The First Division engaged in guarding the Nashville and Chattanooga Railroad from Wartrace Bridge, Tenn., to Bridgeport, Ala., etc. Maj.-Gen, H. W. Slocum, the corps commander, had his headquarters at Tullahoma, Tenn.

FIRST DIVISION (TWELFTH CORPS).

Brig.-Gen. ALPHEUS S. WILLIAMS.

First Brigade.

Brig.-Gen. JOSEPH F. KNIPE.
5th Connecticut, Col. Warren W. Packer.
20th Connecticut, Col. Samuel Ross.
3d Maryland, Col. Joseph M. Sudsburg.
123d New York, Lieut.-Col. James C. Rogers.
145th New York, Capt. Samuel T. Allen.
46th Pennsylvania, Lieut.-Col. William L. Foulk.

Third Brigade.

Brig.-Gen. THOMAS H. RUGER.
27th Indiana, Col. Silas Colgrove.
2d Massachusetts, Col. William Cogswell.
13th New Jersey, Col. Ezra A. Carman.
107th New York, Col. Nirom M. Crane.
150th New York, Col. John H. Ketcham.
3d Wisconsin, Col. William Hawley.

This division was not engaged, but was active and successful in the more important work of keeping open the lines of supply.

SECOND DIVISION TWELFTH CORPS.

Brig.-Gen. JOHN W. GEARY.

First Brigade.

Col. CHARLES CANDY.
Col. WILLIAM R. CREIGHTON.
Col. THOMAS J. AHL.
5th Ohio, Col. John H. Patrick.
7th Ohio:
   Col. William R. Creighton.
   Lieut.-Col. Orrin J. Crane.
   Capt. Ernst J. Krieger.
29th Ohio, Col. William T. Fitch.
66th Ohio:
   Lieut.-Col. Eugene Powell.
   Capt. Thomas McConnell.
28th Pennsylvania:
   Col. Thomas J. Ahl.
   Capt. John Flynn.
147th Pennsylvania, Lieut.-Col. Ario Pardee, Jr.

Second Brigade.

Col. GEORGE A. COBHAM, JR.
29th Pennsylvania, Col. William Rickards, Jr.
109th Pennsylvania, Capt. Frederick L. Gimber.
111th Pennsylvania, Col. Thomas M. Walker.

Third Brigade.

Col. DAVID IRELAND.
60th New York, Col. Abel Godard.
78th New York, Lieut.-Col. Herbert von Hammerstein.
102d New York, Col. James C. Lane.
137th New York, Capt. Milo B. Eldredge.
149th New York:
   Col. Henry A. Barnum.
   Lieut.-Col. Charles B. Randall.

Artillery.
Maj. JOHN A. REYNOLDS.
Pennsylvania Light, Battery F, Lieut. James D. McGill.
5th United States, Battery K, Capt. Edmund C. Bainbridge.

This division fought the battle at Wauhatchie, October 28th, the troops dispatched to his relief from Brown's Ferry being engaged to the north of the railroad crossing of Lookout Creek. November 24th, it was prominent in the battle of Lookout Mountain. November 25th, it assaulted the west slope of Missionary Ridge, carrying it about three-quarters of a mile north of Rossville.

ARMY OF THE TENNESSEE.
Maj.-Gen. WILLIAM T. SHERMAN.[○]

FIFTEENTH ARMY CORPS.[†]
Maj.-Gen. FRANK P. BLAIR, JR.

FIRST DIVISION (FIFTEENTH CORPS).
Brig.-Gen. PETER J. OSTERHAUS.

First Brigade.
Brig.-Gen. CHARLES R. WOODS.
13th Illinois:
  Lieut.-Col. Frederick W. Partridge.
  Captain George P. Brown.
3d Missouri, Lieut.-Col. Theodore Memann.
12th Missouri:
  Col. Hugo Wangelin.
  Lieut.-Col. Jacob Kaercher.
17th Missouri, Col. John F. Cramer.
27th Missouri, Col. Thomas Curly.
29th Missouri:
  Col. James Peckham.
  Maj. Philip H. Murphy.
31st Missouri, Lieut.-Col. Samuel P. Simpson.
32d Missouri, Lieut.-Col. Henry C. Warmoth.
76th Ohio, Maj. Willard Warner.

Second Brigade.
Col. JAMES A. WILLIAMSON.
4th Iowa, Lieut.-Col. George Burton.
9th Iowa, Col. David Carskaddon.
25th Iowa, Col. George A. Stone.
26th Iowa, Col. Milo Smith.
30th Iowa, Lieut.-Col. Aurelius Roberts.
31st Iowa, Lieut.-Col. Jeremiah W. Jenkins.

Artillery.
Capt. HENRY H. GRIFFITHS.
Iowa Light, 1st Battery, Lieut. James M. Williams.
2d Missouri Light, Battery F, Capt. Clemens Landgraeber.
Ohio Light, 4th Battery, Capt. George Froehlich.

November 24th, held the left of the line in storming Lookout Moun-

---

[○] Gen. Sherman had under his immediate command at the battle of Chattanooga the Eleventh Corps and the Second Division, Fourteenth Corps, of the Army of the Cumberland; the Second and Fourth Divisions, Fifteenth Corps, and the Second Division, Seventeenth Corps, Army of the Tennessee.

[†] The Third Division, Brig.-Gen. James M. Tuttle, commanding, at Memphis, La Grange, and Pocahontas, Tenn.

tain. November 25th, cleared Rossville Gap of the enemy, and turning north along the eastern base of Missionary Ridge assaulted and carried it about a mile north of Rossville, bivouacking on the east slope at Bragg's Headquarters.

SECOND DIVISION (FIFTEENTH CORPS).

Brig.-Gen. MORGAN L. SMITH.

First Brigade.

Brig.-Gen. GILES A. SMITH.
Col. NATHAN W. TUPPER.
55th Illinois, Col. Oscar Malmborg.
116th Illinois:
   Col. Nathan W. Tupper.
   Lieut.-Col. James P. Boyd.
127th Illinois, Lieut.-Col. Frank S. Curtiss.
6th Missouri, Lieut.-Col. Ira Boutell.
8th Missouri, Lieut.-Col. David C. Coleman.
57th Ohio, Lieut.-Col. Samuel R. Mott.
13th United States, 1st Battalion, Capt. Charles C. Smith.

Second Brigade.

Brig.-Gen. JOSEPH A. J. LIGHTBURN.
83d Indiana, Col. Benjamin J. Spooner.
30th Ohio, Col. Theodore Jones.
37th Ohio, Lieut.-Col. Lewis Von Blessingh.
47th Ohio, Col. Augustus C. Parry.
54th Ohio, Maj. Robert Williams, Jr.
4th West Virginia, Col. James H. Dayton.

Artillery.

1st Illinois Light, Battery A, Capt. Peter P. Wood.
1st Illinois Light, Battery B, Capt. Israel P. Rumsey.
1st Illinois Light, Battery H, Lieut. Francis De Gress.

November 24th, the division occupied the detached range north of the extremity of Missionary Ridge. November 25th, Giles A. Smith's Brigade, with most of Lightburn's, was engaged in the attack on the north point of Missionary Ridge, approaching it from the northeast.

FOURTH DIVISION (FIFTEENTH CORPS).
Brig.-Gen. HUGH EWING.

First Brigade.
Col. JOHN M. LOOMIS.
26th Illinois, Lieut.-Col. Robert A. Gillmore.
90th Illinois:
  Col. Timothy O'Meara.
  Lieut.-Col. Owen Stuart.
12th Indiana, Col. Reuben Williams.
100th Indiana, Lieut.-Col. Albert Heath.

Second Brigade.
Brig.-Gen. JOHN M. CORSE.
Col. CHARLES C. WALCUTT.
40th Illinois, Maj. Hiram W. Hall.
103d Illinois, Col. Willard A. Dickerman.
6th Iowa, Lieut.-Col. Alexander J. Miller.
15th Michigan,° Lieut.-Col. Austin E. Jaquith.
46th Ohio:
  Col. Charles C. Walcutt.
  Capt. Isaac N. Alexander.

Third Brigade.
Col. JOSEPH R. COCKERILL.
48th Illinois, Lieut.-Col. Lucien Greathouse
97th Indiana. Col. Robert F. Catterson.
99th Indiana, Col. Alexander Fowler.
53 Ohio. Col. Wells S. Jones.
70th Ohio, Major William B. Brown.

Artillery.
Capt. HENRY RICHARDSON.
1st Illinois Light, Battery F, Capt. John T. Cheney.
1st Illinois Light, Battery I, Lieut. Josiah H. Burton.
1st Missouri Light, Battery D, Lieut. Byron M. Callender.

November 25th, Cockerill's Brigade remained on the crest of detached hills north-west of Missionary Ridge. Corse's Brigade descended their slope, assaulted and carried the north point of Missionary Ridge at the Moon House. This point was held till near night, Corse being wounded early, and Col. C. C. Walcutt commanding thereafter. Loomis' Brigade assaulted to the left of the Tunnel, and fought till late in the afternoon.

° Detached at Scottsborough, Alabama.

SECOND DIVISION (SEVENTEENTH CORPS).

Brig.-Gen. JOHN E. SMITH.

First Brigade.
Col. JESSE I. ALEXANDER.
63d Illinois, Col. Joseph B. McCown.
48th Indiana, Lieut.-Col. Edward J. Wood.
59th Indiana, Capt. Wilford H. Welman.
4th Minnesota, Lieut.-Col. John E. Tourtellotte.
18th Wisconsin, Col. Gabriel Bouck.

Second Brigade.
Col. GREEN B. RAUM.
Col. FRANCIS C. DEIMLING.
Col. CLARK R. WEVER.
56th Illinois, Maj. Pinckney J. Welsh.
17th Iowa:
  Col. Clark R. Wever.
  Maj. John F. Walden.
10th Missouri:
  Col. Francis C. Deimling.
  Lieut.-Col. Christian Happel.
24th Missouri, Company E, Capt. William W. McCammon.
80th Ohio, Lieut.-Col. Pren Metham.

Third Brigade.
Brig.-Gen. CHARLES L. MATTHIES.
Col. BENJAMIN D. DEAN.
Col. JABEZ BANBURY.
93d Illinois:
  Col. Holden Putnam.
  Lieut.-Col. Nicholas C. Buswell.
5th Iowa:
  Col. Jabez Banbury.
  Lieut.-Col. Ezekiel S. Sampson.
10th Iowa, Lieut.-Col. Paris P. Henderson.
26th Missouri, Col. Benjamin D. Dean.

Artillery..
Capt. HENRY DILLON.
Cogswell's (Illinois) Battery, Capt. William Cogswell.
Wisconsin Light, 6th Battery, Lieut. Samuel F. Clark.
Wisconsin Light, 12th Battery, Capt. William Zickerick.

November 25th, Alexander's Brigade remained on the detached hills. Matthies' and Raum's Brigades assaulted to the left of Tunnel Hill, and gained the crest north of it, but, after severe fighting, were compelled to withdraw.

Organization of the Army of Tennessee, Gen. Braxton Bragg, C. S. Army, Commanding, November 20, 1863.

GENERAL HEADQUARTERS.

1st Louisiana (regulars), Col. James Strawbridge.
1st Louisiana Cavalry, Maj. J. M. Taylor.

DETACHMENT FROM THE ARMY OF NORTHERN VIRGINIA.

LONGSTREET'S ARMY CORPS.*

Lieut.-Gen. James Longstreet.

McLAWS' DIVISION (LONGSTREET'S CORPS).†

Maj.-Gen. Lafayette McLaws.

Kershaw's Brigade.

2d South Carolina, Col. John D. Kennedy.
3d South Carolina, Col. James D. Nance.
7th South Carolina, Col. D. Wyatt Aiken.
8th South Carolina, Col. John W. Henagan.
15th South Carolina, Col. Joseph F. Gist.
3d South Carolina Battalion, Lieut.-Col. William G. Rice.

Wofford's Brigade.

16th Georgia, Col. Henry P. Thomas.
18th Georgia, Col. S. Z. Ruff.
24th Georgia, Col. Robert McMillan.
Cobb's Legion, Lieut.-Col. Luther J. Glenn.
Phillips' Legion, Lieut.-Col. E. S. Barclay.
3d Georgia Battalion Sharpshooters, Lieut.-Col. N. L. Hutchins, Jr.

Humphreys' Brigade.

13th Mississippi, Col. Kennon McElroy.
17th Mississippi, Col. William D. Holder.
18th Mississippi, Col. Thomas M. Griffin.
21st Mississippi, Col. William L. Brandon.

Bryan's Brigade.

10th Georgia, Col. John B. Weems.
50th Georgia, Col. Peter McGlashan.
51st Georgia, Col. Edward Ball.
53d Georgia, Col. James P. Simms.

---

* Detached, November 4th, for operations in East Tennessee.
† Detached, November 4th, and sent to East Tennessee.

Artillery Battalion.
Maj. AUSTIN LEYDEN.
Georgia Battery, Capt. Tyler M. Peeples.
Georgia Battery, Capt. Andrew M. Wolihin.
Georgia Battery, Capt. Billington W. York.

HOOD'S DIVISION (LONGSTREET'S CORPS).

Maj. Gen. JOHN B. HOOD.

Jenkins' Brigade.
1st South Carolina, Col. Franklin W. Kilpatrick.
2d South Carolina Rifles, Col. Thomas Thomson.
5th South Carolina, Col. O. Coward.
6th South Carolina, Col. John Bratton.
Hampton (South Carolina) Legion, Col. Martin W. Gary.
Palmetto (South Carolina) Sharpshooters, Col. Joseph Walker.

Robertson's Brigade.
3d Arkansas, Col. Van H. Manning.
1st Texas, Col. A. T. Rainey.
4th Texas, Col. J. C. G. Key.
5th Texas, Col. R. M. Powell.

Law's Brigade.
4th Alabama, Col. Pinckney D. Bowles.
15th Alabama, Col. W. C. Oates.
44th Alabama, Col. William F. Perry.
47th Alabama, Col. Michael J. Bulger.
48th Alabama, Col. James L. Sheffield.

Anderson's Brigade.
7th Georgia, Col. W. W. White.
8th Georgia, Col. John R. Towers.
9th Georgia, Col. Benjamin Beck.
11th Georgia, Col. F. H. Little.
59th Georgia, Col. Jack Brown.

Benning's Brigade.
2d Georgia, Col. Edgar M. Butt.
15th Georgia, Col. Dudley M. DuBose.
17th Georgia, Col. Wesley C. Hodges.
20th Georgia, Col. J. D. Waddell.

Artillery Battalion.
Col. E. PORTER ALEXANDER.
South Carolina Battery, William W. Fickling.
Virginia Battery, Capt. Tyler C. Jordan.
Louisiana Battery, Capt. George V. Moody.
Virginia Battery, Capt. William W. Parker.
Virginia Battery, Capt. Osmond B. Taylor.
Virginia Battery, Capt. Pichegru Woolfolk, Jr.

Law's Brigade was picketing Brown's Ferry when the latter was captured. Jenkins' Brigade attacked Geary at Wauhatchie the night of October 28th, supported by Benning's, Laws', and Robertson's Brigades on the heights at and north of the railroad crossing of Lookout Creek. November 4th, the division was sent to East Tennessee.

HARDEE'S CORPS.

Lieut.-Gen. WILLIAM J. HARDEE.

CHEATHAM'S DIVISION (HARDEE'S CORPS).

Maj.-Gen. B. F. CHEATHAM.

Jackson's Brigade.
1st Georgia (Confederate), Maj. James C. Gordon.
5th Georgia, Col. Charles P. Daniel.
37 Georgia, Capt. J. J. Harper.
65th Georgia, Lieut.-Col. Jacob W. Pearcy.
2d Georgia Battalion Sharpshooters, Lieut.-Col. Richard H. Whitely.
5th Mississippi, Maj. John B. Herring.
8th Mississippi, Maj. John F. Smith.

Moore's Brigade.
37th Alabama, Col. James F. Dowdell.
40th Alabama, Col. John H. Higley.
42d Alabama, Lieut.-Col. Thomas C. Lanier.

Walthall's Brigade.
24th and 27th Mississippi, Col. William F. Dowd.
29th and 30th Mississippi, Capt. W. G. Reynolds.
34th Mississippi, Col. Samuel Benton.

Wright's Brigade.
8th Tennessee, Col. John H. Anderson.
16th Tennessee, Col. D. M. Donnell.
28th Tennessee, Col. Sidney S. Stanton.
38th Tennessee, Lieut.-Col. Andrew D. Gwynne.
51st and 52d Tennessee, Lieut.-Col. John G. Hall.
Murray's (Tennessee) Battalion, Lieut.-Col. Andrew D. Gwynne.

Artillery Battalion.
Maj. MELANCTHON SMITH.
Alabama Battery, Capt. William H. Fowler.
Florida Battery, Capt. Robert P. McCants.
Georgia Battery, Capt. John Scogin.
Mississippi Battery (Smith's), Lieut. William B. Turner.

Walthall's Brigade fought the battle of Lookout Mountain until the Craven House was carried by Hooker. Moore's Brigade then supported his right, and Pettus' Brigade of Stevenson's Division came up to Walthall's line. Wright's Brigade was at Chickamauga Station. November 25th, Cheatham's Division was on Missionary Ridge just north of the DeLong Tower. When the enemy carried the Ridge at the latter point, Walthall's Brigade checked his further advance, supported by Brown's Brigade of Stevenson's Division on his left.

CLEBURNE'S DIVISION (HARDEE'S CORPS).

Maj.-Gen. PATRICK R. CLEBURNE.

Liddell's Brigade.

2d and 15th Arkansas, Maj. E. Warfield.
5th and 13th Arkansas, Col. John E. Murray.
6th and 7th Arkansas, Lieut.-Col. Peter Snyder.
8th Arkansas, Maj. Anderson Watkins.
19th and 24th Arkansas, Lieut.-Col. A. S. Hutchison.

Polk's Brigade.

1st Arkansas, Col. John W. Colquitt.
3d and 5th Confederate, Lieut.-Col. J. C. Cole.
2d Tennessee, Col. William D. Robison.
35th and 48th Tennessee, Col. Benjamin J. Hill.

Smith's Brigade.

6th and 10th Texas Infantry and 15th Texas (dismounted) Cavalry, Col. Roger Q. Mills.
7th Texas, Col. Hiram B. Granbury.
17th, 18th, 24th, and 25th Texas Cavalry (dismounted), Maj. William A. Taylor.

Lowrey's Brigade.

16th Alabama, Maj. Frederick A. Ashford.
33d Alabama, Col. Samuel Adams.
45th Alabama, Lieut.-Col. H. D. Lampley,
32d and 45th Mississippi, Lieut.-Col. R. Charlton.
15th Mississippi Battalion Sharpshooters, Capt. Daniel Coleman.

Artillery Battalion.

Maj. T. R. HOTCHKISS.

Arkansas Battery (Calvert's), Lieut. Thomas J. Key.
Texas Battery, Capt. James P. Douglas.
Alabama Battery (Semple's), Lieut. Richard W. Goldthwaite.
Mississippi Battery (Swett's), Lieut. H. Shannon.

November 23d, this division returned from Chickamauga Station. November 24th, until 2 P. M., it was constructing earthworks on the Ridge north from Bragg's Headquarters to the Shallow Ford Road. At that hour it was ordered to Tunnel Hill, reaching it at 2:30 P. M. November 25th, it resisted Sherman and fought the battle of Tunnel Hill, assisted at various points of the line by Cumming's, Pettus', and Brown's Brigades of Stevenson's Division, and Maney's of Walker's.

STEVENSON'S DIVISION (HARDEE'S CORPS).

Maj.-Gen. CARTER L. STEVENSON.

Brown's Brigade.*
3d Tennessee,† Col. Calvin H. Walker.
18th and 26th Tennessee, Lieut.-Col. William R. Butler.
32d Tennessee, Capt. Thomas D. Deavenport.
45th Tennessee and 23d Tennessee, Battalion, Col. Anderson Searcy.

Cummings' Brigade.†
34th Georgia, Col. J. A. W. Johnson.
36th Georgia, Lieut.-Col. Alexander M. Wallace.
39th Georgia, Col. J. T. McConnell.
56th Georgia, Lieut.-Col. J. T. Slaughter.

Pettus' Brigade.‡
20th Alabama, Capt. John W. Davis.
23d Alabama, Lieut.-Col. J. B. Bibb.
30th Alabama, Col. Charles M. Shelley.
31st Alabama, Col. D. R. Hundley.
46th Alabama, Capt. George E. Brewer.

Vaughn's Brigade.|
3d Tennessee (Provisional Army).
39th Tennessee.
43d Tennessee.
59th Tennessee.

Artillery Battalion.¶
Capt. WILLIAM W. CARNES.

Tennessee Battery, Capt. Edmund D. Baxter.
Tennessee Battery, Capt. William W. Carnes.
Georgia Battery, Capt. Max Van Den Corput.
Georgia Battery, Capt. John B. Rowan (Maryland Battery).

November 24th, held the top of Lookout. At 1:30 P. M. Pettus' Brigade assisted Walthall. November 25th, it reached the Tunnel at 9 A. M., occupying the high ground south of it. Cummings', Pettus', and Brown's Brigades assisted Cleburne's forces. About 5 P. M. Brown's Brigade returned to the center to assist in checking Baird, reaching Baird's line just as Walthall's Brigade of Cheatham's Division had stopped his northward advance along the crest of the Ridge.

---

* Transferred from Stewart's Division, November 12, 1863.

† In Gregg's Brigade, October 31, 1863.

‡ Regimental commanders not reported in original, are supplied from Stevenson's roster.

§ Reassigned to division, November 12, 1863.

| Note on original: "Exchanged prisoners; but few reported."

¶ According to Stevenson's return, his artillery battalion consisted at this date of Carnes', Corput's, and Rowan's Batteries, and the 20th Alabama Battalion, viz.: Company A, Capt. Winslow D. Emery; Company B, Capt. Richard H. Bellamy, and Company C, Capt. T. J. Key.

WALKER'S DIVISION * (HARDEE'S CORPS).

Maj.-Gen. W. H. T. WALKER.

Maney's Brigade.†

1st and 27th Tennessee, Col. Hume R. Field.
4th Tennessee (Provisional Army) Capt. Joseph Bostick.
6th and 9th Tennessee, Lieut.-Col. J. W. Buford.
41st Tennessee,‡ Col. Robert Farquharson.
50th Tennessee,‡ Col Cyrus A. Sugg.
24th Tennessee Battalion (Sharpshooters), Maj. Frank Maney.

Wilson's Brigade.

25th Georgia, Col. Claudius C. Wilson.
29th Georgia, Col. William J. Young.
30th Georgia, Col. Thomas W. Mangham.
26th Georgia Battalion, Maj. John W. Nisbet.
1st Georgia Battalion Sharpshooters,§ Maj. Arthur Shaaff.

Gist's Brigade.

46th Georgia, Lieut.-Col. William A. Daniel.
8th Georgia Battalion Lieut.-Col. Leroy Napier.
16th South Carolina, Col. James McCullough.
24th South Carolina, Col. Clement H. Stevens.

Artillery Battalion.

Maj. ROBERT MARTIN.
Missouri Battery, Capt. Hiram M. Bledsoe.
South Carolina Battery, Capt. T. B. Ferguson.
Georgia Battery, Capt. Evan P. Howell.

November 23d, the division was sent from the base of Lookout to a point on Missionary Ridge, a mile south of Tunnel Hill. November 25th, Maney's Brigade reported to Cleburne at the latter point and supported it in the engagement.

---

* Transferred from Longstreet's Corps, November 12, 1863, and regiments of Gregg's Brigade distributed to Bate's, Maney's, and Smith's Brigades.

† Transferred from Cheatham's Division, November 12, 1863.

‡ From Gregg's Brigade.

§ Assigned, November 12, 1863.

BRECKINRIDGES' ARMY CORPS.
Maj.-Gen. JOHN C. BRECKINRIDGE.

STEWART'S DIVISION (BRECKINRIDGE'S CORPS).
Maj.-Gen. ALEXANDER P. STEWART.

Adams' Brigade.

13th and 20th Louisiana, Col. Leon von Zinken.
16th and 25th Louisiana, Col. Daniel Gober.
19th Louisiana, Col. W. P. Winans.
4th Louisiana Battalion, Lieut.-Col. John McEnery.
14th Louisiana Battalion Sharpshooters, Maj. J. E. Austin.

Clayton's Brigade.

18th Alabama, Maj. Shep. Ruffin.
32d Alabama, Capt. John W. Bell.
36th Alabama, Col. Lewis T. Woodruff.
38th Alabama, Col. Charles T. Ketchum.
58th Alabama, Lieut.-Col. John W. Inzer.

Strahl's Brigade.

4th and 5th Tennessee, Col. Jonathan J. Lamb.
19th Tennessee, Col. Francis M. Walker.
24th Tennessee, Col. John A. Wilson.
31st Tennessee, Col. Egbert E. Tansil.
33d Tennessee, Lieut.-Col. Henry C. McNeill

Stovall's Brigade.

40th Georgia, [Col. Abda Johnson].
41st Georgia, [Col. William E. Curtiss].
42d Georgia, [Col. R. J. Henderson].
43d Georgia, [Col. Hiram P. Bell].
52d Georgia, [Maj. John J. Moore].

Artillery Battalion.
Capt. HENRY C. SEMPLE.

Georgia Battery (Dawson's), Lieut. R. W. Anderson.
Arkansas Battery (Humphrey's), Lieut. John W. Rivers.
Alabama Battery, Capt. McDonald Oliver.
Mississippi Battery, Capt. Thomas J. Stanford.

November 24th, at night, Stewart withdrew from the earthworks and occupied Missionary Ridge from Bragg's Headquarters to Rossville. November 25th, his line was carried, being assaulted in front by the right of Sheridan's Division and all of Johnson's and Geary's, on its left flank by Cruft's, and its rear by Osterhaus'.

BRECKINRIDGE'S DIVISION (BRECKINRIDGE'S CORPS).

Brig.-Gen. WILLIAM B. BATE.

Lewis' Brigade.

2d Kentucky, Lieut.-Col. James W. Moss.
4th Kentucky, Maj. Thomas W. Thompson.
5th Kentucky, Col. H. Hawkins.
6th Kentucky, Lieut.-Col. W. L. Clarke.
9th Kentucky, Lieut.-Col. John C. Wickliffe.
John H. Morgan's dismounted men.

Bate's Brigade.*

37th Georgia, Col. A. F. Rudler.
4th Georgia Battalion Sharpshooters, Lieut. Joel Towers.
10th Tennessee,† Col. William Grace.
15th and 37th Tennessee, Lieut.-Col. R. Dudley Frayser.
20th Tennessee, Maj. W. M. Shy.
30th Tennessee,† Lieut.-Col. James J. Turner.
1st Tennessee Battalion,† Maj. Stephen H. Colms.

Florida Brigade.‡

1st and 3d Florida, Capt. W. T. Saxon.
4th Florida, Lieut.-Col. F. Badger.
6th Florida, Col. Jesse J. Finley.
7th Florida, Lieut.-Col. Tillman Ingram.
1st Florida Cavalry (dismounted), Col. G. Troup Maxwell.

Artillery Battalion.

Capt. C. H. SLOCOMB.
Kentucky Battery (Cobb's), Lieut. Frank P. Gracey.
Tennessee Battery, Capt. John W. Mebane.
Louisiana Battery (Slocomb's), Lieut. W. C. D. Vaught.

The night of November 24th, the division withdrew from the earthworks and occupied the line on Missionary Ridge next north of Bragg's Headquarters. It fought stubbornly until both of its flanks were exposed to the fire of heavy forces, when it withdrew to the next Ridge in the rear, and there checked the advance of Sheridan's Division.

---

* Transferred from Stewart's Division, November 12, 1863.
† Transferred from Gregg's Brigade, November 12, 1863.
‡ Organized, November 12, 1863.

BUCKNER'S DIVISION* (BRECKINRIDGE'S CORPS).

Brig.-Gen. BUSHROD R. JOHNSON.

Johnson's Brigade.

17th and 23d Tennessee, Lieut.-Col. Watt W. Floyd.
25th and 44th Tennessee, Lieut.-Col. John L. McEwen, Jr.
63d Tennessee, Maj. John A. Aiken.

Gracie's Brigade.

41st Alabama, Lieut.-Col. Theodore G. Trimmier.
43d Alabama, Col. Young M. Moody.
1st Battalion, Alabama (Hilliard's) Legion, Maj. Daniel S. Troy.
2d Battalion, Alabama (Hilliard's) Legion, Capt. John H. Dillard.
3d Battalion, Alabama (Hilliard's) Legion, Lieut.-Col. John W. A. Sanford.
4th Battalion, Alabama (Hilliard's) Legion, Maj. John D. McLennan.

Reynolds' Brigade.

58th North Carolina, Col. John B. Palmer.
60th North Carolina, Capt. James T. Weaver.
54th Virginia, Lieut.-Col. John J. Wade.
63d Virginia, Maj. James M. French.

Artillery Battalion.

Maj. SAMUEL C. WILLIAMS.
Mississippi Battery (Darden's), Lieut. H. W. Bullen.
Virginia Battery, Capt. William C. Jeffress.
Alabama Battery, Capt. R. F. Kolb.

This division, with the exception of Reynolds' Brigade, was absent in East Tennessee. Reynolds was sent to the trenches, and retired to the Ridge in the face of the general assault of the Army of the Cumberland, and formed on the line of Bate's Division.

HINDMAN'S DIVISION (BRECKINRIDGE'S CORPS).

Brig.-Gen. PATTON ANDERSON.

Anderson's Brigade.

7th Mississippi, Col. William H. Bishop.
9th Mississippi, Maj. Thomas H. Lynam.
10th Mississippi, Capt. Robert A. Bell.
41st Mississippi, Col. W. F. Tucker.
44th Mississippi, Lieut.-Col. R. G. Kelsey.
9th Mississippi Battalion Sharpshooters, Capt. W. W. Tucker.

Deas' Brigade.

19th Alabama, Col. Samuel K. McSpadden.
22d Alabama, Capt. Harry T. Toulmin.
25th Alabama, Col. George D. Johnson.
39th Alabama, Col. Whitfield Clark.
50th Alabama, Col. J. G. Coltart.
17th Alabama Battalion Sharpshooters, Capt. James F. Nabers.

---

* Detached, November 22d, for operations against Burnside in East Tennessee. Reynolds' Brigade and the artillery were recalled.

Manigault's Brigade.
24th Alabama Col. N. N. Davis.
28th Alabama, Maj. W. L. Butler.
34th Alabama, Maj. John N. Slaughter.
10th and 19th South Carolina, Col. James F. Pressley.

Vaughan's Brigade.
11th Tennessee, Col. George W. Gordon.
12th and 47th Tennessee, Col. William M. Watkins.
13th and 154th Tennessee, Lieut.-Col. R. W. Pitman.
29th Tennessee, Col. Horace Rice.

Artillery Battalion.
Maj. ALFRED R. COURTNEY.
Alabama Battery, Capt. S. H. Dent.
Alabama Battery, Capt. James Garrity.
Tennessee Battery (Scott's), Lieut. John Doscher.
Alabama Battery (Waters'), Lieut. William P. Hamilton.

November 25th, Anderson's Division, having withdrawn from the earthworks at the foot of the Ridge during the night before, was on the right of Bate's, and extended nearly to the DeLong Tower. His line was carried in the general assault by the left of Wood's Division and the right of Baird's.

WHEELER'S CAVALRY CORPS.

Maj.-Gen. JOSEPH WHEELER.

The Confederate cavalry was not engaged at the battle of Chattanooga. After the battle of Chickamauga, it made effective raids north of the Tennessee upon the Union lines of communication, and operated in East Tennessee. Kelley's Division was stationed about Calhoun and Charleston at the time of the battle, and a portion of it attacked Col. Eli Long's Brigade of cavalry at Cleveland, November 27, and followed it back toward Chattanooga.

WHARTON'S DIVISION (WHEELER'S CORPS).

Maj.-Gen. JOHN A. WHARTON.

First Brigade.
Col. THOMAS HARRISON.
3d Arkansas, Lieut.-Col. M. J. Henderson.
65th North Carolina (6th Cavalry), Col. George N. Folk.
8th Texas, Lieut.-Col. Gustave Cook.
11th Texas, Lieut.-Col. J. M. Bounds.

Second Brigade.
Brig.-Gen. HENRY B. DAVIDSON.
1st Tennessee, Col. James E. Carter.
2d Tennessee, Col. Henry M. Ashby.
4th Tennessee, Col. William S. McLemore.
6th Tennessee, Col. James T. Wheeler.
11th Tennessee, Col. Daniel W. Holman.

MARTIN'S DIVISION (WHEELER'S CORPS).
Maj.-Gen. WILLIAM T. MARTIN.

First Brigade.
Brig.-Gen. JOHN T. MORGAN.
1st Alabama, Lieut.-Col. D. T. Blakey.
3d Alabama, Lieut.-Col. T. H. Mauldin.
4th Alabama (Russell's), Lieut.-Col. J. M. Hambrick.
Malone's (Alabama) Regiment, Col. James C. Malone, Jr.
51st Alabama, Capt. M. L. Kirkpatrick.

Second Brigade.
Col. J. J. MORRISON.
1st Georgia, Lieut.-Col. S. W. Davitte.
2d Georgia, Lieut.-Col. F. M. Ison.
3d Georgia, Lieut.-Col. R. Thompson.
4th Georgia, Col. Isaac W. Avery.
6th Georgia, Col. John R. Hart.

ARMSTRONG'S DIVISION (WHEELER'S CORPS).
Brig.-Gen. FRANK C. ARMSTRONG.

First Brigade.
Brig.-Gen. WILLIAM Y. C. HUMES.
4th Tennessee (Baxter Smith's), Lieut.-Col. Paul F. Anderson.
5th Tennessee, Col. George W. McKenzie.
8th Tennessee, (Dibrell's), —— ——.
9th Tennessee, Col. Jacob B. Biffle.
10th Tennessee, Col. Nicholas N. Cox.

Second Brigade.
Col. C. H. TYLER.
Clay's (Kentucky) Battalion, Lieut.-Col. Ezekiel F. Clay.
Edmundson's (Virginia) Battalion, Maj. S. P. McConnell.
Jessee's (Kentucky) Battalion, Maj. A. L. McAfee.
Johnson's (Kentucky) Battalion, Maj. O. S. Tenney.

KELLY'S DIVISION (WHEELER'S CORPS).

First Brigade.
Col. WILLIAM B. WADE.
1st Confederate, Capt. C. H. Conner.
3d Confederate, Col. W. N. Estes.
8th Confederate, Lieut.-Col. John S. Prather.
10th Confederate, Col. Charles T. Goode.

Second Brigade.
Col. J. WARREN GRIGSBY.
2d Kentucky, Col. Thomas G. Woodward.
1st Kentucky, Col. J. R. Butler.
9th Kentucky, Col. W. C. P. Breckinridge.
Allison's (Tennessee) Squadron, Capt. R. D. Allison.
Hamilton's (Tennessee) Battalion, Lieut.-Col. O. P. Hamilton.
Rucker's Legion, E. W. Rucker.

Artillery.
Tennessee Battery, Capt. A. L. Huggins.
Tennessee Battery, Capt. Gustave A. Huwald.
Tennessee Battery, Capt. B. F. White, Jr.
Arkansas Battery, Capt. J. H. Wiggins.

RESERVE ARTILLERY.

Maj. FELIX H. ROBERTSON.

Missouri Battery, Capt. Overton W. Barret.
Georgia Battery (Havis'), Lieut. James R. Duncan.
Alabama Battery (Lumsden's), Lieut. Harvey H. Cribbs.
Georgia Battery, Capt. Thomas L. Massenburg.

DETACHED.

Roddey's Cavalry Brigade.

4th Alabama, Col. William A. Johnson.
5th Alabama, Col. Josiah Patterson.
53d Alabama, Col. M. W. Hannon.
Moreland's (Alabama) Battalion, Lieut.-Col. M. D. Moreland.
Georgia Battery, Capt. C. B. Ferrell.

CHAPTER XIII.

GUIDE TO THE CHICKAMAUGA FIELD, APPROACHING FROM CRAWFISH SPRINGS.*

There are three points from which to make the tour of the Chickamauga battle field. The most natural one is to start from Crawfish Springs, thirteen miles from Chattanooga, on the Chattanooga, Rome and Columbus Railroad, and drive over the roads by which Rosecrans' army reached the field. The second is to take the train to Battle Field Station, nine miles from Chattanooga, on the Rome Road, and thence drive about the Park. This station is near the center of the west line of the field, half way between Snodgrass Hill and Widow Glenn's and a few hundred yards west of Dyer's House. The third is to drive from Chattanooga; but those who adopt this method should first study this chapter showing how the armies came upon the battle field, since, in driving from the city, the various positions for the first day are reached in their reverse order.

To the Field from Crawfish Springs.

Those who desire to visit the extreme point of infantry fighting on the Union right and the Confederate left will find it at Glass's Mill, on the Chickamauga, two and three-quarters miles south-east of Crawfish Springs. The first road to the left, about a mile south of the latter point, leads to the mill. The direct road runs to Pond Spring, Davis' Cross Roads, Dug Gap, Blue Bird Gap, Bailey's Cross Roads, Stevens' Gap, and other points of the campaign in McLemore's Cove.

The road to Glass' Mill emerges from the woods on high

---

* See maps, pages 1, 30, and 42.

CRAWFISH SPRING—THE OLD WHEEL. (See page xviii.)

ground overlooking the Valley of the Chickamauga. It descends into the low ground and runs direct to the mill.

Breckinridge's Division occupied the south bank of the river opposite the mill at daylight, September 19th. Helm's Brigade crossed to the west side at the mill, and attacked John Beatty's Brigade of Negley's Division. The latter was drawn up on the crest to the left of the road as it comes out of the woods. The fighting was chiefly between the artillery. Beatty's Brigade was supported by Stanley's. After two hours engagement between the batteries of each side, Breckinridge's troops were withdrawn, and proceeded to the vicinity of Lee and Gordon's Mill. The casualties were: Union, 2 killed and 17 wounded; Confederate, 22 killed and wounded.

On the 20th, Wheeler's cavalry crossed at Glass' Mill, dismounted, and attacked Eli Long's Brigade of Crook's Division, driving it back to the vicinity of Crawfish Springs, with a loss of 127 killed, wounded, and missing. The Union cavalry was operating in the vicinity of and at the fords above Glass' Mill throughout the 19th and 20th of September.

On the afternoon of the 20th, the Union cavalry was massed in the fields to the right and left of the road for a half mile or more south of the Park Hotel, at Crawfish Springs.

The old undershot wheel and mill stood at the upper side of the present pool nearest the road. The dam had not been constructed at the time of the battle, and the stream from the spring ran unobstructed to the Chickamauga. The railroad from Chattanooga was built after the war.

Back of the Park Hotel, on the high ground across the road, stands the Lee Mansion, which was Gen. Rosecrans' headquarters from the morning of September 16th until the forenoon of the 19th, when they were moved to Widow Glenn's. Near it were the Union Field Hospitals.

From the tower of the hotel the principal points in Mc-

Lemore's Cove, such as Stevens', Dougherty's, Blue Bird, Dug, and Wrothen's Gaps, and the Lookout and Pigeon Ranges, are plainly seen.

The observation tower to the north-east marks the ground near Hall's Ford where Bragg concentrated that part of his army which had crossed the Chickamauga during the night of the 18th and early morning of the 19th, and formed to attack Crittenden's Corps. The latter then stretched northward along the La Fayette road for a mile, its right resting at Lee and Gordon's Mill.

The troops of Thomas' Corps (Fourteenth) began to arrive at Crawfish from McLemore's Cove, about 5 o'clock on the afternoon of the 18th. Negley's Division, leading, was turned off toward Glass' Mill. The other divisions pressed on through the night, following the road along which the railroad now runs to the Widow Glenn's, and thence along the present Park Road skirting the east of the Dyer Fields, thence to the La Fayette Road in the vicinity of Kelly's. The broad road east of the railroad running from Crawfish Springs to the Viditoe House did not exist at the time of the battle. It was built by the Park Commissioners to enable visitors to avoid the seven dangerous railroad crossings on the old Crawfish Springs Road to Widow Glenn's and Viditoe's. This new road between these points does not cross the track after leaving Crawfish Springs. It runs throughout its length east of and nearly parallel to the old road over which a large part of Rosecrans' army advanced on the night of the 18th and during the 19th. Baird's Division, which became the advance when Negley left the column at Crawfish, after crossing the road from Dyer's to Brotherton, took the first road to the right, and reached the La Fayette Road between Kelly's and Poe's at daylight. Brannan passed on to the foot of Snodgrass Hill, and then turning to the right, reached Kelly's, on the La Fayette Road, at sunrise.

Gen. Thomas' field headquarters were then at the cross-

Kelly House and Field—Looking East from Lafayette Road. (See page xv.)

roads at that point, on the west side of the La Fayette Road, and south of the cross-roads.

Brannan's Division lighted fires for breakfast, but before it could be prepared, was ordered forward by Gen. Thomas upon the report from Col. Dan. McCook that a Confederate brigade had crossed at Reed's Bridge, that the bridge had been destroyed, and the brigade could be captured. Brannan marched rapidly north along the La Fayette Road to McDonald's, and there turned eastward with his left brigade, Van Derveer's, while his right, Croxton's, moved eastward from the center of the Kelly Field, and soon after struck Forrest's cavalry in the vicinity of Jay's Mill.

Reynolds' Division, following the same road from Crawfish, came out on the La Fayette Road at Poe's, about 1 o'clock. Johnson's Division of McCook's Corps reached the road just before noon over the same route as Baird's. The latter, about 9 A. M., marched eastward from the La Fayette Road along the road skirting the south side of the Kelly Field, and came into action on Brannan's right and rear between 9 and 10 o'clock.

Johnson's Division, moving along the same road, followed Baird into action soon after noon.

Reynolds' Division was sent in on the right and left of Palmer's Division of Crittenden's Corps. The latter division had been dispatched by Crittenden to Thomas without orders, and had marched from Lee and Gordon's to Poe's by the La Fayette Road, and attacked to the right of Johnson and south-east of Poe's. This move was at once reported to Gen. Rosecrans and approved.

Davis' Division of McCook's Corps followed the column on the Crawfish Springs Road to a point near the Widow Glenn's, where it was turned eastward through the woods to Viniard's, and attacked the Confederate left east of that point between 1 and 2 P. M. The place where Davis left the Crawfish Springs Road is indicated by a tablet.

A short distance north of this point is the site of Widow

Glenn's House, the headquarters of Gen. Rosecrans from Saturday forenoon until Sunday noon. The high shaft to Wilder's Brigade marks the position. Standing here, the line of telegraph poles along the La Fayette Road can be seen across the open ground to the east. Turning back to the railroad, and looking north along its track, the high ground in the distance is the southern point of Snodgrass Hill, immediately above the Viditoe House. A few hundred yards north, and to the right of the railroad, is Bloody Pond. It was the only water on this part of the field during the battle. The low wooded rise across the open ground north of Widow Glenn's is Lytle Hill, upon which is the monument to Gen. William H. Lytle, who was killed there. Following the road around its eastern base, the large fields next beyond are on the Dyer Farm. Through and over these fields streamed Longstreet's columns after they had broken through the Union line on Sunday at Brotherton's, to the east of them.

The last division to pass Saturday over the road from Crawfish Springs to the Dyer Fields was Negley's, which arrived at the latter point at 5 o'clock Saturday evening. It assisted in restoring the line which had been broken at Brotherton by Stewart's Division, one of whose brigades penetrated to the Tan Yard in the Dyer Fields.

To follow the rest of the Union troops into battle on Saturday, upon reaching the southern boundary of the Park from Crawfish Springs, take the right-hand road, which forms this southern limit, and drive to Lee and Gordon's Mill, a mile distant on the La Fayette Road at the crossing of the Chickamauga.

Crittenden's Corps occupied the line of the La Fayette Road during Friday night from Lee and Gordon's Mill northward for more than a mile. The right of Wood's Division rested on the bluff above and west of the mill. Van Cleve's was in the field west of Scott's, and Palmer's Division, on the left of it, reached into the woods beyond.

Bloody Pond—Widow Glenn's—Looking East. (See page xvi.)

The observation tower to the north-east stands on the ground where Bragg's army began at daylight to form for an attack on Crittenden, then supposed by Bragg to be the Union left, as the night march of the center and right from McLemore's Cove to the La Fayette Road at Kelly's had not been discovered.

At 11 o'clock A. M. of Saturday, Palmer's Division was dispatched along the La Fayette Road to Poe's, where it formed and moved at once into action in the woods to the south-east of that point. Two brigades of Van Cleve's Division followed Palmer about 1 o'clock, and attacked 400 yards south-east of Brotherton's, on Palmer's right.

Soon after Van Cleve had passed Viniard's, as he was moving north, Davis' Division, marching from the vicinity of Widow Glenn's, reached that point, and, moving into the fields east of the La Fayette Road, was soon heavily engaged with Hood's troops advancing from the forest east of the Viniard Fields. Wilder's Brigade of Mounted Infantry, which had occupied the line of forest west and north of Viniard's since daylight, assisted Davis. Wood's Division next moved up from Lee and Gordon's, reaching Viniard's about 4 o'clock, followed soon by Barnes' Brigade of Van Cleve's Division, and next by Bradley's and Laibolt's Brigades of Sheridan's, Lytle's Brigade being left at Lee and Gordon's. The battle at Viniard's lasted from 2 o'clock till sundown, and was one of the most desperate of the whole engagement. The opposing Confederate troops were the divisions of Law and Bushrod Johnson of Hood's Corps, and Trigg's Brigade of Preston's Division.

Riding north on the La Fayette Road from Viniard's, to the left is seen the shell monument to mark the spot where Col. Heg, commanding a brigade of Davis' Division, was killed. He was attempting to rally his line, which had been forced across the road from the north-east.

To the right, and further north, in the open ground which was then in timber, Harker's Brigade of Wood's Division engaged a part of Gregg's and McNair's Brigades of Bushrod Johnson's Division. A little further north, upon the first road to the left, part of Harker's command struck the rear of Fulton's Brigade, the right of Johnson's Division, which had crossed the La Fayette Road and wheeled north toward Brotherton's. Fulton was attacking the right of Van Cleve's Division, then rallying on the high ground south of Brotherton's in the face of Stewart's advance. Four regiments of Law's Brigade, under command of Col. W. C. Oates, Fifteenth Alabama, were engaged on the right of Fulton.

Brotherton's House is next reached. It marks both the point where Clayton's Brigade of Stewart's Division penetrated the Union line on Saturday, and where Johnson's Division, followed by Law's and Kershaw's, these being the center of Longstreet's column, pierced the Union line on Sunday. The tablets marking Longstreet's lines before this advance will be found on the road leading east from Brotherton's, and about 700 yards from the latter point.

Poe's House, known in the Confederate reports as the "burning house," is next north of Brotherton's on the left. From the north end of the Poe Field, Gen. Reynolds, with his own troops, and part of Palmer's, assisted by twenty guns which he had collected, repulsed the extreme advance of Bate's Brigade of Stewart's Division about 5 o'clock Saturday evening.

The first road to the left, north of Poe's, is the one upon which Baird's Division, the head of Rosecrans' turning column, reached the La Fayette Road at daylight, September 19th, from Crawfish Springs. The second road to the left is the one upon which Brannan's Division reached the La Fayette Road at sunrise, while Reynolds reached the Poe House about 1 o'clock by the road upon which Baird had moved.

The best route for visiting the whole line of the first day's battle is to follow Brannan's advance from the McDonald House to the vicinity of Jay's Mill, and then drive from the latter point to Brotherton's. This will cover the whole, except the battle about Viniard's, the general features of which have already been given (page 175).

Soon after sunrise, Brannan's left Brigade (Van Derveer's) turned eastward opposite the McDonald House toward Reed's Bridge. At the same time, Croxton took a road leading from the center of the east side of Kelly's Field to the same point by way of Jay's Mill. The Reed's Bridge Road, a few rods north of the McDonald House, leads directly to the ground of Van Derveer's engagement, though his brigade took a farm lane that led through the grounds opposite McDonald's, and reached the true Ringgold Road a short distance before it went into action. This latter point is at the cross-roads on the crest of the Ridge a mile east of McDonald's.

Arriving at the cross-roads, with deployed lines on each side of the Reed's Bridge Road, Van Derveer swung his front toward the south-east, descended the slope a hundred yards, and became hotly engaged about 8 o'clock with Forrest's dismounted cavalry, soon re-enforced by Ector's Infantry Brigade of Walker's Division.

The crest to the north of the cross-roads running nearly parallel to the Reed's Bridge Road marks the line of Van Derveer's Brigade at the close of the fighting on Brannan's front, when Forrest's command was repulsed in a final attempt to turn Van Derveer's left.

The trace passing along the rocky glade to the right from the cross-roads leads in rear of Van Derveer's first position up to the tower which stands just in rear of his right. Here, part of Connell's Brigade with its battery re-enforced Van Derveer. From a point a short distance to the right (south) of the tower, the Ninth Ohio charged forward from Van Derveer's right to recapture the battery of the regular brigade of Baird's Division, which had lost its guns and been driven back over Van Derveer's troops by an attack on its right flank from Walthall's Brigade of Liddell's Division. At this point of recapture now stands the monument to Battery H, Fifth U. S. Artillery.

Passing along the road by the observation tower toward Jay's Mill, 600 yards beyond it the position is reached where the regular brigade (J. H. King's), which came to the relief of Croxton about 10 A. M., was broken later by the sudden appearance of Walthall's Brigade of Liddell's Division on its right flank. A few hundred yards beyond that is the position where Croxton's Brigade, advancing from the Kelly Field on the right of Van Derveer, opened the battle of Chickamauga. The right of Croxton's line, marked by the Seventy-fourth Indiana, is beyond the monument to Battery H, in the edge of the first field reached, and near the Brotherton Road. Croxton became engaged at 7:30 A. M.; Van Derveer, at 8.

Across this latter road, and some hundred yards beyond it in the wood's Wilson's Infantry Brigade of Walker's Division appeared on Croxton's right flank. Croxton's line was then changed to face toward Wilson, and stretched westward in the general direction of the Brotherton Road a full brigade front.

It is an interesting fact that Wilson's Infantry Brigade was hurried forward to Forrest's support with the statement to its officers that a Federal brigade had been discovered in the woods near Reed's Bridge, which could be captured by prompt work. It will be remembered that Brannan had been dispatched toward Reed's Bridge upon a similar report from Dan. McCook in regard to an isolated Confederate brigade.

Driving east on the Brotherton Road, the site of Jay's Steam Saw-mill is soon reached. It stood at the junction of this road with the one from Alexander's to Reed's Bridge. Here the battle of Chickamauga began.

Forrest's Cavalry, coming early from Alexander's Bridge, was formed in the general direction of the road facing toward the positions afterward occupied by Brannan's Division.

Dan. McCook's Brigade of J. D. Morgan's Division of Granger's Corps, supported by Mitchell's Brigade of Steedman's Division, had bivouacked the night of the 18th across the road from Reed's Bridge to McDonald's at the first frame house seen on the north side of the clearing. At daylight, McCook made an attempt to burn the bridge, and his skirmishers tried to reach the spring at Jay's Mill for water, but were sharply attacked by Forrest's men. McCook and Mitchell were withdrawn at sunrise toward Rossville, passing the left flank of Van Derveer's Brigade as it was advancing.

At 7:30, Croxton's skirmishers had advanced nearly to the mill, and soon after the main lines were heavily engaged, Forrest's men fighting dismounted.

From a point a few paces north of the spring the observation tower can be plainly seen which marks the right of Van Derveer's first position. At the time of the battle, the present clearing was woods, with the exception of a field extending two or three hundred yards west of the spring.

Soon after 10 o'clock Ector's Infantry Brigade came to the assistance of Forrest, formed east of the spring, and advanced westward against Van Derveer.

Forrest's last offensive movement was to throw a strong column into the ravine north of Van Derveer's left, and advance against that flank of Brannan's line. The movement was discovered, and Van Derveer rapidly changed his front to meet it. After a severe engagement, Forrest withdrew, and the fighting in the vicinity of the mill ceased about 1 o'clock.

Returning westward along the Brotherton Road the drive is across the Alexander's Bridge Road, and on to the Brock Field, nearly between the Union and Confederate lines. After passing through the first open field, and the woods to the west of it, the higher ground to the right in the field beyond is the position of Scribner's Brigade, the right of Baird's Division. To the left, and back along the line of road just traversed, the troops of Wilson's Brigade, and Forrest's dismounted men operating with them, attacked Croxton's line north of the road. The fighting was prolonged and severe.

Site of Jay's Mill—Forrest's Line at Opening of the Battle. (See page xvi.)

About 11 o'clock, Liddell's Division, with Walthall's Brigade on its right, and Govan's on its left, marching from the south, struck Scribner in flank, Govan capturing his battery (Van Pelt's First Michigan). Walthall, passing further to the right, marched northward to the next crest, striking the right flank of King's Regular Brigade (the left of Baird), on the ground where the monument to Battery H, Fifth U. S. Artillery, stands. Here Walthall captured this battery, and drove King to his left, and over Van Derveer's Brigade. The troops of the latter line, in turn, repulsed Walthall. Govan and Walthall then retired, before a movement on their flank, to the ground near where Wilson first came into action.

Riding on to the junction of the Alexander's Bridge Road, we reach the right flank of Cheatham's Division, which advanced next after Liddell. The right of Jackson's Brigade, as it advanced into action, was near the culvert next east of the Alexander's Bridge Road. From this point Cheatham's line extended southwesterly, passing west of the Winfrey House (now Reed's), which is the first one to the east on the Alexander's Bridge Road, and through the Brock Field to a point near its south-west corner, where the left of Wright's Brigade rested. Between Jackson's and Wright's Brigades, on the front line, was Preston Smith's. Maney's and Strahl's Brigades constituted the second line. Upon advancing, Jackson struck a line believed to have been Starkweather's Brigade of Baird's Division, and pushed it over the crest a quarter of a mile north-west of the Brotherton Road. Just beyond this crest, Willich's Brigade of Johnson's Division was encountered. After two hours' fighting Jackson was relieved on the crest by Maney's Brigade. By 3 P. M., Johnson's Division had advanced across the Brotherton Road nearly to the Winfrey (Reed) House, Dodge being on the right, Willich in the center, and Baldwin on the left in the field where Scribner's Brigade of Baird's Division first had position. Cheatham's Division retired before Johnson's attack to the rear of the high ground next south of the Winfrey House, establishing its batteries on that elevation.

The ground south of the Brotherton Road from the eastern edge of the Brock Field to the first crest west of Jay's Mill is the scene of the furious night fight Between Johnson's Division and Scribner's and Starkweather's Brigades of Baird's Division on the Union side, and Cleburne's Division and Jackson's and Preston Smith's brigades of Cheatham's Division on the Confederate. This engagement was brought on by Cleburne. Crossing the Chickamauga at Thedford's Ford, reaching Jay's Mill at 6 o'clock, and forming his line along the Jay's Mill and Alexander's Bridge Road, with his right brigade (Polk's) at the mill, Wood's in the center, and Deshler's on the left, he advanced in a north-west direction, encountering Baird's two brigades on the left of Johnson, and soon after Johnson's whole division. Jackson's and Smith's Brigades of Cheatham's Division advanced, in rear of Cleburne's left. Preston Smith, riding through an opening in Cleburne's line, came upon Dodge's Brigade of Johnson's Division and was killed. The shell monument which marks the spot will be found within sight, and west of the Winfrey (Reed's) House.

The next point of interest on the road toward Brotherton's is the Brock Field. Hazen's Brigade, the left of Palmer's Division, marching from the direction of the Poe House, came into its eastern half. It became engaged to the right, or north of the road, forced its way well toward the center of the field, and faced its eastern border. Cruft's Brigade, the center of Palmer's Division, entered the western side of the Brock Field from the north of the road, and Grose's Brigade, the right of the division, from the same direction, occupying a position south of the road, and half way between the western edge of the Brock Field and the Brotherton House.

About 4 o'clock, Hazen's Brigade was withdrawn to the

Poe House to replenish ammunition, and Turchin's Brigade of Reynolds' Division took its place in the Brock Field.

Shortly before 2 o'clock, S. Beatty's and Dick's Brigades of Van Cleve's Division advanced from the La Fayette Road at Brotherton's, and went into action to the right of Grose's line, about 400 yards east of the La Fayette Road.

Cheatham's line having been forced considerably to the rear, Stewart's Division was dispatched from the vicinity of the Park House to its assistance. It entered the Brock Field at its south-west corner, moving north in column of brigades, and at once wheeled to the left, advancing in the general direction of Brotherton's and Poe's Houses. Clayton's Brigade attacked first, and, after persistent fighting, was replaced by Brown's, and the latter in turn by Bate's. A small part of Law's Brigade (Sheffield's), marching from east of Viniard's, joined in the attack on Cruft in the Brock Field, and the whole was charged by Turchin, who wheeled upon these lines from the north-eastern portion of the field, and, with the help of Cruft, repulsed them. King's Brigade of Reynolds' Division came from the Poe Field, and reinforced both Grose and Van Cleve.

At 4 P. M., Clayton pushed Van Cleve across the La Fayette Road at Brotherton's, and at 4:30 drove him west of the Dyer Field. Bate turned north into the Poe Field, and was repulsed at 5 o'clock by troops and guns collected by Gen. Reynolds from his own and Palmer's commands.

From a short distance south of Brotherton's, neither line of battle was continuous toward the south, but both soon began again, and were as described (p. 175) where the movements and positions about Viniard's are given.

To follow the movements of the Confederate forces into Saturday's battle, it will be necessary to start in succession from Reed's Bridge, Alexander's House, and the Hall's Ford Tower.

Bushrod Johnson's Division and Robertson's Brigade of Hood's (Law's), marching from Ringgold early in the morning of September 18th, had forced a crossing of the Chickamauga at Reed's Bridge about 3 o'clock in the afternoon of that day. Here Hood arrived and took command. There was stubborn resistance from Minty's cavalry and a portion of Wilder's mounted infantry. The latter, at Alexander's Bridge, had prevented the attempted crossing of Walker's Corps by sharp resistance and final dismantling of the bridge. Walker then crossed at Byram's Ford, passed Alexander's on the road to Viniard's, and bivouacked west of the great bend in the river. Hood bivouacked still further in advance on the same road, three-quarters of a mile east of Viniard's.

During the night of the 18th and morning of the 19th, Buckner's Corps, consisting of Stewart's and Preston's Divisions, crossed the Chickamauga, the former at Thedford's. and the latter at Dalton's (Hunt's) Ford, and early formed line on the ground now marked by the observation tower near Thedford's House. Preston's left rested just west of and to the left of the tower. Stewart formed to the right of Preston, near the Park House. Hood's Corps moved forward from its bivouac to the crest in front, which during the night had been occupied by Wilder's Brigade, and formed line of battle with Bushrod Johnson's Division on the right of Stewart, and Law's Division on Johnson's right.

Cheatham's Division crossed early on the 19th at Dalton's Ford, and formed in reserve in rear of Buckner's Corps. All this ground is best seen from the Hall's Ford Tower. Walker's Corps was near the great bend in the river, as described, about to move forward to form on Hood's right. Forrest's cavalry had bivouacked near Alexander's, and very early had marched to Jay's Mill to observe in that direction.

Such was the Confederate position early on September 19th, with lines deployed toward Lee and Gordon's, ready to advance on Crittenden's Corps, when Brannan's Division attacked Forrest at Jay's Mill. Forrest himself soon went for infantry assistance, and finding Wilson's Brigade at Alexander's on the march toward its corps (Walker's), he took it in haste

Reed's Bridge, Looking Upstream—Bragg's First Crossing. (See page xviii.)

to the aid of his troops. Ector's Brigade, also of Walker's Division, was dispatched soon after to the same point. About 11 o'clock, Liddell's Division started northward. At noon, Cheatham's Division followed, and at 1 o'clock Stewart was on the march to the Brock Field to assist Cheatham. At 2 o'clock, Hood's Corps, assisted by Trigg's Brigade of Preston's Division, moved westward into battle at Viniard's. Hindman's Division crossed at Dalton's Ford at 4 o'clock, and advanced toward Viniard's, but did not become engaged.

The Lines Sunday Morning, September 20th.

During the night of the 19th, the lines of both armies were re-arranged. Before the battle re-opened, at 9:30 A. M. the Union line extended from the north-east corner of the Kelly Field along it eastern and southern borders. Over this part of the line it was protected by roughly constructed logworks. It crossed the La Fayette Road on the northern side of the Poe Field, ran along its western side and in rear of Brotherton's Field to the vicinity of the Tan-Yard, and thence to Widow Glenn's. The line to the Tan-Yard was protected by a rough barricade of rails, stumps, and stones.

The Confederate lines at the time of attack began with Forrest's cavalry on their extreme right in the woods east of the Cloud House, facing the La Fayette Road. The right division of infantry was Breckinridge's. Two of its brigades and half of the third reached beyond the left of the Union line. Following thence toward the Confederate left, the front line ran about 600 or 700 yards east of the Union position. Its divisions next on the left of Breckinridge were Cleburne, Stewart, Bushrod Johnson, and Hindman. Walker's Corps was in reserve to the right and rear of Breckinridge. Cheatham's Division was in reserve behind Cleburne and Stewart, and Preston's to the left and rear of Hindman. In the center, east of the Brotherton House, Law's Division was in rear of Bushrod Johnson's, and Kershaw's in rear of Law's.

As the attack opened on the Union left and extended to its right, the most satisfactory route by which to examine the lines is to follow the movements of the battle.

Forrest's position will be most easily reached by riding eastward from McDonald's on the Ringgold Road to the first glade, a distance of about 700 yards. The left of Forrest's line will be found on this glade about 100 yards north.

Breckinridge's position, where the attack of the Confederate infantry began, is best found by following the Alexander Bridge Road, the first to the left south of McDonald's, to the glade east of this road. Here, on the right, will be found the monuments marking the Union left. Breckinridge assaulted the crest on the east side of this glade, and from this crest, at the foot of the slope beyond it, can be seen the pyramidal monument of shells marking the spot where Helm, commanding his left brigade was mortally wounded. To the north of the Helm monument is one to Colquitt, killed while commanding a brigade in Gist's (Walker's) Division, which, after Breckinridge's repulse, attacked nearly on the same ground. To the south of the Helm monument, and on the same ridge, but nearly opposite the south end of the Kelly Field, will be found a monument to Deshler, killed there in command of the left brigade of Cleburne's Division.

Baird's Division held the left of the Union line around the north-east corner of the Kelly Field, including the eastern and northern salients of the logworks, and the reverse extending toward the La Fayette Road. This reverse is marked by the monuments of the regular brigade. Before the attack began, Grose's Brigade of Palmer, Dodge's of Johnson, and part of John Beatty's of Negley, strengthened the reverse, and extended it nearly to the La Fayette Road. Proceeding along the eastern side of the Kelly Field, on the right of Baird's, came Johnson's Division, and next Palmer's, while

Reynolds' extended the line around the south-east corner and south side of the field, his line crossing the La Fayette Road and joining Brannan's Division north of the Poe Field. The latter was formed along the west side of the Poe Field; its right extended toward the west side of the Brotherton Field, and nearly reaching it, at which point it joined Negley, whose line along the west side of the Brotherton Field reached to the Tan-Yard.

Just before the attack opened at the Brotherton House, Negley's Division had been sent to the left, and its place taken by Wood's Division. This being also sent to the left, almost at the moment the Confederate attack was delivered, Longstreet's column marched into the gap, and, in spite of considerable fighting from the flanks of the opening, forced its way into the Dyer Field. At this moment, Davis' Division, from about the Tan-Yard, was attempting to close to the left, and fill the space vacated by Wood. Sheridan was hastening toward the same point from his position in front of Widow Glenn's. While thus moving, these two divisions were attacked from the front and right by Hindman, and by Bushrod Johnson on their left, forced off the field and over the ridge west of the Crawfish Springs Road.

Wilder's mounted infantry held the Union right at the opening of the action, being posted on the ridge next west of the Widow Glenn's, and from that line with Harrison's regiment of mounted infantry, charged the left of Hindman's advance, and pushed it back across the La Fayette Road.

At daylight four Union divisions and Wilder's Brigade occupied the ridge west of and overlooking the Crawfish Springs Road. Next to Wilder's troops, which formed the right, was Sheridan's Division nearly opposite the Bloody Pond, next Davis', reaching nearly to a point opposite Lytle Station, then Wood's with his left on the road to Dyers' and Van Cleve's with his right on this road and his left overlooking the Viditoe Fields.

Just before the break in the lines back of Brotherton's,

Van Cleve had been sent forward to Dyer's Field, and then diagonally to the left, being nearly in rear of Brannan's line back of Poe's at the time of the break. Wood, with Barnes' Brigade of Van Cleve, had been moved forward into Negley's line back of Brotherton's. Davis had moved forward to the vicinity of the Tan-Yard, and Sheridan to the widow Glenn's.

When the break first occurred, Gen. Rosecrans, with part of his staff, and the Fifteenth Pennsylvania Cavalry, was on the crest next east of Lytle's Station, and in front of the grove on the right of the road to Dyer's. At the first signs of trouble on the lines he rode to Widow Glenn's to hasten Sheridan to the left.

From the La Fayette Road near the Poe House, the position of Stewart's Division, which was next on the left of Cleburne, can be seen. It occupied the first low ridge in the woods to the east. Its right joined Cleburne, and its left rested on Bushrod Johnson's Division.

The Brotherton House at the La Fayette Road marks the spot where Longstreet's central column pierced the Union center. The position of this line at the time of its advance can be seen from the La Fayette Road. Its front, Bushrod Johnson's Division, was on the same ridge with Stewart's line. In rear of Johnson was Law's Division of Hood's Corps, with Kershaw's Division in the third line. The center of each of these was on the road leading east from Brotherton's. Hindman's Division was on the left of Johnson's, its left nearly reaching the La Fayette Road at a point half way between Brotherton's and Viniard's. Trigg's Brigade, the right of Preston's Division, was on the east line of the Viniard Field, and the left of the division rested at the observation tower near Hall's Ford.

Snodgrass Hill.

The Snodgrass Hill position can be most readily understood by approaching it from the direction taken by the Union troops when falling back to occupy it.

When Bushrod Johnson's Division, advancing from the forest east of the La Fayette Road at the Brotherton House, forced its way through the gap in the Union lines west of Brotherton's caused by the sending of Wood to the left, it turned to the right upon reaching the Dyer Field, and moved forward to the ridge on its western edge.

Law's Division followed by Kershaw moved against Brannan's lines in the western edge of the Poe Field. Being forced back, Brannan directed his two brigades—Connell's and Croxton's, Van Derveer's having been sent to Baird before the break—toward the Snodgrass House.

Harker's Brigade of Wood's Division, having passed to the rear of Brannan and to his left, finding that the enemy was marching northward in the Dyer Field, moved back rapidly by the left flank, and formed across the field upon the first high ground toward its northern limits. From this point it repulsed Law's Division, and was in turn pushed back by Kershaw's Division, which passed over Law, and attacked Harker in force. This checking of Hood's column greatly assisted Brannan in forming a line of troops, of his own and various other commands, reaching from the Snodgrass House to the high point of the hill at the present observation tower. Battery I, Fourth U. S. Artillery, Lieut. Frank G. Smith, already held position at the house. Stanley's Brigade of Negley formed next on the right of this battery, Croxton's Brigade and portions of Connell's next, and the Twenty-first Ohio of Sirwell's Brigade of Negley on the extreme right.

Standing at the Snodgrass House, and looking north, the open country is the ground over which Gordon Granger advanced on Sunday to the assistance of Gen. Thomas. His troops, upon arriving, marched rapidly into the ravine back of the house, attacked the force which had gained Brannan's rear, pushed it back over the ridge and extended Thomas' line.

When Harker was forced back by Kershaw, he took position on the low open crest to the north of the Snodgrass barn.

Front of the Snodgrass House. (See page xvi.)

Later in the afternoon, Hazen's Brigade of Palmer's Division joined Harker from the Kelly Field line.

Harker's position was unsuccessfully assaulted at 2 o'clock by Humphrey's Brigade of Kershaw's Division, and Brannan's line by Kershaw's Brigade of the same division.

At 2 P. M., Johnson's Division, with Anderson's Brigade of Hindman's Division on his right, assaulted Snodgrass Hill from the direction of Viditoe's House, and a portion of his line passed over the crest beyond Brannan's right, and at 2:30 P. M. had gained the northern slope in his rear below the observation tower.

At that point he was met by Whitaker's Brigade, followed by Mitchell's, both of Steedman's Division of Gordon Granger's Corps. The latter had been marched rapidly by Gen. Granger from McAfee's Church to the assistance of Gen. Thomas, who was then in command of the army, with headquarters at the Snodgrass House.

Whitaker charged Johnson's advance, regained the crest, and prolonged Brannan's right, which was still further extended by Mitchell's Brigade fighting its way to the summit and taking position on Whitaker's right. A portion of the Ninety-sixth Illinois, belonging to Whitaker, was upon the right of Mitchell, and held the extreme right of the army. Gen. Thomas' line was then solid from the edge of the woods north-east of the Snodgrass House to a point beyond the ravine through which the road leads down to the Viditoe House.

Van Derveer's Brigade returned intact from an engagement with Breckinridge's troops in the Kelly Field at the same time that Granger's troops arrived. It formed on the left of Steedman's Division, moved to the crest of the ridge with it, and strengthened Brannan's line from the tower to the right of Stanley's Brigade.

At 6 o'clock, Steedman, being out of amunition, withdrew to the next ridge in his rear, the Confederates following to the bottom of the ravine on the northern side of the ridge.

Three regiments on the left of Whitaker which had not received notice to withdraw were mostly captured by Trigg's and Kelly's Brigades of Preston's Division. These were the Twenty-first and Eighty-ninth Ohio and the Twenty-second Michigan. Their place of capture was upon the next knoll 150 yards south-west of the observation tower.

The withdrawal to McFarland's Gap from Wood's and Brannan's lines was from left to right, beginning on the left of Wood at 7 P. M.; after fighting had ceased, and ending on the right of Brannan, at the tower, at 8 o'clock.

The road at the base of Snodgrass Hill, beginning a few hundred yards south of the Snodgrass House, follows the base to the Viditoe House. It passes along the line of Confederate assault. Humphrey's Brigade of Kershaw's Division faced Harker's position on the open crest. The right of Kershaw's Brigade rested upon and not far from the beginning of this road to Viditoe's. Anderson's Brigade of Hindman's Division was on the left of Kershaw, and the three brigades of Bushrod Johnson's Division, Sugg, Fulton, and McNair, next in line, reached Viditoe's, and Manigault's and Deas' of Hindman's Division were on the extreme left. Deas' Brigade was directed against the high spur to the left of the road, leading from the railroad up the gorge to the Union right. The point of the spur to the right of this road was carried early in the action by Fulton's Brigade, assisted by Manigault's, and held until the close of the battle.

The Union line on Snodgrass Hill can be reached by the road up the gorge near the Viditoe House. This road crosses the crest on the line of Mitchell's Brigade, the right of Granger's line. The brigades as they succeeded this one toward the Union left were Whitaker's of Steedman, Van Derveer's of Brannan, with portions of Croxton's and Connell's of the same division, Stanley's of Negley, Harker's of Wood, and Hazen's of Palmer.

Division and Brigade Positions on Snodgrass Hill.

Wood's Division held the line on the open crest from the Snodgrass barn to the woods, Hazen's Brigade of Palmer's Division being sent to re-enforce it about 3 o'clock. Stanley's Brigade of Negley's Division, which was under the command of Brannan after Negley left the field, extended from the Snodgrass House to the first high point south of it. Brannan's Division reached thence to the observation tower, and Steedman's Division from the tower to the top of the ravine running down to the Viditoe House. The two companies of the Ninety-sixth Illinois, posted across the high ridge beyond, acted there throughout the afternoon as sharpshooters, checking the advance of Deas' left.

An Incident at Widow Glenn's.

This position was held Sunday forenoon by portions of two companies of the Twenty-first Michigan under Lieut. Charles E. Belknap, assisted by Lieut. A. E. Barr, when enveloped by the left of Hindman's Division. This was one of the brilliant lesser affairs of the battle. The plucky command was finally saved by a charge of Wilder's Brigade.

CHAPTER XIV.

VISITING CHICKAMAUGA FROM CHATTANOOGA.*

Those who decide to visit the Chickamauga Park by driving from Chattanooga, should first read Chapter XIII, presenting in detail the movements of both Rosecrans' and Bragg's armies to the field. As these reached it from the south instead of from the direction of Chattanooga, those who drive from the latter point reverse the more natural order of approaching the field as the armies did.

The direct route is by Rossville, and thence through the Gap by the La Fayette Road. It is four miles to Rossville, and four and a half thence to Kelly's, which is central on the field.

If the desire is to see as much as possible of Missionary Ridge and Chickamauga the same day, by driving on McCallie Avenue to the Ridge, a distance of about three miles, the visitor can then pass along upon the Crest Road above the greater part of the line of assault of the Army of the Cumberland, and overlook the scenes of nearly all the battles about Chattanooga. The added distance to Chickamauga by this plan is about five miles.

This route takes the visitor to Bragg's Headquarters on Missionary Ridge. Here the government has purchased between three and four acres, and erected one of the steel observation towers. Each of these is seventy feet to the upper platform.

Upon reaching Rossville Gap, it is not necessary to descend to Rossville, as a cut-off along the crest runs direct to the La Fayette Road at the top of the Gap.

---

* See pages 1, 30 and 42.

Tower, Bragg's Headquarters, Missionary Ridge. (P. xvi.)

At Rossville the roads of the Park are reached. About this position, and on the ridges and in the Gap just beyond it, the Army of the Cumberland went into line again after withdrawing from Chickamauga at nightfall of September 20th. Crittenden's Corps occupied Missionary Ridge to the north of the Gap, Thomas' Corps held the Gap, and the ridge south of it, and McCook's Corps was in position across Chattanooga Valley. These dispositions continued until midnight of Monday, September 21st, when, the enemy not attacking, the army marched into Chattanooga. The road to the right, at Rossville, runs to McFarland's Gap, two and three-quarters miles distant, and thence to Crawfish Springs, six miles and a quarter from the Gap, the road from that point forming the western boundary of the Park.

The first road to the left in descending from the Gap, after passing the crest road, leads to McAfee's Church and Ringgold. As the tablet at the junction shows, Gordon Granger's Corps, after a forced march of thirty-five miles from Bridgeport, moved over it to Ringgold, and was subsequently established in the vicinity of McAfee's Church. From that point, it marched, shortly before noon of Sunday, September 20th, to the assistance of Gen. Thomas on Snodgrass Hill.

The first Union force to pass over the La Fayette Road in the Chickamauga campaign was Harker's Brigade of Wood's Division of Crittenden's Corps, which left Rossville Gap the morning of September 10th, reaching Lee and Gordon's Mill at 4:30 P. M., skirmishing, at intervals, with Armstrong's Division of Forrest's cavalry from a point three-quarters of a mile south of the Gap. The marks of this affair can still be easily detected on the larger trees. About a mile from the Gap a tablet will be found pointing out McAfee's Church.

Two miles and a half from the Gap the north line of the Park is reached. It is marked with a small tablet. The first house beyond on the left of the road is the site of the church, which, with its horse-sheds, was used as a hospital by the Fourteenth Corps, as was the Cloud House, which stood on the slope of the hill opposite. The mounting-block of the church can still be seen in the door yard. The low ground to the west of the road, a short distance beyond, about the Cloud Spring, was an extensive field hospital. All these were captured by Forrest's cavalry, which advanced from the east about 11 o'clock Sunday morning. They were re-captured at noon by Whitaker's Brigade, the advance of Steedman's Division of Granger's Reserve Corps, as it was hastening from McAfee's Church to Snodgrass Hill.

This column reached the La Fayette Road in the low ravine next north of the Cloud Church site. Whitaker's Brigade deployed on the west of the road and at right angles to it, and, advancing rapidly, drove Forrest from the hospitals and pressed on in the lead toward Snodgrass Hill, followed by Mitchell's Brigade of Steedman's Division, and Dan McCook's of J. D. Morgan's Division. About the present Dixon House, the first frame with fine grounds on the right after leaving Cloud's, the column left the road and moved to the right across the fields to Snodgrass Hill. McCook's Brigade was put in position on the ridge north-west of Dixon's, and about 700 yards from it. In this position it remained until 10 P. M., engaged at frequent intervals with Forrest's cavalry, which held a line about as far east of the La Fayette Road as McCook was west of it.

Arriving at Dixon's, many features of Sunday's battle are to be seen from the high point in the road. The edge of the low woods and glade to the east mark the position of Armstrong's Division of dismounted cavalry, which was on the right of the Confederate infantry line at the time the battle of Sunday opened. Breckinridge's Division was on the left of Armstrong's with Adams' Brigade as its right, Stovall's its center, and Helm's its left. The latter brigade extended half its front south of the north salient of the Union log-works north-east of the Kelly Field. The high pines to the south, beyond the first woods, mark the location of Snodgrass Hill.

Riding to the clump of cedars on the right, and near the foot of the slope, the site of the McDonald House (called, also, in the Confederate reports, Glenn's) is found. This was one of the landmarks of the battle. Through the farmyard opposite, the head of Thomas' Corps, after marching all night, September 18th, turned eastward toward Jay's Mill soon after sunrise on Saturday, the 19th, and opened the battle of Chickamauga near that point. The distance to the mill is a little over two miles. The frame house now opposite McDonald's has been built since the battle. The log stables were there at the time.

The ground about McDonald's, and east of it, was the scene of the opening of the engagement on Sunday morning, and of its close on the Confederate right flank Sunday evening.

Looking south along the road, the position of the Kelly Field can be seen beyond the first woods. This field extends a quarter of a mile to the east of the road and three-quarters of a mile along it. The Union line, Sunday morning, ran entirely around that part of it east of the road at a distance of about 150 yards from its border; except that the line along the northern side did not extend to the La Fayette Road by about 300 yards. The front was protected by rough low logworks. Breckinridge's Division, formed as above described, moved first to the attack. Its left brigade (Helm's) struck the Union logworks around Baird's left, and was shattered. Adams' and Stovall's Brigades, with the right of Helm's, moved directly forward to the La Fayette Road, forcing back John Beatty's Brigade of Negley's Division, which, under orders, was attempting, with four regiments, to fill out the gap from the left of Baird's Division north of the Kelly Field to the McDonald's House. Two guns of Beatty's Battery (Bridge's) were captured by Helm's regiments on the west side of the La Fayette Road where the Crawfish Springs Road leaves it.

Upon reaching the road, Adams' and Stovall's Brigades changed direction to the left until their lines were perpendicular to it, the former on the right at McDonald's, the latter on the left, with the road between them. Placing Slocomb's (Louisiana) Battery on the knoll to the west of the road, these two brigades marched directly toward the Kelly Field to strike the Union left and gain its rear. Adams was stoutly resisted upon entering the woods west of the road, first by the remnants of John Beatty's Brigade, and then checked by Stanley's Brigade, also of Negley's Division. Adams was wounded and Col. Randall R. Gibson took command. Stanley's Brigade being withdrawn by its left toward Snodgrass Hill, in pursuance of a call from that direction, both Adams and Stovall advanced beyond the north line of the Kelly Field. Moving forward, Stovall was met and repulsed by a charge of Van Derveer's Brigade of Brannan's Division, which had been hastily dispatched from the Dyer Field to the assistance of the Union left. Breckinridge's troops were then pushed back to their original position before their advance.

Sunday Evening Movements About McDonald's.

Between 5 and 6 o'clock, Liddell's Division of Walker's Corps advanced from the glade east of McDonald's as the right flank of the general Confederate attack delivered at that time. This division, with Walthall's Brigade on the right and Govan's on the left, crossed the road and advanced to the low crest in the fields beyond. The guns now mounted upon it represent Fowler's and Swett's Batteries. While Dan. McCook's Battery opened an oblique fire upon these lines and threw forward some guns which enfiladed their right, Turchin's Brigade of Reynolds' Division, the latter then in the act of withdrawing from the south line of the Kelly Field, suddenly rushed out of the woods west of the La Fayette Road and swept north along the front of

Liddell's line, capturing its skirmishers and forcing it to retire in haste across the La Fayette Road.

Those wishing to drive around the whole line of Saturday's battle can do so by starting eastward at the McDonald House. A full description of the route, and of the engagement at the various points of it, will be found, beginning on page 177. The whole drive eastward to Jay's Mill and westward from that point to Brotherton's, on the La Fayette Road, a mile and a half south of McDonald's, is four miles and a half. From that point, by the La Fayette Road to the right of the Union line, near Viniard's, September 19th, is a mile and a quarter further.

Instead of riding directly to the Kelly Field, which is Sunday's center of interest on the La Fayette Road after leaving McDonald's, time will be saved by taking the Alexander's Bridge Road, which is the first to the left, and riding along the front of the Union line east of the Kelly Field, following it back to the La Fayette Road at the south border of the field. This drive and the points of interest upon it are described on page 186.

It is well to remember that the first road to the right, after leaving McDonald's, leads to McFarland's Gap, and is the main road over which the Union army withdrew from the field on Sunday night; and that the road opposite the intersection of the Alexander Bridge Road leads direct to Snodgrass Hill and the Dyer Field.

But a more satisfactory way of reaching Snodgrass, when driving from Chattanooga, unless the purpose be to omit the lines east of the Kelly Field, is to take the Alexander Bridge Road and follow the Union line around the field to the Kelly House, and then, crossing the La Fayette Road there, drive direct to the Snodgrass House.

The most satisfactory route, however, to those who wish to study all the outlines of the position and the movements against Snodgrass, is to drive to it from the La Fayette Road at Brotherton's, as set forth on page 189. This can be done either after driving around the line of Saturday's battle, as explained on page 177, and reaching the La Fayette Road from Jay's Mill, or by driving direct on the La Fayette Road to Brotherton's.

The Kelly Field Operations.

Before leaving the Kelly Field, the position there can be best understood by driving to the Goodspeed Monument, Battery A, First Ohio, just north of the Kelly House, from or near which point the best general view of the field can be had.

There was no fighting in or around this field on Saturday. The nearest was in the Poe Field, next south. It was, however, a base of operations for the battle east and south-east of it. The early movements of Saturday morning are detailed on page 170.

During the night of the 19th, the Union left was withdrawn from its fighting ground of Saturday, and formed about the north, east, and south sides of Kelly Field. The line was about 150 yards inside the timber surrounding it. Baird's Division was around the north-east corner, Johnson's and Palmer's covered nearly all the eastern side, while Reynolds' ran around the south-east corner and reached across the La Fayette Road north of the Poe Field. When the break occurred in the Union line at Brotherton's, Reynolds brought his right brigade (King's) to the east side of the La Fayette Road and posted it in front of the south edge of the field, facing toward Poe's House. To the left of Baird's line, around the north-east corner of the fields, the brigades of Grose, Dodge, Barnes, and John Beatty were sent just before the Confederate attack, for the purpose of extending the line to the La Fayette Road at the McDonald House.

Before this was formed, Breckinridge's Division, the right of the Confederate infantry, attacked Baird's position. The Union line was protected by hastily constructed obstructions of stumps, stones, rails, and logs. Only the left of Breckinridge's line struck Baird's eastern front. This was Helm's Brigade. It assaulted three times, and was badly broken up, Gen. Helm being mortally wounded. But its two right regiments, which cleared Baird's works, kept on to the La Fayette Road and captured two guns from John Beatty's Brigade at that point. A shell monument just over the slope east of the glade marks the spot where Helm fell. Adams' and Stovall's Brigades pushed forward to the La Fayette Road at the McDonald House, and there, changing direction to the left, marched, with the La Fayette Road between them, directly toward the Kelly Field, as already described, and Stovall's Brigade burst out of the woods on its northern edge, covering the ground from the road to the low ravine half way across the field. The line of Adams' Brigade at the same moment was abreast of it in the woods west of the road. Portions of John Beatty's Brigade, in very attenuated line, had vainly attempted to resist this advance. Stanley's Brigade had checked Adams, the left of it, and then had been withdrawn by its left toward Snodgrass Hill.

It seemed at the moment as if the Union left must be enveloped. Johnson, Palmer, and Reynolds were hotly engaged, and could not leave their lines east of the field to resist a flank or rear attack. Cleburne was assaulting the first two, and Stewart was attacking Reynolds. Bullets flying over these lines from the east reached the La Fayette Road, and those from Stewart's troops were falling half way to Stovall's front. Goodspeed's Battery, from behind Johnson's Division, whirled toward this advance and opened upon it with canister. But Stovall and Adams were moving rapidly, and the situation was growing desperate.

Just then the deployed lines of Van Derveer's Brigade, which Brannan had sent from the Dyer Field to assist Baird, dashed into the field from a point a little north of the Kelly House. There were two regiments in his front line and two in the second, both parallel to the road. Before it had cleared the thicket of pines, which then lined the west side of the road, the Confederates, then only two hundred yards from its left flank, opened a heavy enfilading fire upon it. The men in the ranks could not see the enemy. Van Derveer took in the situation at a glance, rushed his brigade into the open field, changed front toward Stovall on a run, and laid both lines down almost in the face of the advancing enemy, fired a full volley, sent his second line over the first in a charge which the first followed and took part in. Stovall and Adams, being unsupported, were repulsed and forced back around the Union left, and the position was saved.

By 1 o'clock the persistent but unsuccessful assaults of the Confederates upon the Kelly Field line had diminished to affairs between skirmishers.

About 5:30 P. M., orders were received from Gen. Thomas to withdraw the line, beginning with Reynolds. His two brigades moved by the right flank to the La Fayette Road and marched northward. Arriving near the north line of the field, Turchin's Brigade filed to the left, and, facing by the rear rank, all started north on a charge through the McDonald Field. Its right flank passed close to the fronts of Govan's and Walthall's Brigades, capturing a portion of their skirmishers, and forcing their main line with its batteries to withdraw eastward across the La Fayette Road.

Palmer's Division marched directly back toward the Kelly House and reached the middle of the field before it was subjected to fire. Here it received a sharp artillery fire from the Poe Field, and also from beyond the north-east corner of the Kelly Field. However it reached the woods west of the road in organized condition, and proceeded toward McFarland's Gap. Johnson and Baird were hotly attacked just as the order came to retire. They withdrew under this attack in considerable confusion, but immediately reorganized when once in the cover of the woods west of the La Fayette Road. At dusk the field and edge of the woods west and north of it were filled with the Confederate lines of Breckinridge, Gist, Cleburne, Cheatham and Stewart.

In Rear of the Snodgrass House—Thomas' Headquarters at the Left. (See page xvii.)

The Withdrawal from Snodgrass Hill.

At sundown, Gen. Steedman's Division being out of ammunition, withdrew to the next ridge in rear of the one upon which they had fought during the afternoon. The Confederates followed to the crest and some distance down its northern slope. Above half of three regiments, the Twenty-First and Eighty-ninth Ohio, and the Twenty-second Michigan, attached to the left of Whitaker's Brigade, not receiving notice to withdraw, were captured at dusk by Trigg's and Kelly's Brigades of Preston's Division. At 7 o'clock the rest of the Snodgrass Hill line began to withdraw, commencing with the left of Wood's, and ending about 8 o'clock with Van Derveer's Brigade, the right of Brannan's line, which then rested at the present observation tower. The divisions as they withdrew, both from Snodgrass Hill and the Kelly Field, passed through McFarland's Gap to Rossville, and immediately took positions in Rossville Gap and upon Missionary Ridge, to the right and left of it, and across the valley nearly to Lookout Mountain. They thus remained in line of battle throughout September 21st. During the night of that day they moved on to Chattanooga and established their lines about the city on the morning of the 22d. These were immediately covered by rifle-pits, which in a few days grew into formidable field works.

CHAPTER XV.

GUIDE TO THE CHATTANOOGA FIELDS—LOOKOUT MOUNTAIN, WAUHATCHIE, ORCHARD KNOB, MISSIONARY RIDGE.

Arriving in Chattanooga in clear or fair weather, it is best to take advantage of it and first visit Lookout Mountain. From this point all the general features, and many of the details of the various campaigns and battles which resulted in the capture of Chattanooga, can be readily understood.

The view presented of the ranges over which Rosecrans marched makes it easy to comprehend the strategy of his campaign.

The electric cars from the city connect at the base of the mountain with the Incline, which is a cable road to the foot of the palisades, connecting with steam cars that run along the western bluff, overlooking the Wauhatchie Valley, and the whole scene of Hooker's operations there, up to and including the battle of Lookout Mountain. The train then runs across the top of the mountain to its eastern side, and, turning again toward the point, stops at Lookout Inn, to which station it is best to purchase a round trip ticket at the foot of the Incline. From the Inn a short walk brings the visitor to the jutting point of the mountain, which is so plainly seen from Chattanooga. From this open rocky floor above the palisades, one of the most interesting views which any land affords spreads widely in all directions. Points in seven states are within the range of vision when the day is absolutely clear. Large areas of Alabama, Georgia, and Tennessee are close at hand. The mountains of South Carolina and North Carolina can be seen in ordinary conditions of the atmosphere, and on exceptionally clear days the eye reaches northward across Tennessee to the mountains about Cumberland Gap in Kentucky and Virginia.

Standing on the point and facing Chattanooga, Wauhatchie Valley, with the Raccoon Range beyond it over which Rosecrans' army marched from Bridgeport, are at the left. Wauhatchie Station is at the forks of the railroad toward the upper end of the valley. The branch to the right runs to Bridgeport, the one to the left to Trenton and Valley Head, at which points the Fourteenth Corps, and the Twentieth and Cavalry Corps, respectively, crossed Lookout, before the battle of Chickamauga, into the rear of Chattanooga.

The little church and farm house a short distance toward the river from Wauhatchie Station is the ground of the night attack of Longstreet's troops on Geary's Division. (See Chapter X.)

Looking down the Tennessee, in its last bend lies Williams' Island. Just above it on the left bank is a low range of hills parallel to the river. Brown's Ferry is opposite the first gap in this range above the island. To this point the flotilla of 52 boats carrying 1,600 men floated from behind Cameron Hill, the highest point in the city, before daylight of October 27th, and, landing there, captured the hills on either side of the road to the ferry. A bridge was then thrown, and a short way opened across the narrow neck to Chattanooga out of range of the guns on Lookout. This movement, in conjunction with Hooker's forces, which marched simultaneously from Bridgeport, re opened the Tennessee. The first crest in the range to the right of the railroad where it crosses Lookout Creek is Tyndale's Hill, and the next to the right of that is Smith's Hill, so called after the brigades of the Eleventh Corps, which captured them in the night fight of October 28th. For full details, see Chapters IX and X.

Turning toward Wauhatchie Station, a short distance beyond it and to the left, is seen a low range running parallel to the mountain. Through the first gap in that range Geary's forces passed to cross Lookout Creek and ascend to the foot of the palisades, as the first move in the battle of Lookout Mountain.

The Confederate works, held by the brigade of Gen. E. C. Walthall, were parallel to the palisades along the western side of the mountain and upon the first bench of the mountain below their foot. They are still well preserved. The left of these works was some 1,500 feet south of the point of the mountain. Directly under this north point lies the Craven House plateau, where the Union line, advancing from the west side of the mountain during the battle, first came into view from Chattanooga. The Craven House, known at the time of the battle as the White House, was the headquarters of Gen. Walthall. The great bend in the river opposite Lookout is Moccasin Point, the heel of the moccasin being near Brown's Ferry. The Union batteries were on the highest ground, and so swept the north face of the mountain that troops could not move upon it in daylight with safety. At its base, to the left and across Lookout Creek, is the ground from which Osterhaus' Division of Sherman's army crossed to take part under Hooker in the assault on the mountain. One brigade crossed from the open ground to the right of the railroad bridge, and one through the gap to the left of it. One brigade of Cruft's Division crossed with Geary, and the other near Osterhaus' upper crossing. For full details of the battle of Lookout Mountain, which was the second of the three day's battle of Chattanooga, see page 116.

Looking toward the city, and to the extreme right of it, a large, low stand-pipe can be seen. It marks the site of Fort Wood (afterward Creighton), a strong work which was the eastern salient of the Union line. Upon the slope under its eastern face the Union forces formed on the afternoon of November 23, 1863, for the movement on Orchard Knob, which lies half way between Fort Wood and Missionary Ridge. The Knob can be seen just beyond the National

Chattanooga from Lookout—Sherman Heights on the Extreme Right. (See page xvii.)

Cemetery. For the details of this engagement, the first of the three days' battle of Chattanooga, see page 113.

Fort Sheridan, the strong work of the city defenses upon the Union right, is still nearly perfect. It is upon the point of the Cameron Hill Ridge nearest Lookout. The circular road plainly seen at the base of the slope under it, marks its position. Fort Lytle was near the large schoolbuilding on the next height in the city east of Fort Sheridan, and Fort Negley (afterward Phelps) stood about half a mile south-east of the Public Building. It was also known as the Star Fort, and by the Confederates as Fort Cheatham, it having been begun by them. It was the strongest outer work at the center of the line.

To the right across the plain, is Missionary Ridge. Rossville Gap, through which the main road runs across the Chickamauga Field to La Fayette, is the low depression directly east of the point of the mountain. The distance from Rossville to the north end of Missionary Ridge is eight miles. The first tower north of the Gap marks the site of Bragg's Headquarters. It is four miles from Rossville. The second tower marks the point where Baird's Division, the left of Gen. Thomas' assaulting column, gained the Ridge. The right of the storming line of the Army of the Cumberland reached nearly half way between Bragg's Headquarters and Rossville.

The small town in the gap of Missionary Ridge near its northern point marks the ground of Gen. Sherman's fighting in the battle of Missionary Ridge. For the details of his crossing of the river, see page 120, and for the account of the battle of Missionary Ridge, see page 123.

The next depression south of Rossville is McFarland's Gap. The battle field of Chickamauga lies about two and one-half miles east of Missionary Ridge and between Rossville and McFarland's Gap. Through the latter, the Union army withdrew at the close of the battle, and, passing out again through Rossville Gap, formed its lines at its southern

SCALING THE PALISADES—LOOKOUT, NOV. 25. (See p. xvii.)

opening, and on each side of it, upon Missionary Ridge, and across the valley to Lookout. Here it remained during September 21st. The night of that day, and the morning of the 22d, it moved forward to Chattanooga, and for the first time occupied the city in force.

From the summit, stairs on the west lead down the palisades to the Incline. These stairs have replaced rude ladders and ropes by which the summit could be reached in war times, and they mark the line over which a company from the Eighth Kentucky of Whitaker's Brigade of Cruft's Division clambered before daylight of November 25th, and at sunrise displayed their flag in the sight of both armies. From the wide porches at the hotel at the base of the palisades, the same view heretofore described, spreads below the observer, and the conveniences for studying it are all that could be desired.

Orchard Knob, Sherman Heights, and Bragg's Headquarters.

There are two lines of electric cars to Orchard Knob. One of these passes the National Cemetery, and runs to Bragg's Headquarters on Missionary Ridge, and thence along the Ridge about half way to Rossville. If the visitor has not time to drive on the Ridge, or does not care to take a carriage, this trip, with the scene from the observation tower at Bragg's Headquarters, gives a very satisfactory idea of the Ridge and the battle fields about it.

A line of steam cars runs by way of Orchard Knob to Sherman Heights, the station at the latter point being in the center of Gen. Sherman's operations against the north end of Missionary Ridge. The positions of Hardee's troops on the summit of Tunnel Hill, and the ground of the assaults of Corse's, Loomis', Matthies', Raum's, and Bushbeck's Brigades are within fair walking distance. The fares by all these lines are the ordinary street car rates.

Orchard Knob.

Standing on the Knob, and looking back toward the city, the position of Fort Wood is marked by the low, black standpipe. The slope in front of it is where the Union army formed for the advance on Orchard Knob and the adjacent lines. For details, see page 113.

Looking toward Missionary Ridge, the tower to the left stands at the point where Van Derveer's Brigade of Baird's Division went up the Ridge. This was the left division of the line of assault of the Army of the Cumberland. The tower to the right is on the site of Bragg's Headquarters and also marks the point where the center of Sheridan's Division gained the crest. A division and half front of the assaulting line was south of this tower. The storming column started across the plain from the line of Orchard Knob. Its front was two miles and a half, and the lines diverging somewhat as they advanced, the length of the crest carried by the assault was three miles, excluding the south end toward Rossville, where a mile was carried by Hooker's troops.

For the details of the battle of Missionary Ridge, see page 123.

As has been elsewhere explained, a visit to the Ridge and to Chickamauga may be combined by driving first to Bragg's Headquarters, or even to the tower at the De Long place, and then taking the Crest Road to Chickamauga. Or, this may be reversed, driving first by Rossville to Chickamauga and returning by the Crest Road. This, however, is too long a drive to allow of any thing more than a glance at the prominent points of interest.

The Drive upon the Crest Road.

The most satisfactory method of visiting Missionary Ridge is to take a carriage from Chattanooga and drive its entire length. The grades are such toward the northern end as to make Rossville the better point of approaching the Ridge than Sherman Heights. From the latter point the return can then be by the Harrison Turnpike through the valley.

At Rossville, the ground of Hooker's advance from Lookout Mountain is reached. The tablets through the Gap explain the movements of his division. Osterhaus, leading, passed through, and, marching northward along the eastern side of the Ridge, assaulted it from that direction, gaining the crest about a mile north of Rossville.

Cruft marched into the Gap, faced the southern extremity of the Ridge and carried it. Geary turned along its western base from Rossville, and finally assaulted and carried the crest about three-quarters of a mile north.

Leaving these positions, which are indicated by the tablets on the Crest Road, a short drive suffices to reach the right of the assault of the Army of the Cumberland. This point is about opposite East Lake, which is plainly seen near the base of the Ridge.

The Confederate divisions on the crest, running from the left at Rossville to the right at Tunnel Hill, were as follows: Stewart's, stretched from Rossville Gap to Bragg's Headquarters. As Gen. Breckinridge took Stewart's strongest brigade (Clayton's) to resist Hooker in Rossville Gap, the left of Gen. Stewart's line was exceedingly thin, and all of it was much attenuated. Next north of Bragg's Headquarters was Reynolds' Brigade of Bushrod Johnson's Division, followed on the line by Breckinridge's Division, commanded by Bate. Beyond Bate, came Hindman's Division, commanded by Patton Anderson, reaching to the vicinity of the tower at the De Long place. North of that, and beyond the left of the assaulting lines of Gen. Thomas, were the divisions of Cheatham, Walker, and Stevenson, the latter supporting Cleburne at the Tunnel, and, lastly, the division of Cleburne strongly posted on the first high hill north of it.

Beginning at the right of Johnson's line of the Army of the Cumberland, which rested nearly as far south as East Lake, the force of Gen. Thomas which moved from its central line in the plain to storm the Ridge was arranged from right to left as follows: Johnson, Sheridan, Wood, and Baird. Sheridan's center moved against Bragg's Headquarters; Wood's right crowned the Ridge about the crossing of the Bird's Mill Road—the point where the electric road at the extreme end of McCallie Avenue now reaches the summit. Baird's center gained the crest at the De Long Tower, and his left brigade (Phelps') at the next jutting spur north of it.

All these positions are clearly designated by tablets. In reading them, it should be remembered that at nearly all points the Confederate line was established upon the summit, and did not follow the present road, although near it throughout its extent.

From the towers can be seen both Orchard Knob, the headquarters of Gens. Grant, Thomas, and Gordon Granger during the battle of the 25th November, and Fort Wood, before which the lines were formed for the first day's advance to Orchard Knob. The place of Sherman's crossing is also visible.

The open ground behind the crest, some 600 yards north of the De Long Tower, is where Walthall's Brigade of Cheatham's Division formed to resist the northward advance of Baird's Division, after the latter had reached the summit of the Ridge. Jackson and Moore's Brigades, which constituted the left of Cheatham's Division, were rushed to the left to oppose Baird as his movement up the Ridge began, but were unsuccessful. Walthall's line, however, held until darkness ended the contest. Meantime, before the action closed, Brown's Brigade of Stevenson's Division had arrived from the Tunnel. Forming on the left of Walthall, it participated in the final checking of Baird's northward advance along the Ridge.

Contrary to prevailing impressions, no Confederate troops left the front of the Army of the Cumberland to oppose Gen. Sherman, after the battle of Tunnel Hill opened. It is true,

Missionary Ridge.—Center of Baird's Assault—Van Derveer's Brigade. (See page xviii.)

instead, that troops left Sherman's front soon after the movement of Gen. Thomas' line began, and reached Cheatham's position in time to take part in the effort to resist Baird's advance on the Ridge.

After leaving the ground of Walthall's fight, the drive passes beyond the left of the Union troops in the center. Cheatham's and Walker's Divisions had no enemy in their front until Cheatham's moved to resist Baird. Stevenson's Division, which came next on their right, but with a considerable interval intervening, reached to the left of Sherman's lines, and joined Cleburne's Division at the Tunnel.

Tablets along this section of the Crest Road designate all these positions.

For a full account of Sherman's crossing and advance against Tunnel Hill, and Hardee's defense of the latter, which was chiefly executed by Gen. Cleburne, see pages 120, 126, and following.

The most convenient way of returning to the city is to leave the Ridge at the Tunnel, and drive down through Sherman Heights, over the ground of Gen. Sherman's formations for attack, and thence to the city by the Harrison Turnpike.

CHAPTER XVI.

ORIGIN AND DEVELOPMENT OF THE PARK PROJECT—THE CHICKAMAUGA MEMORIAL ASSOCIATION.

The first steps in the development of the National Military Park embraced only the battle field of Chickamauga. This part of the project had its origin in a visit to the field, in June, 1888, of Gen. Ferd. Van Derveer, a noted officer of the Army of the Cumberland; and the author of this work, then Washington correspondent of the *Cincinnati Commercial Gazette*.

In a series of letters to that newspaper describing the condition of the field, and reviewing the campaign and the battle, the Park scheme was thus suggested:

"The survivors of the Army of the Cumberland should awake to great pride in this notable field of Chickamauga. Why should it not, as well as eastern fields, be marked by monuments, and its lines be accurately preserved for history? There was no more magnificent fighting during the war than both armies did there. Both sides might well unite in preserving the field where both, in a military sense, won such renown."

It will thus be seen that from the first the plan differed essentially from that of Gettysburg, where, up to that time, only the Union lines, that is, only one side of the battle, had been marked. The suggestion was received with much favorable comment at the North.

At the next annual meeting of the Society of the Army of the Cumberland, held at Chicago a few weeks later, on motion of Gen. Henry M. Cist, then corresponding secretary of the society, a resolution was adopted providing that a committee of five be appointed by the chair for the purpose of taking the necessary steps to inaugurate a movement for the purchase of the ground on which the battle of Chickamauga was fought, that monuments be placed thereon to mark the location of the troops that fought there, and that it be preserved similar to the plan of the battle field of Gettysburg. Gen. Rosecrans, president of the society, appointed as members of this committee Gen. Henry M. Cist, Gen. Charles F. Manderson, Gen. Russell A. Alger, Gen. Absalom Baird, Gen. Henry V. Boynton.

This committee met in Washington City, February 13, 1889. Gen. Manderson presided. It was agreed to invite such Confederate veterans of the battle of Chickamauga as were in Washington to unite in forming a Chickamauga Memorial Association. This joint conference was held February 14th, in the room of the Senate Committee on Military Affairs. Those present were Gens. Rosecrans, Baird, Reynolds, Cist, Manderson, and Boynton, and Col. Kellogg, of the Union officers; and Gens. Bate, of Tennessee; Colquitt, of Georgia; Walthall, of Mississippi; Morgan and Wheeler, of Alabama; Wright, of Tennessee; and Cols. Bankhead, of Alabama; and Morgan, of Mississippi.

The plan of preserving and marking the field of Chickamauga, under the auspices of a joint memorial corporation representing all the states that had troops there, patterned in general after the organization of the Gettysburg Association, was cordially approved. Gens. Cist and Colquitt were appointed a committee, with power to add four to their number, to prepare an act of incorporation and correspond with leading officers from each state whose troops fought at Chickamauga, with a view of securing a proper list of incorporators. The sub-committee was completed by adding Gens. Baird, Boynton, Walthall, Wheeler, Wright, and Col. S. C. Kellogg. It was agreed that each side should name fifty of the leading veterans of that field and some civilians, North and South, who had prominently identified themselves with the project, as incorporators of a Joint Chickamauga Memorial Association for preserving and marking the battle field.

At a subsequent meeting, a list of incorporators and the outlines of a charter were agreed upon, and Senator Colquitt was appointed to take the necessary steps to secure the incorporation. He placed the matter in the hands of Julius Brown, Esq., of Atlanta, who, declining compensation, gave the subject prompt attention, and prepared a petition for a charter, which he secured from the Superior Court of Walker county, Georgia, on the 4th of December, 1889.

The objects of the Association were declared in the charter to be "to mark and preserve the battle field of Chickamauga, on which were fought the actions of September eighteenth, nineteenth, and twentieth, Anno Domini, one thousand eight hundred and sixty-three, together with the natural and artificial features, as they were at the time of said battle, by such memorial stones, tablets, or monuments as a generous people may aid to erect, to commemorate the valor displayed by American soldiers on that field."

On the 19th of September, 1889, a joint meeting of Union and Confederate veterans was called, to be held in the tent at Chattanooga erected for the annual reunion of the Society of the Army of the Cumberland, to consider the subject of the Chickamauga Park. The meeting was under the auspices of the following local committee: on Chickamauga Memorial Association—Adolph S. Ochs, chairman, Maj. A. G. Sharp, Gen. S. B. Moe, Capt. J. F. Shipp, Maj. W. J. Colburn, Maj. H. S. Chamberlain, Maj. C. W. Norwood, J. B. Nicklin; on Chickamauga Barbecue—Gordon Lee, chairman, W. P. McClatchey, secretary.

The large tent was crowded to its capacity by strong representations of both armies and leading citizens interested with them. Addresses, setting forth the features of the Park project and indorsing it with great enthusiasm, were made by Gen. Rosecrans and other Union veterans, and by ex-

Governor A. S. Marks, of Nashville, and Hon. W. A. Henderson, of Knoxville.

Nothing can give a better idea of the spirit which marked the inauguration of the Park project than extracts from these speeches:

Upon calling the vast assembly to order, Gen. Rosecrans said:

Ladies and Gentlemen and Comrades of the Blue and the Gray:
This occasion is one for which you will look through history in vain to find a second. To-day twenty-six years ago began the great bloody battle of Saturday, the 19th day of September, 1863, within twelve miles of this place, and the survivors of that battle, both Blue and Gray, and the people who to-day enjoy the fruits which grew out of that battle, are assembled together to consider how they shall make it a national memorial ground, which people of all time shall come and visit with the interest due to the greatness of the events which occurred on that battle ground. One of the most noble features to me of the occasion is this: It is very difficult to find in history an instance where contending parties in after years meet together in perfect amity. It took great men to win that battle, but it takes greater men still, I will say morally greater, to wipe away all the ill feeling which naturally grows out of such a contest. [Applause.]

To me there is another feature of peculiar interest, and that is that there has been no time since the war when the respect felt by the people of the South for the men who fought and fell in their cause could be shown by systematically undertaking to commemorate the deeds they performed, and to keep alive their memories by the erection of monuments, without incurring the criticism that they were keeping up the memories of the war and the feelings of hatred which ought to perish as peace returns.

On the soil of Georgia both the Blue and the Gray can unite in obtaining control over the grounds, laying out the roads and marking sites where the men entitled, in their opinion, to special respect and special veneration, may have monuments erected to their memories, where the organizations who choose to do so can put up monuments to the heroism displayed on those fields without criticism and with rather the feeling of comradeship. That to me is a very noble thing, and I believe that the spirit which brings you here on this occasion, and the foundation upon which your views of that thing rests, conspire to produce a result very wonderful, indeed.

You will be told a great many things by those who will follow me to show how strong the foundation of our expectation is that we are commencing a national event at this meeting this afternoon.

As I am quite unfitted for public speaking and heartily detest the task, I think what I have said will be enough to show to you how thankful I am to be with you and to be called upon to preside over this meeting.

The first exercise in order will be some remarks from Gen. H. V. Boynton, who deserves the thanks of every body, and especially of the comrades of the Army of the Cumberland, for his work in studying up this subject, and he will tell you a great deal more than I can about it.

Gen. Boynton spoke as follows:

My Friends:

I have been asked to make a statement of the objects which those members of the Society of the Army of the Cumberland who conceived the idea of a Joint Chickamauga Memorial Association have in view, the motives which actuate them, and the methods by which they hope to attain the desired ends. These I will attempt to set forth in brief form.

Perhaps, if I take a few moments in going over the path which led some of us to a deep interest in this project, it may suggest to you strong reasons in support of it.

A year ago last summer, it was my privilege to revisit Chickamauga in company with my old commander, Gen. Van Derveer. The ride was the more impressive because the day was Sunday. On reaching the Cloud House, on the northern boundaries of the field, there came to us from a country church near by the voice of solemn song.

The last music which had fallen on our ears, as we left that field a quarter of a century before, was the screech, the rattle, the roar, the thunder of that hell of battle which had loaded the air with horror through all that earlier and well-remembered Sabbath.

In a moment, as with a flash, memory peopled those scenes for us with the actors of that other day. We gloried in Rosecrans, and mourned that Thomas did not still live to enjoy his ever-increasing renown.

We saw Baird's and Johnson's and Palmer's and Reynolds' immovable lines around the Kelly Farm. We recalled Wood on the spur of Snodgrass Hill, and Brannan, and Grosvenor and Steedman under Granger on the Horseshoe.

There rolled back on the mind the unequaled fighting of that thin and contracted line of heroes; and the magnificent Confederate assaults which swept in upon us time and again, and ceaselessly, as that service of all the gods of war went on throughout those Sabbath hours.

Then—thinking of our Union lines alone—we said to each other: "This field should be a western Gettysburg—a Chickamauga memorial."

It was but a flash forward in thought to our present plan, and the proposition became—"Aye, it should be more than Gettysburg, with its monuments along one side alone; the lines of both armies should be equally marked."

We went over the ground where Forrest's and Walker's men had marched on Saturday into the smoke of our rifles and the very flame of our batteries. Again we saw their ranks melt as snowflakes disappear over the heat of conflagration.

We stood on Baird's line, where Helm's Brigade went to pieces, but not till one man out of every three—think of that!—not till one out of every three—was dead or wounded.

We saw Longstreet's men roll in on the difficult slopes of the Horseshoe, dash wildly and break there, and recede, only to sweep on again almost with the regularity of the ocean surges, and ever marking a higher tide.

We looked down again on those slopes, slippery with blood, and strewn thick as the leaves with all the horrible wreck of battle, over which, and in spite of repeated failure, these assaulting columns still formed, and reformed, and came on.

And then, thinking of this as fighting alone—grand, awe-inspiring, magnificent fighting—the project of a Joint Chickamauga Battle Field Assciation was born in the mind.

I stood silent, thinking of that unsurpassed Confederate fighting, and in my heart thanked God that the men who were equal to such endeavors on the battle field were Americans. Behold the essentials and the essence of our project!

Let all the lines be marked. Let the whole unbroken history of such a field be carefully preserved.

So thinking, on my return home I wrote of Chickamauga to the *Cincinnati Commercial Gazette*, of August 17th, thus publicly suggesting the scheme:

"The survivors of the Army of the Cumberland should awake to great pride in this notable field of Chickamauga. Why should it not, as well as Eastern fields, be marked by monuments, and its lines be accurately preserved for history? There was no more magnificent fighting during the war than both armies did there. Both sides might well unite in preserving the field where both, in a military sense, won such renown."

The idea received much and only favorable comment in the North.

Twenty-six years ago to-day the thunders of the deadliest battle of modern times were rolling over the low lands and re-echoing from the mountains which look down upon Chickamauga. Many great battles shook our continent and attracted the attention of the world as our war went on; but the splendid facts of the bitter, stubborn, and desperate contest along the unknown stream, in the thick forests which lined it, and on the ridges which dominated them, were, for years, almost as completely hidden from the public as were the armies which operated over this obscure and tangled field.

But, as the publication of the official records of both armies has progressed, and made intelligent study of the strategy and the fighting of Chickamauga possible, the battle has been gradually revealed to the public until it stands to-day where those of us who participated knew so well that it deserved to rank—for both armies—as the most stubbornly contested battle of the war. And not only this, but the percentage of its casualty lists are found to exceed those of Napoleon's most noted battles, as well as those of all the later fields of modern Europe. This conclusively appears from some facts which I have heretofore presented in print in regard to Chickamauga, and which are pertinent here.

The marvel of German fighting in the great battle of Mars la Tour was performed by the Third Westphalian Regiment. It suffered the heaviest loss in the German army during the Franco-Prussian war. It went into battle 3,000 strong, and its loss was 49.4 per cent. There was nothing in the campaigns of which this formed a part which exceeded these figures, and they became famous throughout the German army. And yet in our war there were over sixty regiments whose losses exceeded this. Seventeen of them lost above 60 per cent, and quite a number ranged from 70 to 80.

There were over a score of regiments on each side at Chickamauga whose loss exceeded that of the Westphalian Regiment. The percentage of loss in the charge of the Light Brigade at Balaklava, of world-wide celebrity, was only 36.7.

The battle was desperate from the moment it opened till its close. For the most part the lines fought at close range, and, in the countless assaults, often hand to hand. On the first day there were no field works of any kind. On the second, Thomas was protected on the Kelly Farm by such rude logworks as could be hastily thrown together. Brannan, after the break on Sunday, and Steedman were without a semblance of works. The battle, in the main, on both sides, was dogged, stand-up fighting far within the limits of point-blank range. For the second day, on the Confederate side, the contest was one continued series of brave and magnificent assaults.

A reference to the losses on each side will show that there has been no exaggeration in the description of the fighting. Rosecrans' loss was 16,179. This included 4,774 missing, of which a large number were killed or wounded. Bragg's losses, as compiled and estimated at the War Records office, were 17,804. Thus the total loss for each army was over 25 per cent of the entire force of each, and it will be found to average about 33 per cent on each side for the troops actually engaged.

Longstreet's wing of the Confederate army lost 44 per cent, nearly all of this on the second day, and the largest part of that in an hour and a half on Sunday afternoon.

Steedman's and Brannan's Divisions, which confronted a portion of Longstreet's assault, lost, the first, 49 per cent in four hours, and all these were killed or wounded but one, and the second an average of 38 per cent, while one brigade, Van Derveer's, of Brannan, lost only a small fraction less than 50 per cent

For the entire Union army the losses ranged from these

maximum figures down to 33 per cent, a terrible minimum of one in three.

Bushrod Johnson's Division lost 44 per cent, Patton Anderson's Brigade, of Hindman's, 30 per cent, and most of this on Sunday afternoon. Bate's Brigade, of Stewart's Division, lost 52 per cent. Preston's division, in an hour and a half before sunset on Sunday, lost 33 per cent, and Gracie's Brigade nearly 35 per cent in a single hour while assaulting Brannan's position on the Horseshoe. The Brigade losses in Cheatham's Division ranged from 35 to 50 per cent. The aggregate loss in Breckinridge's Division was 33 per cent. Cleburne's loss was 43 per cent.

These figures become the more significant when compared with the statement of losses of the world's noted battles. Gen. Wheeler, the distinguished Confederate cavalry commander, thus vividly presented this question at the gathering of the Society of the Army of the Cumberland and Confederates in Chattanooga in 1881, first premising that:

"Waterloo was one of the most desperate and bloody fields chronicled in European history." Gen. Wheeler showed that Wellington's casualties were much below the rate for either side at Chickamauga or Gettysburg. "At Shiloh, the first great battle in which Gen. Grant was engaged, one side lost in killed and wounded 9,740 out of 33,000, while their opponents reported their killed and wounded at 9,616, making the casualties about 30 per cent. At the great Battle of Wagram, Napoleon lost but about 5 per cent. At Würzburg the French lost but $3\frac{1}{2}$ per cent, and yet the army gave up the field and retreated to the Rhine. At Racour, Marshal Saxe lost but $2\frac{1}{2}$ per cent. At Zurich, Massena lost but 8 per cent. At Lagriz, Frederick lost but $6\frac{1}{2}$ per cent. At Malplaquet, Marlborough lost but 10 per cent, and at Ramillies the same intrepid commander lost but 6 per cent. At Contras, Henry of Navarre was reported as cut to pieces, yet his loss was less than 10 per cent. At Lodi, Napoleon lost $1\frac{1}{4}$ per cent. At Valmy, Frederick lost but 3 per cent, and at the great battles of Marengo and Austerlitz, sanguinary as they were, Napoleon lost an average of less than 14½ per cent. At Magenta and Solferino, in 1859, the average loss of both armies was less than 9 per cent. At Worth, Specheran, Mars la Tour, Gravelotte and Sedan, in 1870, the average loss was 12 per cent. At Linden, Gen. Moreau lost but 4 per cent, and the Archduke John lost 7 per cent in killed and wounded. Americans scarcely call this a lively skirmish. At Perryville, Murfreesboro, Chickamauga, Atlanta, Gettysburg, Missionary Ridge, the Wilderness, and Spottsylvania, the loss frequently reached, and sometimes exceeded, 40 per cent, and the average of killed and wounded on one side or the other was over 30 per cent."

When it is considered that this degree of bitter fighting was persistently maintained by both sides throughout two days, without any defensive works deserving the name, and for the most part without any at all except as the natural features of the ground supplied them in part to the Union side, it is readily seen that there is no other field of the war which more fully illustrates the indomitable courage and all the varied fighting qualities of the American veteran. A large number of organizations on both sides in that battle came out of it with a loss of every other man who entered it, killed or wounded.

The assaults on the Confederate side were without parallel in the war. Pickett's charge at Gettysburg was a single effort. But Longstreet's entire wing at Chickamauga assaulted time and again on far more difficult ground than the slopes of Cemetery Hill. There were three general assaults which each deserved to rank with Pickett's charge, while the Union defense of the Horseshoe Ridge is also without parallel in the war. So thin a line never before successfully withstood such tremendous assaults. Of the whole battle, from opening to close, there was never truer thing written than Gen. Hindman's words in regard to his conflict with Granger's troops: "I have never known Federal troops to fight so well. It is just to say, also, that I never saw Confederate soldiers fight better." And Kershaw, of Longstreet's Virginia troops, who had seen all the fighting in the army of Northern Virginia, said of one of the Confederate assaults which Brannan repulsed: "This was one of the heaviest attacks of the war on a single point."

Surely the ground of such fighting deserves to be preserved for pilgrimages and historic study. To illustrate the attainments of soldierly endeavor with which the veterans of each army distinguished themselves in our war, there is no spot of fighting ground in which each can take a greater pride, or where each can lay stronger claims to victory. While the Confederates secured and held the field, Gen. Rosecrans gained his objective—Chattanooga.

Chickamauga is, then, beyond question, the most noted battle field of modern times, when measured by the stubborn and undaunted fighting done upon it—a standard whose fairness there will be none to dispute.

We meet here, surviving veterans of that field, ranged once in confronting lines, fringed with all that made war horrible or gilded its horrors with glory. We, who fought as iron veterans fight, gather here to-day under one flag, citizens of one country, to celebrate and take measures to perpetuate the memory of the fighting which will cause Chickamauga to take first rank among the battles of the world.

So far as I understand it, this is in no sense a political move. Nor need it be regarded as non-partisan. Speaking for myself, I do not desire to be misunderstood. I yield to no man an iota of my convictions. They are as dear to me, and as clear to my mind, as when we fought for them. On the other hand, for the purposes which we seek here, I ask no one of the brave men who fought for their convictions under a different flag to yield them in any degree to me. These differences we do not discuss, nor do they properly enter into our project.

That contemplates mainly American fighting as fighting—

the celebrating in enduring bronze and marble the achievements of American manhood as illustrated in the unsurpassed pluck and endurance, the stubborn, desperate, and magnificent fighting performed by each side on this field of Chickamauga.

We propose to take a very important, very necessary, and eminently practical step beyond the far-famed Gettysburg Memorial Association, and ascertain and permanently designate all the lines of both armies, and set up tablets to mark the lines of advance and the extreme points reached by each squadron, battery, or regiment, be it Union or Confederate, and to state their strength and losses, to the end that the ordinary visitor and military student shall be able, one and all, to understand our great object lesson of American prowess on the field of battle.

As to the ways and means of our project, we propose to go before Congress at its coming session and ask it to appropriate a sufficient sum to buy the entire field from Rossville Gap to Crawfish Springs, or so much thereof as the directors, when our organization is complete, may deem expedient to secure. This purchase, of course, must be contingent upon the State of Georgia ceding jurisdiction to the government for the sole purpose of maintaining a National Military Park.

There is no intention of dispossessing the present owners and occupants of the field. It would be better that they should remain, upon conditions advantageous to themselves, to preserve its roads and its outlines of field and forest, and its farm houses, as they were at the time of the fight. But these things belong to the details of the project, and it will doubtless be easy to arrange them all so as to give general satisfaction.

Eleven northern and eleven southern states had organizations in the battle, and Kentucky, Missouri, and Tennessee had troops on each side. The United States were represented by nine organizations. The general government will without doubt appropriate liberally, as it has done for the Gettysburg Field, to mark the positions of the regular regiments and batteries. The purpose is to ask each state to erect monuments to mark the ground where its troops distinguished themselves. There must, therefore, be a joint management of the Park by the government and the states interested, the manner of which must be left to Congress and those charged with working out the details of the plan.

To our proposed Park, ending at Rossville Gap, the city of Chattanooga and its immediate surroundings, Lookout, Orchard Knob, and Missionary Ridge, properly attach themselves, enlarge the dimensions of our scheme, and make it unsurpassed and unsurpassable as a place for interesting pilgrimages or military study. Here the natural features, which for all time will clearly mark the lines of battle, are such that scarcely any thing is needed except tablets to mark the position of forts and headquarters, to complete the project we are here considering. The roads now exist leading from Rossville to the extreme north point of Missionary Ridge, and from Chattanooga to all other points of chief interest in the noted fields about the city.

No words from me to you who can, with vivid memory, re-people the fields and the surroundings of Chattanooga with the battle pageants which will make them illustrious for all time, are necessary to enforce our project, or make it clear that when once established it must excite universal and continuing interest.

ADDRESS OF EX-GOV. A. S. MARKS.

When Gen. Boynton concluded his remarks, ex-Gov. Albert S. Marks, of Tennessee, was introduced and spoke as follows:

Ladies and Gentlemen and Old Soldiers Who Wore the Blue and the Gray:

In the name of the soldiers of the South, soldiers of the

North, I salute you and welcome you among us—welcome you to the fields of Chickamauga.

It has been a long time ago since the men of the North fronted the men of the South on the bloody, stricken field of Chickamauga. By a common impulse—with one mind and one heart—the men of the South and the men of the North have here met again to-day to unite in celebrating the twenty-sixth anniversary, and to unite in a testimonial to posterity, that both have a common interest and a common heritage in the glories of the field of Chickamauga.

When we met before, thousands of men, from Maine to Texas—from every state of the Union—came to Chickamauga and heard the long roll beat off for the last time. They died that Chickamauga might live forever, and so it was twenty-six years ago—in the blood of tens of thousands of brave men—Chickamauga was baptized into immortality.

Where we stand to-day, then the firm earth trembled with the roar and crash of the great Lutzen of the civil war. That day when the guns were sounding and blood was running, was heard the rebel yell, ringing out as clear and sharp as the bray of ten thousand trumpets. Up from the field of Chickamauga it rose and rolled up the mountains, and now but a memory—now like an echo which has lost itself amid distant hills—it has gone forever sounding down the ages of history, poetry, and song. From the same field to-day rises the sweet anthem of peace. It swells up and away from the field of Chickamauga, swells over the sentineling mountains, and floats away to the lakes and oceans, its sweet strains telling that the men of the North and of the South will learn war no more; telling that the battle cloud of Chickamauga has lifted, and above that glorious field the bow of promise and concord is gently bending, telling that peace, like a sweet benediction, shall rest upon the land forever.

When we met here before we saw the rude, red hand of war work universal desolation upon the lovely plain of Chickamauga. Returning to-day, we see that nature, the gentle priestess of a loving God, has painted out with her sweet and beautiful colors the last vestige of war's desolation. We see that she has re-clothed its naked, war-plowed fields with her verdant robe, and over them the gentle flocks and herds roam again unvexed. We then saw its forests—leafless, branchless—tossed and torn by the hurricane of war, but feeling her touch again they lift aloft their leafy crowns. Again she has made the beautiful flowers bloom and laden the air with their sweet perfume. She has brought the songbird back, and again its sweet notes fill its forests with melody. Again she has restored the crystal waters to its streams, and now they flow so pure and limpid they give no sign they once ran red with the blood of the brave.

Since we see that the beasts of the field, the birds of the air, and the inanimate earth heard her gentle voice and obeyed her sweet influence, can we wonder that when the soldiers of the North and the South meet again to-day on the field of Chickamauga, and look down into their hearts, that there, too, they find she has painted out every enmity, every resentment, every vestige of war, and deep down in the rich soil of mutual respect planted a concord and friendship which must endure as long as the men live who made the field of Chickamauga immortal.

Speaking for my comrades, we frankly declare that we now regret, and have always regretted, that in the fertile soil of the tremendous differences between the North and the South the horrid seeds of war were ever sown. All our dead are buried and all our wounds are healed. Our backs are to war and our faces to peace. We recognize the sovereignty of the constitution, of the Union. We esteem, respect, and honor you men of the North. With you we have one common country—a common destiny. Still we have memories which are surprisingly dear to us as a people.

We glory in the recollection that, when hope was dying in the great Revolutionary heart, our ancestors, with their sabers in their teeth, climbed King's Mountain, and on its summit raised Independence to its feet, placed on its head the crown of political freedom, and put in its hand the scepter of American destiny.

We glory in the recollection that, in the second war for independence, on the plains of New Orleans, that our ancestors with their bayonets dug up by the roots the willow of defeat and planted the oak of victory so firmly that since that day the foot of a foreign enemy has never polluted the soil of the Union.

We glory in the recollection that when in the fullness of time we came to fight out the great quarrel of North and South, which came to us by inheritance, fronting conditions which, in the judgment of the world, made miraculous success alone possible, we boldly threw down the gage of battle in the face of a people among the most powerful, the most courageous, and most warlike of all the peoples under the sun, and for four long years waged the unequal conflict, and by our sublime courage and fortitude, in the very teeth of fate, time and again moved up and stood in the very shadow of triumph.

When you remember that the Confederate soldiers marched and fought for four years in hunger and rags, you will not be surprised when I tell you that they, too, are drawing a pension. It is a pension which costs no man any thing, and the man who would take it away from them is too low to aspire to the dignity of being contemptible. The pension they draw is a proud consciousness of stern duty done in the light the great God gave to them to see and the undying love and reverence they bear to their dead comrades—their glorious dead, who never heard of the lost cause—who never saw the fallen banner, for when they fell it was floating proudly over them—who never surrendered—who never passed under the yoke—but caught up from the field of their glory—now beyond the river—under the martial trees,

"On fame's eternal camping ground,
    Their silent tents are spread,
While glory guards with solemn round
    The bivouac of the dead."

Men of the North, we stand face to face with you to-day. We will not speak to each other with forked tongues. There has been much babblement about whether the South was right or wrong. I take leave to say in this presence it is still an open question. Accomplished facts put it in the power of the North to decide it. If the event shall prove that the fear of the people of the South was groundless, that the people of the North meant to take away from them their country and their government, inherited from their fathers, and to rule and ruin them through the agency of an alien race, then it will follow that the people of the South were in the wrong. But as certain as the sun shines and the grass grows, if the time shall come (which God forbid!) that the people of any one of the Southern States shall be discrowned by the North, then the eternal verdict will be that the South was right when she struck in defense of the birthright of her people.

This occasion affords me a fit opportunity to say what I think about your distinguished chairman. In my judgment, in comparison with his merits, he is the most underrated of all the Federal generals. We now have all the evidence before us, and when we impartially measure him in its light, we can not fail to see that he is entitled to stand first among the Federal generals.

Reviewing the summer and fall campaign of 1862, we find the general result was disastrous to the Federal armies. Aside from the repulse of Price and Van Dorn by Rosecrans at Corinth, the Confederate armies suffered no material reverse.

The result of those campaigns had the effect to bring more than one of the foreign powers to a serious consideration of the question of recognizing the Confederacy. It had the further effect of so alarming the people of the states of the

Mississippi Valley as to the final result of the war, that they were considering whether the time had not come for them to surrender the Union to secure the free navigation of the Mississippi. Both governments were apprised of the probable action of the foreign powers. We now know that in the month of October, 1862, Gen. McClernand went to Washington and acquainted the general government with the fact that the states of the Mississippi Valley were ripe for a revolt, and that it would inevitably come unless that government immediately manifested its ability to overthrow the Confederacy. The Federal government saw its danger.

To prevent the recognition of the Confederacy and the revolt of the states of the Mississippi Valley it determined to press a winter campaign from Virginia to Vicksburg. McClellan was relieved, and Burnside pushed on to defeat at Fredericksburg in December 1862. In as many days sixty new regiments were raised in the states of the Mississippi Valley and pushed on to Grant and Sherman, and they were ordered to move on Vicksburg and take it. Their army was divided, Sherman to move by the river to Vicksburg and Grant to support him by moving on a parallel line. The Confederate government, seeing the crisis, took order accordingly. About the middle of December, Forrest penetrated West Tennessee, and blazing like a meteor so dazed and paralyzed Gen. Grant that Gen. Sherman was left to move unsupported to an overwhelming defeat at Vicksburg on the 25th of December.

It was on the 30th of December that Rosecrans formed his line in front of Murfreesboro. Up to that hour every battle fought in that winter campaign to prevent the recognition of the Confederates and to prevent the revolt of the Mississippi Valley had resulted in the overwhelming defeat of the Federal armies. Events had made Murfreesboro the hinge upon which the fortunes of the Confedaracy must turn. That battle won by the Confederates, the paper blockade would be torn to tatters and the independence of the Confederacy assured. Gen. Rosecrans understood far better than the government at Washington the gravity of the task assigned him. But a few days before his march began, Gen. Rosecrans had given his deposition in the Buell commission case, in which he had said upon oath that Bragg's Army, for its numbers, was the best army he ever saw. It was flushed with its brilliant victory at Perryville. He knew that in a fair field, man to man, the defeat of that army was impossible. His plan of battle was to move a heavy column upon his left, push it over Stone's River, turn the Confederate right, divided as it was from the Confederate left and center by Stone's River, and occupy Murfreesboro in the rear of the Confederate center, and by this maneuver win the battle. While this movement was in progress, Hardee, with the Confederate left, struck his right and ground it to powder. His center could not gain an inch of ground, and all it could do was to hold its ground by the most desperate fighting. His whole right was in full retreat, and Hardee driving to his rear like a tempest. By all the rules of war the Confederates had gained the day. They had raised the blockade. They had won the independence of the South.

At this supreme moment the genius of Rosecrans struck the fatal blow to the Confederacy. He immediately recalled his left, formed it on a line perpendicular to his center, and there he stood with a line of battle the like of which had never before been seen on land or sea, waiting for Hardee and the Confederate left. When at last it fronted his new line, it had been cut to pieces by a half day's fighting. Its ammunition was spent. The men were worn down by a rush over two miles of fighting ground. Their artillery was far in their rear. They threw themselves upon the new line with the fury of heroes. The struggle was terrific, but the genius of Rosecrans had assigned them a task impossible for men to perform, and so it was not written in the book of fate that the Confederate left should have the glory of crushing both the right and left of the Federal army on the same field.

On that field the genius of Rosecrans turned the paper blockade into one of adamant and doomed the Confederates to fight on to the end in hunger and rags, without pay and without the appliances for war. On that field his genius destroyed the Confederacy and re-established the Union. While on the arrow that struck us down we see the feather of Rosecrans, yet there is not a Confederate in the South who does not honor him, for, while in war he was our deadliest enemy, in peace he has been our constant, unfaltering friend.

General Rosecrans, with one voice, the soldiers of the South welcome you among them and salute you as first among the Federal generals!

ADDRESS OF HON. W. A. HENDERSON.

Hon. W. A. Henderson, of Knoxville, who was observed to be present, was next called upon by the Chairman, and, after repeated calls, he came on the platform and spoke, in part, as follows:

Ladies, and Comrades of both Armies:

I am proud to be selected for such an occasion as this. I came to listen and not to speak. I stopped on my way from my work in the mountains to my home in the hill country, to see what was being done and hear what was being said in this city of Chattanooga * * *.

Now, if there is any man in the North who would like to carry back with him an absolute knowledge of what a rebel soldier thinks, representing that class which is the class that carried a musket and smelled gunpowder, I will tell you what the main body of them think on this subject. I don't speak for all, for in a pile of apples they are n't all sound [laughter], but I can tell you what, in my opinion, a backbone of the South thinks about this question, and you may carry it home with you and it will be verified. That is this: I believe it as strongly as any thing that was ever written by St. John, that the South, in material progress, has made more by the war than has the North. [Great cheering.] Some people thought the question of slavery was the bone of contention which brought on and which carried out the war. Rather in apposition than in opposition to what Gen. Marks has just said, that question is settled now, and settled forever, and in that settlement of the question the South has gained more than the North. While those men who wore the blue were settling that question against us, in our teeth, I am of the opinion that they themselves did not know, and may not now know, how much good they were doing. [Applause.]

While it is true that they set 4,000,000 slaves free, they did not know so well then, as we know now, that they also set free 4,000,000 of the young white men of the South [great applause] whose hands were bound down, chained by the prejudices that we were then living under. It may have been involuntarily done, but they have, for us, made it respectable to work, and it is this work by the young white men of the South, the mixing of brain with muscle, which never could have been done by slave labor, or her cousin-germain, convict labor. It is that which is rebuilding our temple more glorious than that which was originally constructed by King Solomon. [Applause.]

In the providence of God, this thing never could have been done in any other way. It was not a question for argument. It was not a question for lawyers or courts. It was a question for the sword, and shot, and shell, and bayonet. [Turning to Gen. Rosecrans.] You, sir, won the lawsuit, but we got the mule. [Great and prolonged cheers.]

This is what you can tell them when you go back to your homes, and you can tell them you have seen the facts of it working now. Look around you where we now stand. What old soldier who was here twenty-six years ago can go without the greatest difficulty around this city of Chattanooga and find the place even where his camp stood? He is looking for a mud hole and he finds a palace there. He is looking for an old field, and he finds improvements there. You find that the rock has given way to the vineyard, and the thistle is gone in the presence of the roses.

The young white men of the South have done this and will do more. They never could have done it had it not been for the war. Now, this enterprise of yours, in attestation of this idea, I heartily bid God-speed. If heartily pressed, it will be a success beyond question. Let this Chickamauga of yours and ours be made eternal and holy as the Mecca of the Musselman and the Jerusalem of the Jew, where both sides can come, and where the descendants of the gray and blue may look upon it with mutual pride; where, as it was before stated, the coming young man may study the art of war with the proudest battle field before his face that, in my opinion, is on this round world of ours; and these coming young men from both sides, standing side by side on this historic place, will become cemented firmer and stronger as the days go by; and let me give warning to my friend, the chairman of this meeting, that the young men of the South are watching their opportunity, day by day, to show to the world how true the Southern man is to the constitution and to our flag of the stars and stripes. I am persuaded that they are watching national issues, which will lead to disruption with other countries, closer than are the men of the North.

The farmers talk to each other about the fishery question with England, and the internal policy of France, and the national questions that are involving other countries. If a foreign government should break the confines of the soil of the United States, I give you warning to look well to your laurels, that the men of the South don't outstrip you in the contest in devotion to our Union. They look upon this flag as their flag, as it is their flag, because, while this war ended as it did, we left the questions that were involved in it behind us, and have returned to our own country. You may trust the man of the South as he trusts you. He will be hand to hand with you in other questions as, when he thought he was right, he was bravely face to face against you. When such a time comes, then they will stand hand to hand and side by side. God speed your Chickamauga enterprise. I foretell that it will be successful, and we on our side will further its interests as far as it will be in our power to do so.

Previous to this meeting, in pursuance of a joint invitation issued by Maj. W. J. Colburn, Chairman Executive Committee Army of the Cumberland, Adolph S. Ochs, Chairman Local Committee Chickamauga National Park Association, and Capt. J. F. Shipp, Commander of Forrest Camp Confederate Veterans, a preliminary meeting of Confederate veterans was held, at which Captain Shipp briefly outlined the object of the meeting and the proposed plan of organizing the Chickamauga National Park Association. The following associations were represented:

*Army of the Tennessee Veteran Association, New Orleans—*Gen. Jno. Glynn, Jr., E. T. Manning, Jno. McCoy, Capt. J. A. Chalaron, Lieut. Jno. B. Ballard, R. D. Scriven, Col. Fremaux, C. L. Sinclair, Capt. Eugene May, Col. Thos. H. Handy.

*Confederate Cavalry Association, New Orleans—*Dr. Y. R. Lemonnier, Col. Jos. H. Duggan, Col. Robt. W. Gillespie.

*Washington Artillery, Army Northern Virginia, New Orleans—*Gen. Wm. J. Beham, Col. Wm. Miller Owen.

*Tennessee State Association Confederate Veterans—*Capt. Thos. F. Perkins, President, Franklin, Tenn.

*Frank Cheatham Bivouac, Nashville, Tenn.—*Col. Thos. Claiborn, Maj. J. W. Morton, Capt. Geo. B. Guild, Capt. Pat Griffin, Wm. Allen, John Shields.

*Confederate Veteran Association, Chicago, Ill.—*Maj. Geo. Forrester, Capt. R. H. Stewart.

*Forbes Bivouac, Clarksville, Tenn.—*Capt. C. W. Tyler, Chas. H. Bailey, Clay Stacker, Cave Johnson.

ORIGIN AND DEVELOPMENT OF THE PARK PROJECT.

Frierson Bivouac, Shelbyville, Tenn.—Hon. E. Shepard, H. C. Whitesides, J. L. Burt, Dr. Samuel M. Thompson.

The J. B. Palmer Bivouac, Murfreesboro, Tenn.—Hon. J. W. Sparks.

F. K. Zollicoffer Camp, Knoxville, Tenn.—Frank A. Moses, Chas. Ducloux.

Veteran Confederate States Cavalry Association, New Orleans—Maj. D. A. Given.

N. B. Forrest Camp Confederate Veterans, Chattanooga, Tenn.—Capt. J. F. Shipp, Capt. L. T. Dickinson, Capt. J. L. McCollum, Capt. M. H. Clift, Col. T. M. McConnell, Judge W. L. Eakin, Col. Tomlinson Fort, Capt. Milton Russell, Dr. G. W. Drake.

Capt. Geo. B. Guild, of Nashville, was elected Chairman, and E. T. Manning, Secretary. After a full explanation of the project, it was enthusiastically indorsed, and officers and directors to represent the Confederate side were elected.

The next day a quorum of incorporators was held at Crawfish Springs, Georgia, for organization under the charter it being agreed that this should take place, as if the court had formally granted it, and that the organization there agreed upon should stand. The occasion was marked by one of the largest barbecues ever held in the South, tables being set for 12,000 people, and all of them filled. This remarkable affair was organized and carried through by the active work of the committee of which Gordon Lee, Esq., was Chairman, and W. P. McClatchey Secretary.

The formal exercises preceding the barbecue were opened by Gov. John B. Gordon, of Georgia, who said :

Mr. Chairman and Fellow Soldiers of both Armies:

On this anniversary morning the South salutes you with uncovered heads, with open arms, and earnest, honest hearts. She can not receive you with costly and imposing ceremonials, but with simplicity of speech and patriotic purpose she gladly greets the brave and generous of each army and of every section.

To this renowned battle ground, made memorable by your prowess and hallowed by American blood, she bids you welcome. The South congratulates the whole country that these historic plains, where twenty-six years ago you met in deadly sectional conflict, are now to become the scene and witness of your joint pledge of restored and enduring fraternity. She congratulates the Republic that here where the North and the South marshaled their hosts for battle, these hosts now meet in living, lasting brotherhood, united in the bonds of mutual respect and confidence—a brotherhood made better, braver, and grander by mutually cherished and imperishable memories.

The people of this section hail with pleasure the coming of all men who have borne themselves bravely on the field of duty, but they fling wide their open doors and greet with a thousand welcomes those who in war were brave, and in peace are both generous and just.

True courage, always and every-where, challenges the respect and homage of mankind; but the truest and highest courage is that which is born of lofty convictions, and is elevated in its aspirations, gentle, loving, and tender.

True courage cherishes generosity as its noblest characteristic, conquers prejudice and passion as its highest achievement, and thus brings to the victor the greatest possible glory, to the vanquished the least possible detriment, and to both the utmost possible harmony, happiness, and peace.

To you, General Rosecrans, and soldiers of the Army of the Cumberland, I come with a soldier's greeting on my lips, and a soldier's sympathy in my heart.

Speaking of those whom I am called to represent, I pledge their earnest co-operation in the sacred mission which convenes you, and in all things which pertain to the peace, welfare, and unity of the American people.

In their name I proclaim their eternal fealty to the Ameriican Constitution, which is their protecting shield; to the American Republic, which is the joint work of the Father's hands, and to the American Union of States, from which they withdrew for their safety, but which, now that the causes of dissensions are gone, they would loyally and bravely defend for their future protection. They rest in the assurance that the Union, though restored by arms, is to be preserved and made stronger and perpetual by universal amity and impartial laws. With a love for this whole country which no power can destroy; with a title to its freedom which none will dispute; with ancestral traditions which are dearer than life, we are here to unite with you in the final and eternal sepulture of sectional hostility. The causes which produced alienation were long since engulfed in the vortex of revolution beyond the power of resurrection. Let us therefore bury the passions which these causes evoked in a still deeper grave.

Let us bury the foul spirit of discord so deep that no blast of partisan political trumpet, however wide-sounding and penetrating, can ever wake it to service again.

Gainsay it who will, since slavery is abolished, and the Chinese wall along the line of 36° 38' is broken down, there is absolutely no legitimate barrier of separation and no cause for strife.

Why may not the wide waves of sympathetic Continental patriotism roll from sea to sea, and from Maine to Texas, without a break or a ripple, or a single obstruction? God speed the day when this truth shall command recognition throughout the Republic. God speed the day when unworthy doubt shall give place to universal trust; when unstinted faith in the unimpeachable honor and patriotism of the whole American people shall become an essential passport to public station; when he who fights least for party and most for country shall be proclaimed by press and people as the wisest statesman and the truest friend of liberty.

To this, Gen. Rosecrans made response:

Comrades:

How strange it seems that I am called upon by every reason and every sentiment to call you comrades, to call you fellow-citizens. I never was in a condition to fail to do it— to call the men comrades who, twenty-six years ago to-day, and at this hour, were in deadly conflict with my Northern soldiers over in those fields yonder. I see that I shall not be able to reach this audience; I see that my voice will be as inadequate to reach this vast crowd as my words will be to express the gratification with which I return thanks to the Governor of this great State—to this gallant soldier who has given us such a splendid welcome, and in so doing has uttered such noble, patriotic, and far-reaching sentiments.

Soldiers of the Army of the Cumberland! See this vast crowd. It greets us through the Governor of the State to which they belong. It greets us with all this preparation, and I presume this entire affair was planned and paid for by the very men we used to call Confederates. [A voice—Right you are!] What does this signify? The eloquent orator who had just taken his seat spoke of the magnanimity of the truly brave. What words can express the magnanimity of the Confederate soldiers who fought on this battle field twenty-six years ago, against the soldiers of the Army of the Cumberland who were here at that time, in a great contest for life. Great souls are those who fight for liberty; who sacrifice their property, their lives, and every thing that man holds dear; but greater souls, still, are those who now uphold with unrelenting vigor the principles of friendship and fraternal greeting. Your eloquent Governor says why. I know not; I am unable to answer. I say they should fraternize. We assembled to-day to carry out a project for making this a National Memorial Battle Field, a National Memorial Battle Park, dedicated to the bravery of the soldiers of the

United States—I wish I had a word that would cover it—American bravery. [Applause.]

I believe that the work you have begun will be carried auspiciously through. If it is done, there will be no equal in these United States, nor will there be in the tide of time, fellow-citizens, a record of such a thing as this grand work which we propose to undertake, and which I have just mentioned. I know of nothing in history comparable to it. I know of nothing which would inspire the soul or fire the heart of an American soldier as much as to see this splendid monument to American patriotism.

I am sure that Gov. Gordon has so far expressed the feelings and sentiments of the noble soldiers of the Army of the Cumberland, that it is wasting words for me to undertake to gild fine gold, and I therefore proceed to say: If we can carry out the purpose for which this assemblage has met here, we can make this battle field a monument to national courage, pluck, endurance, and bravery. We know, fellow citizens, that this ground was watered by the blood of twenty-seven of the States of this Union, and I feel that it is the Union that will aid in maintaining this splendid memorial to the bravery of her sons.

As an eloquent speaker said, yesterday, in the big tent at Chattanooga, "the project is a good one, if it don't die a-bornin." Now, fellow citizens, I am sorry that I am not able to fittingly express the feelings I have on this occasion, nor to entertain you with the kind thoughts that come before my mind as I stand here. I am sure I have not the words, neither have I the voice, to appropriately do so, but I hope and pray that the future may see the eminent success of our fraternal undertaking.

After the barbecue, a joint meeting of veterans was held in the Baptist Church on the battle field at Chickamauga, at which a full organization was effected and incorporators and directors elected. Gen. H. M. Cist was elected Chairman and E. T. Manning, Secretary.

In making up the list of incorporators, each State was given representation as nearly as possible in proportion to the troops it had in the battle. These were as follows:

Alabama—William H. Forney, J. T. Holtzclaw, W. C. Oates, Joseph Wheeler, and S. M. A. Wood.

Arkansas—James H. Berry, Clifton R. Breckinridge, Evander McNair, and L. H. Mangum.

Colorado—G. C. Symes.

District of Columbia—Absalom Baird, H. V. Boynton, and W. S. Rosecrans.

Florida—Wilkinson Call, Robert H. M. Davidson, and Jesse J. Finley.

Georgia—Joseph M. Brown, Alfred H. Colquitt, J. B. Cummings, James Longstreet, Lafayette McLaws, and E. B. Tate.

Illinois—S. D. Adkins, Lyman Bridges, A. C. McClurg, E. A. Otis, John M. Palmer, and P. S. Post.

Indiana—Joseph B. Dodge, W. Q. Gresham, J. J. Reynolds, M. S. Robinson, G. W. Steele, and J. T. Wilder.

Iowa—Frank Hatton and W. P. Hepburn.

Kansas—John A. Martin.

Kentucky—C. D. Bailey, J. C. S. Blackburn, R. M. Kelly, G. C. Kniffin, Joseph H. Lewis, Alfred Pirtle, and W. J. Stone.

Louisiana—Randall L. Gibson and Felix Robertson.

Michigan—H. M. Duffield and A. W. Wilber.

Minnesota—J. W. Bishop and R. W. Johnson.

Mississippi—Charles E. Hooker, J. Bright Morgan, Jacob M. Sharp, J. A. Smith, and Edward C. Walthall.

Missouri—Joseph S. Fullerton, William Henry Hatch, Robert McCulloch, John S. Melton, and W. H. Wade.

New York—C. A. Dana and A. G. McCook.

North Carolina—William R. Cox, David H. Hill, Charles W. McClammey, and Matt W. Ransom.

Ohio—H. M. Cist, W. F. Goodspeed, Charles H. Grosvenor, P. P. Lane, J. G. Mitchell, J. G. Taylor, and Ferd. Van Derveer.

Pennsylvania—William J. Palmer, John Tweedale, and John G. Vale.

South Carolina—Ellison Capers and E. M. Law.

Tennessee—Frank C. Armstrong, William B. Bate, John C. Brown, S. B. Moe, Adolph S. Ochs, Lucius E. Polk, Alexander P. Stewart, Gates P. Thruston, and Marcus J. Wright.

Texas—C. B. Kilgore, Roger Q. Mills, and William B. Sayers.

Virginia—R. A. Brock, I. M. French, and George D. Wise.

Wisconsin—H. C. Hobart and John L. Mitchell.

United States Army—J. M. Brannan, H. C. Cushing, S. C. Kellogg, Frank G. Smith, and Thomas J. Wood.

The following were chosen Directors:
Alabama—Gen. Jos. Wheeler.
Arkansas—Capt. C. R. Breckinridge.
Florida—Gen. T. Finley.
Georgia—Gen. Alfred H. Colquitt, Gen. James Longstreet.
Illinois—Gen. A. C. McClurg.
Indiana—Gen. J. J. Reynolds.
Kentucky—Col. G. C. Kniffen, Gen. Jos. H. Lewis.
Louisiana—Gen. Randall L. Gibson.
Minnesota—Gen. J. W. Bishop.
Mississippi—Col. Chas. E. Hooker.
Missouri—Gen. F. M. Cockrell, Gen. J. S. Fullerton.
North Carolina—Gen. D. H. Hill.
Ohio—Gen. Henry M. Cist, Gen. C. H. Grosvenor, Gen. Ferd. Van Derveer.
South Carolina—Gen. E. M. Law.
Tennessee—Gen. Marcus J. Wright, Gen. Gates P. Thruston, Gen. J. T. Wilder.
Texas—Gen. Roger Q. Mills.

U. S. Army—Gen. A. Baird, Col. S. C. Kellogg.
Virginia—Hon. Geo. D. Wise.
Washington, D. C.—Gen. W. S. Rosecrans, Gen. H. V. Boynton.

An election for officers resulted as follows, the vote for each being unanimous:

President,
JOHN T. WILDER, Johnson City, Tenn.

Vice President,
JOSEPH WHEELER, Wheeler's Station, Ala.

Secretary,
MARCUS J. WRIGHT, Washington, D. C.

Treasurer,
J. S. FULLERTON, St. Louis, Mo.

The charter of the Association has a life of twenty years.

Such was the organization under which the project of a Military Park at Chickamauga first took shape. While this plan was soon superseded by a more comprehensive project, those active in the former have remained prominent and influential supporters of the latter.

NOTE.—The reports of speeches and meetings in this chapter are mainly from the account of the Chickamauga Memorial Association, published by the Chattanooga Army of the Cumberland Entertainment Committee.

CHAPTER XVII.

DEVELOPMENT OF THE PARK PROJECT—PLAN CHANGED TO A NATIONAL MILITARY PARK.

When the question arose in the winter following the organization of the Chickamauga Memorial Association, of asking the aid of Congress in the purchase of the battle field, the author of the project conceived the idea of enlarging the scope of the scheme so as to embrace the notable fields of Lookout Mountain and Missionary Ridge, and the lesser affairs of the battle of Chattanooga, and establishing the whole as a National Park under the control of the Secretary of War.

He therefore drew a bill authorizing the purchase by the Government of the entire field of Chickamauga, and the acquirement of the main roads leading to and through that field, and those along Missionary Ridge, and thence over Lookout Mountain, as "Approaches." Under the bill, the Secretary of War, acting through a commission of his own selection, was authorized to establish the Park. It was to be known as the Chickamauga and Chattanooga National Military Park.

After consultation with leading men of the Army of the Cumberland, the bill was put into the hands of Gen. Charles H. Grosvenor, an influential member of the House of Representatives, who served with signal distinction at Chickamauga, and is prominent in the Society of the Army of the Cumberland. He introduced the measure, and followed it with unremitting attention through all its stages in both houses, meeting at every step with the most remarkable success.

The House Committee on Military Affairs, by unanimous vote, made a favorable report. This paper is worthy of preservation, and the more so, since the Senate Committee on Military Affairs subsequently adopted it as their own. It was as follows:

March 5, 1890, Mr. Lansing, from the Committee on Military Affairs, submitted the following report:

The Committee on Military Affairs, to whom was referred the bill (H. R. 6454) to establish a National Military Park at the battle field of Chickamauga, having had the same under consideration, respectfully report the same with an amendment, and recommend that the bill as amended do pass.

The bill under consideration establishes as a National Military Park the Approaches which overlook and the ground upon which occurred some of the most remarkable tactical movements and the deadliest fighting of the war of the rebellion, namely, the fields of Chickamauga and Chattanooga.

The preservation for national study of the lines of decisive battles, especially when the tactical movements were unusual both in numbers and military ability, and when the fields embraced great natural difficulties, may properly be regarded as a matter of national importance.

This your committee understands to be the underlying idea of that noted organization of Union soldiers, the Society of the Army of the Cumberland, with whom the pending project originated. Interested with them and supporting them in the movement, we find leading representatives of all the Eastern and of all the Western armies; and for this we find ready explanation in the fact that all the armies and nearly every State of the North and each State of the South had troops on one or both these fields.

The proposition to mark the lines on both sides is held to be absolutely necessary to a clear understanding of the fields and to the sufficient illustration of the persistent, stubborn, and deadly fighting of American soldiers, which made the field of Chickamauga for both sides, as the statistics show, one of the bloodiest, if not the bloodiest battle field, for the numbers engaged and the time of their fighting, of any of the great battles of the modern world, from the days of the first Napoleon to the close of the war for the Union.

The corresponding field for Eastern operations is Gettysburg, where every State in the Union is interested, and the necessity of marking both lines to an intelligent study of the field has been recognized in a proposition before this Congress to provide for marking the Confederate lines upon that noted field.

The proposed Chickamauga and Chattanooga National Park consists of two features—the Approaches and the Park proper. It is expected that title to the former will be obtained by the United States, without cost, through cession of jurisdiction by the States of Tennessee and Georgia, respectively, of the public roads now in existence, and which it is proposed to utitilize as Approaches to the Park. No appropriation is therefore made for their purchase, and informal assurances have been given of their prompt cession to the United States.

The battle field of Chickamauga proper forms the body of the Park. As described in the bill, it embraces about 7,600 acres. It is proposed to obtain title to this by condemnation under the general act. In order that no resident on the tract may feel himself driven from home or from his possessions, it is provided that the Secretary of War may arrange with all who desire to remain to lease their lands at a nominal rent, the conditions on their side being that they will aid in the care of the grounds and in preserving all the natural features of the field as they now exist.

The Approaches to the field form most important adjuncts to the proposed National Park. The Approach from Chattanooga begins at or near Sherman Heights, at the north end of Missionary Ridge. This is the battle field of the Army of the Tennessee, under Gen. W. T. Sherman, during the operations about Chattanooga, November 23, 24, and 25, 1863. From this point, this Approach runs along the crest of Missionary Ridge to Rossville Gap. Throughout its whole length, it overlooks the battle field of Gen. Hooker's troops from the Army of the Potomac on Lookout Mountain, and terminates where these troops, after the battle on the mountain, reached and crossed Missionary Ridge. This Approach also overlooks the ground of the first day's operations about Orchard Knob, and coincides throughout its length with the lines of Gen. Bragg's army, and thus passes along the entire front of the famous assault of the Army of the Cumberland, under Gen. Thomas, upon Missionary Ridge.

The continuation of this first-described Approach is the La Fayette or State Road from Rossville, Georgia, passing through the center of the battle field of Chickamauga, and being the axis and the prize of the fight, to Lee and Gordon's Mills, on the Chickamauga River, which was opposite the center of the Confederate army at the opening of the battle, and thence to Crawfish Springs, the point from which the Union army advanced to the battle, and thence to Glass' Mills, on the Chickamauga, the left of the Confederate line of battle. The third Approach is the road from the junction of the first two at Rossville, Georgia, along the northern base of Missionary Ridge, to McFarland's Gap, being the road over which the Union army advanced to Chattanooga after the battle, and forming the entrance to the northern portion of the proposed Park. These are all roads which, for the most part, like those of the battle field itself, have a stony or flinty foundation, and which require comparatively little care, and all of them are to be obtained without cost to the United States.

The following are the lengths of the Approaches and roads thus to be ceded to the United States without cost:

	MILES.
Sherman Heights to Rossville	6
Rossville to Lee and Gordon's	7
Rossville to McFarland's Gap	2
McFarland's Gap to Crawfish Springs Road	6
Lee and Gordon's Mills to Crawfish Springs	2
Crawfish Springs to Glass' Mills	2
Total	26

The purpose is to maintain the body of the Park, which embraces the fields of Chickamauga, as near as may be in its present condition as to roads, fields, forests, and houses. There have been scarcely any changes in those respects since the battle, except in the growth of underbrush and timber. Almost the only work of any consequence in the restoration of the entire field to its condition at the time of the battle will be the cutting away of underbrush over a very limited area.

The roads as they now exist are the same as were used in the battle, and very little road construction will hereafter be necessary to give access to every point of interest on the field. When, therefore, once established, the cost of the care of the Park and its Approaches will be very small.

The area which it is proposed to acquire for the Park by condemnation contains, as near as may be, 7,600 acres. The land is largely forest and ridge land, though there is considerable good farming land in the tract. The average cost of the whole can not, with all improvements, exceed $20 an acre. The sum appropriated by the bill, which is $250,000,* will be ample for the complete establishment of the Park, including preliminary surveys, fixing its boundaries, surfacing its roads, and ascertaining the military positions.

The purpose is to have each State which had troops engaged on the field provide the monuments for marking the positions of the troops, after the general plan heretofore pur-

---

* Reduced to and passed at $125,000.

sued at Gettysburg by the Gettysburg Battle Field Memorial Association. This work will be performed at Chickamauga and Chattanooga by the Chickamauga Memorial Association, acting under the supervision of the Secretary of War. This latter association is incorporated under the laws of Georgia. Its charter specially states that it will not issue stock, and that its objects are not pecuniary gain. Its incorporators number one hundred, half of them ex-Union veterans of prominence in the battle, and the other half ex-Confederate soldiers of equal prominence on their side.

The sole expense to the United States for monuments will be those for marking the positions of the regular regiments and batteries, being only sixteen in number for both fields.

The Approaches to the Park which traverse Missionary Ridge can be cheaply and quickly reached from Chattanooga by four turnpikes, and by steam and electric railroads, upon which the fare is five cents. The Chickamauga Field can be reached by railroad in fifteen minutes from Chattanooga, this road traversing the whole field from McFarland's Gap to Crawfish Springs. Two other railroads will add facilities for reaching other portions of the Park as soon as its establishment is secured.

Your committee finds the interest in this project widespread. To such an extent is this true that it may properly be called national. The recent demands for the new maps of Chickamauga from every section of the Union illustrate this fact. The Union armies of the Tennessee, the Cumberland, and the Potomac, under Gens. Sherman, Rosecrans, Thomas, and Hooker, all finally united under Gen. Grant, are equally interested in preserving the lines of this extended and notable battle ground.

On the Confederate side the armies of Tennessee, of Northern Virginia through Gen. Longstreet's Corps, of the Mississippi through Gen. Johnston's troops, and Gen. Buckner's army from East Tennessee were all engaged.

The regular army had nine regiments and seven batteries

on these fields, while the following eighteen States had troops in the Union army engaged in these movements: Maine, Massachusetts, Connecticut, New York, Pennsylvania, New Jersey, Maryland, Ohio, Indiana, Kentucky, Michigan, Wisconsin, Minnesota, Iowa, Illinois, Kansas, Missouri, and Tennessee. Every Confederate State had troops on these fields, while Kentucky, Missouri, and Tennessee contributed numerously to both armies.

As already stated, the figures show Chickamauga to rank for the numbers engaged and the time of their fighting among the most noted battles of the modern world.

Wellington lost 12 per cent at Waterloo; Napoleon, 14½ per cent at Austerlitz and 14 per cent at Marengo. The average losses of both armies at Magenta and Solferino, in 1859, was less than 9 per cent. At Königgrätz, in 1866, it was 6 per cent. At Wörth, Mars-la-Tour, Gravelotte, and Sedan, in 1870, the average was 12 per cent.

The marvel of German fighting in the Franco-Prussian war was by the Third Westphalian Infantry at Mars-la-Tour. It took 3,000 men into action and lost 40.4 per cent. Next to this record was that of the Garde-Schützen Battalion, 1,000 strong at Metz, which lost 46.1 per cent. There were several brigades on each side at Chickamauga and very many regiments whose losses exceeded these figures for Mars-la-Tour and Metz.

The average losses on each side for the troops which fought through the two days were fully 33 per cent, while for many portions of each line the losses reached 50 per cent, and for some even 75 per cent.

A field as renowned as this for the stubborness and brilliancy of its fighting, not only in our own war, but when compared with all modern wars, has an importance to the nation as an object lesson of what is possible in American fighting, and the national value of the preservation of such lines for historical and professional study must be apparent to all reflecting minds. The political questions which were involved in the contest do not enter into this view of the subject, nor do they belong to it. The proposition for establishing the Park is in all its aspects a purely military project.

The Eastern armies have already the noted field of Gettysburg upon which to mark and preserve the history of their movements and their renowned fighting. To this the Government has already made liberal appropriations to mark the positions of the regular forces there engaged and for other purposes.

It seems fitting that the Western armies should select a field and be assisted in preserving it by the general Government. It is easy to see from the facts presented that there is no other field upon which all the armies were as fully represented. There is probably no other in the world which presents more formidable natural obstacles to great military operations than the slopes of Lookout Mountain and Missionary Ridge, while, as shown, there is no field that surpasses Chickamauga in the deadliness and persistence of its fighting.

The tactical movements were numerous and brilliant on each field and many of them remarkable. Indeed, both are as noted in this respect as in the character of the fighting.

There were present upon one or the other and in the case of most, upon both fields, Grant, Sherman, Thomas, Rosecrans, Hooker, Sheridan; and Granger, of the Union army, and Bragg, Longstreet, Hood, Hardee, Buckner, Polk, D. H. Hill, Wheeler, Forrest, and Johnson, of the Confederate forces. The preservation of these fields will preserve to the nation for historical and military study the best efforts which these noted officers, commanding American veterans, were able to put forth.

The two together form one of the most valuable object lessons in the art of war, and one which, looking solely to the interests of the public, may properly be preserved.

Your committee therefore recommend the passage of the bill with the amendment on page 6, which is inserted for the purpose of enabling the Secretary of War to take advantage of the coming season in expediting the establishment of the Park, it having been made to appear to your committee that such preliminary work can be done while awaiting the process of condemning the land and the action of the state legislatures in ceding jurisdiction. The accompanying map shows the outlines of the proposed Park and the location of the Approaches.

Considering its magnitude, its present and prospective cost, and, in addition, the fact that both sides were to be admitted to equal participation, the smooth movement of the measure through Congress was surprising. There was not a word or a vote in opposition at any stage. The fact that it was approved by Northern and Southern veterans in the House and Senate relieved it of partisan aspects. It had for its active friends the members of the House and the Senate Committees on Military Affairs and Appropriations, the soldiers in Congress, and especially the very considerable number of those who had served at Chickamauga and Chattanooga.

Much careful work was done in preparing for the presentation of the bill to the House and for its subsequent consideration by the Senate. It was not till the rushing days of the session, when appropriation bills had the right of way, that the bill was ready to be brought forward for action. Then Speaker Thomas B. Reed, by his willing aid, earned a debt of gratitude from all soldiers by promptly agreeing to give the bill the chance of recognition. Without this assistance from the Speaker, it could not have secured a hearing until the following session of Congress. Gen. Grosvenor asked for unanimous consent to take up the measure. A single objection would have defeated the request. None were interposed. This was the more remarkable because Gen. Henderson, of Illinois, had given way to Gen. Grosvenor in the midst of the consideration of the River and Harbor Bill, which every member of the House was anxious to complete.

The bill was read; several amendments proposed by Gen. Grosvenor were adopted; Mr. Buchanan, of New Jersey, made a speech not to oppose, but to suggest the claims of the Trenton Monument; it was agreed that those who chose could print speeches in the Record; and the House, dispensing with the reading of the Report of the Committee, passed the bill without dissent. The time occupied was twenty-three minutes.

In the Senate the bill moved with the same promptness and success. The Military Committee gave a hearing, and unanimously made a favorable report. Senator Allison, Chairman of Appropriations, at the request of Senator Hawley, Chairman of Military Affairs, gave way during the consideration of the Sundry Civil Appropriation Bill, and allowed the Park Bill to be taken up. It was read, and, without a call for the Report, passed with not a vote against it. The Senate clerk being a more rapid reader, and a deeply interested and most efficient friend of the measure, namely, Gen. Anson G. McCook, of "the fighting McCooks," one of the most brilliant officers of the Army of the Cumberland, and a participator in the storming of Lookout Mountain, beat the record of the House clerk, and the bill passed the Senate in twenty minutes. In its final shape it provided for the purchase of fifteen square miles of the Chickamauga Field, and the establishment of a National Park upon this area.

The bill was taken the same night to President Harrison by Hon. H. Clay Evans, of Chattanooga, who represented that district in the House, and who, from first to last, like Hon. J. B. Clements, of Georgia, who represented the Chickamauga district, was an untiring and influential worker for the measure. The President promptly signed it, the National Park was authorized, and an appropriation of $125,000 made available to begin the work. Below is the text of the bill:

An act to establish a National Military Park at the battle field of Chickamauga.

Be it enacted by the Senate and House of Representatives of the United States of America in Congress assembled, That for the purpose of preserving and suitably marking for historical and professional military study the fields of some of the most remarkable maneuvers and most brilliant fighting in the war of the rebellion, and upon the ceding of jurisdiction to the United States by the States of Tennessee and Georgia, respectively, and the report of the Attorney-General of the United States that the title to the lands thus ceded is perfect, the following described highways in those states are hereby declared to be Approaches to and parts of the Chickamauga and Chattanooga National Military Park as established by the second section of this act, to wit: First—The Missionary Ridge Crest Road from Sherman Heights at the north end of Missionary Ridge, in Tennessee, where the said road enters upon the ground occupied by the Army of the Tennessee under Maj.-Gen. William T. Sherman, in the military operations of November twenty-fourth and twenty-fifth, eighteen hundred and sixty-three; thence along said road through the positions occupied by the army of Gen. Braxton Bragg on November twenty-fifth, eighteen hundred and sixty-three, and which were assaulted by the Army of the Cumberland under Maj.-Gen. George H. Thomas on that date, to where the said road crosses the southern boundary of the State of Tennessee, near Rossville Gap, Georgia, upon the ground occupied by the troops of Maj.-Gen. Joseph Hooker, from the Army of the Potomac, and thence in the State of Georgia to the junction of said road with the Chattanooga and La Fayette or State Road at Rossville Gap; second, the La Fayette or State Road from Rossville, Georgia, to Lee and Gordon's Mills, Georgia; third, the road from Lee and Gordon's Mills, Georgia, to Crawfish Springs, Georgia; fourth, the road from Crawfish Springs, Georgia, to the crossing of the Chickamauga, at Glass' Mills, Georgia; fifth, the Dry Valley Road from Rossville, Georgia, to the southern limits of McFarland's Gap in Missionary Ridge; sixth, the Dry Valley and Crawfish Springs Road from McFarland's Gap to the intersection of the road from Crawfish Springs to Lee and Gordon's Mills; seventh, the road from Ringgold, Georgia, to Reed's Bridge on the Chickamauga River; eighth, the roads from the crossing of Lookout Creek across the northern slope of Lookout Mountain and thence to the old Summertown Road and to the Valley on the east slope of the said mountain, and thence by the route of Gen. Joseph Hooker's troops to Rossville, Georgia, and each and all of these herein described roads shall, after the passage of this act, remain open as free public highways, and all rights of way now existing through the grounds of the said Park and its Approaches shall be continued.

SEC. 2. That upon the ceding of jurisdiction by the legislature of the State of Georgia, and the report of the Attorney-General of the United States that a perfect title has been secured under the provisions of the act approved August first, eighteen hundred and eighty-eight, entitled "An act to authorize condemnation of land for sites of public buildings, and for other purposes," the lands and roads embraced in the area bounded as herein described, together with the roads described in section one of this act, are hereby declared to to be a National Park, to be known as the Chickamauga and Chattanooga National Park; that is to say, the area inclosed by a line beginning on the La Fayette or State Road, in Georgia, at a point where the bottom of the ravine next north of the house known on the field of Chickamauga as the Cloud House, and being about six hundred yards north of said house, due east to the Chickamauga River and due west to the intersection of the Dry Valley Road at McFarland's Gap; thence along the west side of the Dry Valley and Crawfish Springs Roads to the south side of the road from Crawfish Springs to Lee and Gordon's Mills; thence along the south side of the last named road to Lee and Gordon's Mills; thence along the channel of the Chickamauga River to the line forming the northern boundary of the Park, as hereinbefore described, containing seven thousand six hundred acres more or less.

SEC. 3. That the said Chickamauga and Chattanooga National Park, and the approaches thereto, shall be under the control of the Secretary of War, and it shall be his duty, immediately after the passage of this act, to notify the Attorney-General of the purpose of the United States to acquire title to the roads and lands described in the previous sections of this act under the provisions of the act of August first, eighteen hundred and eighty-eight; and the said Secretary, upon receiving notice from the Attorney-General of the United States that perfect titles have been secured to the said lands and roads, shall at once proceed to establish and substantially mark the boundaries of the said Park.

SEC. 4. That the Secretary of War is hereby authorized to enter into agreements, upon such nominal terms as he may prescribe, with such present owners of the land as may desire to remain upon it, to occupy and cultivate their present holdings, upon condition that they will preserve the present buildings and roads, and the present outlines of field and forest, and that they will only cut trees or underbrush under such regulations as the Secretary may prescribe, and that they will assist in caring for and protecting all tablets, monuments, or such other artificial works as may from time to time be erected by proper authority.

SEC. 5. That the affairs of the Chickamauga and Chattanooga National Park shall, subject to the supervision and direction of the Secretary of War, be in charge of three Commissioners, each of whom shall have actively participated in the battle of Chickamauga or one of the battles about Chattanooga, two to be appointed from civil life by the Secretary of War, and a third, who shall be detailed by the Secretary of War from among those officers of the army best acquainted with the details of the battles of Chickamauga and Chattanooga, who shall act as Secretary of the Commission. The said Commissioners and Secretary shall have an office in the War Department Building, and while on actual duty shall be paid such compensation, out of the appropriation provided in this act, as the Secretary of War shall deem reasonable and just.

SEC. 6. That it shall be the duty of the Commissioners named in the preceding section, under the direction of the Secretary of War, to superintend the opening of such roads as may be necessary to the purposes of the Park, and the repair of the roads of the same, and to ascertain and definitely mark the lines of battle of all troops engaged in the battles of Chickamauga and Chattanooga, so far as the same shall fall within the lines of the Park as defined in the previous sections of this act, and, for the purpose of assisting them in their duties and in ascertaining these lines, the Secretary of War shall have authority to employ, at such compensation as he may deem reasonable and just, to be paid out of the appropriation made by this act, some person recognized as well informed in regard to the details of the battles of Chickamauga and Chattanooga, and who shall have actively participated in one of those battles, and it shall be the duty of the Secretary of War, from and after the passage of this act, through the Commissioners, and their assistant in historical work, and under the act approved August first, eighteen hundred and eighty-eight, regulating the condemnation of land for public uses, to proceed with the preliminary work of establishing the Park and its approaches as the same are defined in this act, and the expenses thus incurred shall be paid out of the appropriation provided by this act.

SEC. 7. That it shall be the duty of the Commissioners, acting under the direction of the Secretary of War, to ascertain and substantially mark the locations of the regular troops, both infantry and artillery, within the boundaries of the Park, and to erect monuments upon those positions as Congress may provide the necessary appropriations; and the Secretary of War in the same way may ascertain and mark all lines of battle within the boundaries of the Park and erect plain and substantial historical tablets at such points in the vicinity of the Park and its approaches as he may deem fitting and necessary to clearly designate positions and movements, which, although without the limits of the Park, were directly connected with the battles of Chickamauga and Chattanooga.

SEC. 8. That it shall be lawful for the authorities of any State having troops engaged either at Chattanooga or Chickamauga, and for the officers and directors of the Chickamauga Memorial Association, a corporation chartered under the laws of Georgia, to enter upon the lands and approaches of the Chickamauga and Chattanooga National Park for the purpose of ascertaining and marking the lines of battle of troops engaged therein; *Provided*, That before any such lines are permanently designated the position of the lines and the proposed methods of marking them by monuments, tablets, or otherwise shall be submitted to the Secretary of War, and shall first receive the written approval of the Secretary, which approval shall be based upon formal written reports, which must be made to him in each case by the Commissioners of the Park.

SEC. 9. That the Secretary of War, subject to the approval of the President of the United States, shall have the power to make, and shall make, all needed regulations for the care of the Park and for the establishment and marking of the lines of battle and other historical features of the Park.

SEC. 10. That if any person shall willfully destroy, mutilate, deface, injure or remove any monument, column, statues, memorial structure, or work of art that shall be erected or placed upon the grounds of the Park by lawful authority, or shall willfully destroy or remove any fence, railing, inclosure, or other work for the protection or ornament of said Park, or any portion thereof, or shall willfully destroy, cut, hack, bark, break down, or otherwise injure any tree, bush or shubbery that may be growing upon said Park, or shall cut down or fell or remove any timber, battle relic, tree or trees growing or being upon such Park, except by permission of the Secretary of War, or shall willfully remove or destroy any breastworks, earthworks, walls, or other defenses or shelter, on any part thereof, constructed by the armies formerly engaged, in the battles on the lands or approaches to the Park, any person so offending and found guilty thereof, before any justice of the peace of the county in which the offense may be committed, shall for each any every such offense forfeit and pay a fine, in the discretion of the justice, according to the aggravation of the offense, of not less that five nor more than fifty dollars, one-half to the use of the Park, and the other half to the informer, to be enforced and recovered before such justice, in like manner as debts of like nature are now by law recoverable in the several counties where the offense may be committed.

SEC. 11. That to enable the Secretary of War to begin to carry out the purposes of this act, including the condemnation and purchase of the necessary land, marking the boundaries of the Park, opening or repairing necessary roads, maps and surveys, and the pay and expenses of the Commissioners and their assistant, the sum of one hundred and twenty-five thousand dollars, or such portion thereof as may be necessary, is hereby appropriated, out of any moneys in the Treasury not otherwise appropriated, and disbursements under this act shall require the approval of the Secretary of War, and he shall make annual report of the same to Congress.

Approved, August 19, 1890.

[By an error in preparing the above act the Crawfish Springs Road was designated as the Dry Valley Road. The latter is quite west of the former, and wholly without the Park.]

It is fitting that the names of the members of the two Committees on Military Affairs and on Appropriations, together with the Chickamauga veterans in Congress at the time, should be given as those to whom the enactment of the Park Bill is largely due. Indeed, no history of the Park would be complete without them:

House Committee on Military Affairs—Byron M. Cutcheon, of Michigan; Francis W. Rockwell, of Massachusetts; Edwin S. Osborne, of Pennsylvania; Henry J. Spooner, of Rhode Island; Elihu S. Williams, of Ohio; Fred. Lansing, of New York; S. P. Snider, of Minnesota; William M. Kinsey, of Missouri; Francis B. Spinola, of New York; Joseph Wheeler, of Alabama; S. W. T. Lanham, of Texas; S. M. Robertson, of Louisiana; Joseph M. Carey, of Wyoming.

House Committee on Appropriations—Joseph G. Cannon, of Illinois; Benjamin Butterworth, of Ohio; Louis E. McComas, of Maryland; David B. Henderson, of Iowa; Samuel R. Peters, of Kansas; William Coggswell, of Massachusetts; James J. Belden, of New York; W. W. Morrow, of California; Mark S. Brewer, of Michigan; William H. Forney, of Alabama; Joseph D. Sayers, of Texas; Judson C. Clements, of Georgia; William C. P. Breckinridge, of Kentucky; Alexander M. Dockery, of Missouri; William Mutchler, of Pennsylvania.

Senate Committee on Military Affairs—Joseph R. Hawley, of Connecticut; James Donald Cameron, of Pennsylvania; Charles F. Manderson, of Nebraska; William M. Stewart, of Nevada; Cushman K. Davis, of Minnesota; Francis M. Cockrell, of Missouri; Wade Hampton, of South Carolina; Edward C. Walthall, of Mississippi; William B. Bate, of Tennessee.

Senate Committee on Appropriations—William B. Allison, of Iowa; Henry L. Dawes, of Massachusetts; Preston B. Plumb, of Kansas; Eugene Hale, of Maine; Charles B. Farwell, of Illinois; Francis M. Cockrell, of Missouri; Wilkinson Call, of Florida; Arthur P. Gorman, of Maryland.

The subsequent Chairmen of Appropriations in the House for the Fifty-second and Fifty-third Congress, Hons. W. S. Holman and J. S. Sayers, with the additional new members, have given the project their continuous and cordial support, and the same is true of the new members of the Senate Committee on Appropriations, Senators Blackburn, Cullom, and Stewart, and Senators Proctor and Palmer, of Military Affairs, and Hon. Joseph H. Outhwaite, Chairman of the House Military Committee.

The following senators who served in the campaign for Chattanooga have given active assistance: Bate, Blackburn, Randall, Gibson, Manderson, Mitchell, of Wisconsin, Moody, Morgan, Pasco, Squire, and Walthall, also Gen. Anson G. McCook, the Secretary of the Senate.

Those in the House who had served on these fields were: Charles E. Belknap, of Michigan; C. R. Breckinridge, of Arkansas; W. C. P. Breckinridge, of Kentucky; William Cogswell, of Massachusetts; Charles H. Grosvenor, of Ohio; C. B. Kilgore and Roger Q. Mills, of Texas; Wm. C. Oates, of Alabama; P. S. Post, of Illinois; Samuel P. Snyder, of Minnesota; W. H. Wade, of Missouri; Joseph Wheeler, of Alabama; and W. C. Whitthorne, of Tennessee.

In fact there has not been at any time an active opponent of the project in either House of Congress from its first introduction until the passage of the bill providing for the National dedication of the Park in September of the present year. From the inception of the project, Maj. George B. Davis, U. S. A., and Hon. J. W. Kirkley, of the War Record Office, have rendered constant and most valuable assistance.

While enumerating the sources of important aid for the Park project, it would be a grave oversight to omit the leading Washington correspondents, editors, and managers of the Press Associations, who made it thoroughly known to the country. This secured the prompt co-operation of all the States whose troops are interested. No more deservedly influential body of men can be found anywhere in the land than the leading press men of the National Capitol. To this company, on account of his valuable and continuing local services, should be added Mr. Adolph S. Ochs, of the *Chattanooga Times*.

The text of the bill providing for the dedication completes the history of the Park to the present time. It was introduced by Gen. C. H. Grosvenor, and after unanimous reports in its favor from the two Committees on Military Affairs, it was passed by unanimous vote in each House:

The National Dedication of the Park.

Be it enacted by the Senate and House of Representatives of the United States of America in Congress assembled, That a national dedication of the Chickamauga and Chattanooga National Military Park shall take place on the battle fields of Chickamauga and Chattanooga, September nineteenth and twentieth, eighteen hundred and ninety-five under the direction of the Secretary of War, who is hereby authorized to fix upon and determine the arrangements, cremonies, and exercises connected with the dedication; to request the participation of the President, Congress, the Supreme Court, the heads of Executive Departments, the General of the Army, and the Admiral of the Navy therein; to invite the governors of States and their staffs, and the survivors of the several armies there engaged, and have direction and full authority in all matters which he may deem necessary to the success of the dedication. He shall have authority to procure such supplies and services, and to call upon the heads of the several staff departments of the Army for such material and stores as he may deem necessary in connection with the dedication.

SEC. 2. That to carry out the purposes of this act, the sum of twenty thousand dollars, or so much thereof as may be necessary, is hereby appropriated, out of any moneys in the Treasury not otherwise appropriated, which shall be expended under the direction of the Secretary of War: Provided, that the amount hereby named, twenty thousand dollars, shall cover all expenses for services, supplies, material, stores, and expenses contemplated by this bill.

Regulations Concerning Monuments, Tablets, and Markers.

The following regulations govern the erection of monuments, tablets, and markers in the Park, except that, under later legislation by Congress, section 3 is so modified that foundations for State monuments are constructed as specified, but without cost to the States:

CHICKAMAUGA AND CHATTANOOGA
NATIONAL MILITARY PARK COMMISSION,
WAR DEPARTMENT, WASHINGTON, D. C.

In accordance with the act of Congress approved August 19, 1890, establishing the Chickamauga and Chattanooga National Military Park, the following regulations are published for the information and guidance of all interested in the erection of monuments, tablets, or other methods of indicating lines of battle or positions within the limits of the said Park:

1. A statement of the proposed dimensions, designs, inscriptions upon, and material for all monuments, tablets, or other markers, must be submitted to the Commissioners of the Park, and, in the case of monuments, plans and elevaitons showing exact measurements, and a close estimate of weight, must be submitted. The Park Commissioners will report upon these to the Secretary of War, and, upon his approval, such monuments, tablets, or other markers may be erected. A duplicate copy of the approved specifications, design, and inscription of each monument, tablet, or marker will be furnished to the Commissioners of the Park for file with their records before a permit to erect will be issued.

2. Monuments of stone must be constructed of granite, or such other durable stone as, after investigation by the Park Commissioners, may be approved by the Secretary of War. Monuments may also be of bronze.

3. The foundations of all monuments will be constructed under the direction of an engineer of the Park, of material, except cement, supplied from the lands of the Park, and by labor employed by the engineer, the cost of the same to be paid by those for whom the foundations are prepared, in such way as the Secretary of War may direct.

4. Inscriptions must be purely historical, and must relate only to the Chickamauga and Chattanooga campaigns. They must also be based upon, and conform to, the official reports of these campaigns; and must be submitted to the Secretary of War, through the Park Commissioners, for his approval, before being adopted or cut into the stones.

5. Brigades, divisions, and corps may be designated, in the inscriptions, by their numbers, where that method was used, and also by the names of their respective commanders; as "First Brigade, First Division, Fourteenth Corps," or "Scribner's Brigade, Baird's Division, Thomas' Corps;" "Polk's Brigade, Cleburne's Division, Hill's Corps." The numerical designations alone would be meaningless to most visitors.

6. Tablets and other markers will be erected under the direction of the Park engineers—if of metal, upon metal posts set in hydraulic concrete; if of stone, upon suitable foundations to be determined by the Park engineers.

For the Commissioners:

J. S. FULLERTON,
Chairman.

Approved, December 19, 1893.

DANIEL S. LAMONT,
Secretary of War.

CHAPTER XVIII.

ESTABLISHING THE PARK—ORGANIZATION AND PROSECUTION OF THE WORK.

The law placed the duty of establishing the Park in the hands of the Secretary of War. Secretary Proctor at once took a deep interest in the matter, and his executive ability and practical knowledge enabled him to organize the extended work with promptness and due regard to its future proportions. He selected as the two civilian members of the Commission, Gen. Joseph S. Fullerton, Chairman, and Gen. Alexander P. Stewart, a leading ex-Confederate, with Capt. and Brevet Col. Sanford C. Kellogg, of the Fourth Cavalry, whom he detailed as the army officer provided by the law, and who was also to be Secretary of the Commission. Gen. H. V. Boynton was appointed Historian. All these gentlemen had served in the battles about Chattanooga. Mr. Hugh B. Rowland has from the first been the clerk. Gen. Fullerton was Chief of Staff to Gen. Gordon Granger, and had a most distinguished record. Gen. Stewart commanded a division in Buckner's Corps of Bragg's army with distinction, and was subsequently lieutenant-general in command of a corps. Col. Kellogg was an aide on the staff of Gen. Thomas at the time of the battle, and was thoroughly familiar with the field.

Throughout his term, Secretary Proctor continued to give most friendly and practical attention to the project. He was aided by the Assistant Secretary, Gen. L. A. Grant, to whom the executive work was entrusted. Gen. Grant continued to give energetic and most valuable attention to all park matters throughout the terms of Secretaries Proctor and Elkins, and for the first year of Secretary Lamont's term. Secretary Elkins also proved a warm friend of the measure, and neglected no opportunity to push it forward.

The advent of Col. Lamont to the Secretaryship found the establishing of the Park well under way. He promptly made himself acquainted with its details, and gave such intelligent attention and cordial support to every branch of the work, as to richly merit the thanks of the veterans of all the armies engaged. The establishment of the Park will be virtually completed under his administration. The new Assistant Secretary of War, Gen. Joseph Doe, upon whom much of the executive work falls, early made personal inspection of the fields, and gives the project most efficient help.

After rendering much exceedingly valuable aid for three years, Col. Kellogg was detailed as the Military Attaché of the American Legation in Paris, and Major Frank G. Smith, of the Second U. S. Artillery, succeeded him. Major Smith commanded Battery I, Fourth U. S. Artillery, at Chickamauga, that had the distinction of losing a greater percentage of men than any battery on the field, of remaining through the battle, and losing neither positions nor guns.

Mr. Atwell Thompson, Civil Engineer, has had charge under Gen. Stewart, of road construction, the erection of towers and bridges, and the general engineering work of the Park.

The topographical engineering, the elaborate maps of the several fields, and the erection of monuments have been executed by Mr. E. E. Betts, Civil Engineer.

The roads are equal to any, if, indeed, they are not the best which the government has built on extended scale, while their cost has fallen much below the usual expenditure for such work. This is owing, in great part, to the abundance of most excellent surfacing material within the Park.

The topographical maps—which are soon to be engraved, and thus made accessible to the public—are of the highest order of merit. Upon one set of these which represents the battle fields as they were in 1863, the positions of the lines as determined by the studies of the Commission, and the painstaking assistance rendered by the State Commissions, are being platted by Major Smith, who has this matter in his especial charge.

The National Commission, through appointment by Secretary Lamont, has been fortunate in securing the assistance of Mr. J. P. Smartt, of Chattanooga, to aid in the location of Confederate lines, and determining the details of Confederate movements. He served in the battles, has long been engaged in the study of the fields about Chattanooga, is an excellent authority, and a most enthusiastic and impartial student.

CHAPTER XIX.

THE STATE COMMISSIONS AND STATE TROOPS.

The general interest developed in Congress for the Park project extended at once to the States which had troops engaged in and around it. There were twenty-eight of these. The National Commission presented the matter to their legislatures where these were in session, and to their governors where they were not. In the latter case the request was made that a commission of veterans who served in the battles might be appointed. This was complied with in nearly all cases, and promised in all. The delay has arisen, where any occurred, in the difficulty of finding those who could serve without pay until their legislatures met.

The governors who rendered prompt and cordial aid were these: William M. Fishback, Arkansas; Henry L. Mitchell, Florida; John B. Gordon and W. J. Northern, Georgia; John P. Atgeld, Illinois; Claude Mathews, Indiana; Horace Boies and F. D. Jackson, Iowa; John Young Brown, Kentucky; M. J. Foster, Louisiana; Wm. E. Russell, Massachusetts; John T. Rich, Michigan; Knute Nelson, Minnesota; John M. Stone, Mississippi; Wm. J. Stone, Missouri; George T. Werts, New Jersey; Roswell P. Flower, New York; Elias Carr, North Carolina; James E. Campbell, Ohio; Robert E. Patteson, Pennsylvania; B. R. Tillman, South Carolina; Peter Turney, Tennessee; James S. Hogg, Texas; Charles T. O'Ferrall, Virginia; George M. Peck, Wisconsin; and E. N. Morrill, Kansas.

Ohio, which had the largest number of organizations, both at Chickamauga and Chattanooga, led off under the active encouragement of Governor James E. Campbell in the appointment of a Commission, and an appropriation for its expenses. In the following session of its legislature, it led in the matter of appropriations, giving $90,000 for monuments on the Chickamauga field alone. Minnesota, which had only three organizations in the battles, followed with the very liberal appropriation of $15,000, and her monuments were the first erected by any state. Massachusetts came next with the beautiful monument to her two organizations, on Orchard Knob, then Ohio, with fifty-five monuments, and fifty-one markers. New York followed, under a bill, the passage of which was largely due to the untiring work of Mr. Hugh Hastings, of the *New York Times*, Col. Lewis Stegman, of the *Brooklyn Standard Union*, and Senator Jacob A. Cantor, of the State Legislature, which provided for an expenditure of $81,000, one-quarter of this being made immediately available.

Most of the State Commissions have conducted careful studies on the ground in company with the National Commission, and, as a result, the general lines of battle, and most of their important details, have been established. This has been an immense work, and, considering the well-known intricacies of the fields, the progress has been remarkable.

The interest taken by the most distant states is shown by these facts: Gen. Cogswell, the Massachusetts Commissioner, has been twice upon the field, and the monument erected by that state under his supervision was the first to mark any eastern position. Gen. Daniel Butterfield twice brought the New York Commissioners and large parties of influential men from that state with them in special cars, and on both occasions went carefully over all the ground where eastern troops were engaged in the vicinity of Chattanooga. Col. L. R. Stegman and Mr. Clinton Beckwith, of that Commission, in addition to these, made a third, and prolonged visit, to the field. Twenty-five members of the Pennsylvania Commission have spent a week upon the fields, performing active and most valuable service. The Texas Commission has had its members at the Park twice; and the Louisiana Commission remained a week upon the occasion of its first visit, locating all positions occupied by troops of that state. The Minnesota Commission has been three times on the field and all its monuments are erected. The Michigan, Iowa, Indiana, and Illinois Commissions have made each two visits. It will thus be seen that the more distant states are among the most active. The State Commissions are as follows:

Alabama—Gen. Joseph Wheeler; Col. Charles M. Shelley; Col. Samuel K. McSpadden. [Gov. Oates, who is actively interested, is completing his commission.]

Arkansas—Gen. D. C. Govan, Mariana; Gen. R. P. Rowley, Carlisle; Col. Geo. F. Baucum, Little Rock; Col. J. W. Colquitt, Little Rock; Maj. J. A. Ross.

Florida—Hon. Samuel Pasco, Monticello.

Georgia—Gen. James Longstreet, Gainesville; Capt. Evan P. Howell, Atlanta; Judge W. T. Newman, Atlanta; Judge J. S. Boynton, Griffin; Col. Jos. B. Cumming, Augusta; Col. J. C. Gordon, Judson; Capt. Tyler M. Peeples, Lawrenceville; Col. T. W. Avery, Atlanta; Hon. John W. Maddox, Rome; Mr. Spillsbee Dyer, Pond Spring; Mr. George W. Kelley.

Illinois—Gen. John M. Palmer, Springfield; Col. J. G. Everest, Chicago; Maj. L. M. Buford, Rock Island; Col. H. E. Rives, Paris; Maj. W. E. Carlin, Jerseyville; Gen. Smith D. Atkins, Freeport; Col. E. D. Swain, Chicago, Gen. J. B. Turchin, Radom; Maj. J. A. Connolly, Springfield.

Indiana—Gen. Morton C. Hunter, Bloomington; Capt. Felix Shumate, Lebanon; Capt. Wm. P. Herron, Crawfordsville; Gen. Jas. R. Carnahan, Indianapolis; Capt. Jas. H. McHugh, Indianapolis; Capt. Milton Garrigus, Kokomo; Capt. D. B. McConnell, Logansport; Capt. R. M. Johnson, Elkhart; Capt. Milton M. Thompson, Fort Wayne; Capt. Geo. H. Puntenney, Rushville.

Iowa—Maj. J. D. Fegan, Clinton; John A. Young, Washington; Alexander J. Miller, Oxford; F. P. Spencer, Randolph; Henry G. Aukeny, Corning.

Kentucky (Union)—Col. R. M. Kelly, Louisville; Maj. John S. Clark, Lexington; Maj. John W. Robbins, Angusta; Capt. John W. Tuttle, Monticello; Capt. S. K. Cox, Hartford.

Kentucky (Confederate)—Col. John W. Caldwell, Russellville; Capt. John H. Weller, Louisville; Captain A. T. Pullen, Pryor; Capt. W. W. Herr, Owensboro; Capt. W. H. May, Lexington.

Louisiana: Col. J. A. Chalaron, New Orleans; Gen. J. B. Vinet, New Orleans; Col. John McGrath, Baton Rouge; Col. Henry P. Kernochan, New Orleans; Dr. Y. R. Le Mounier, New Orleans; Capt. Charles H. Luzenberg, New New Orleans; J. W. Pitts, Mansfield.

Massachusetts—Gen. Wm. Cogswell, Salem.

Michigan—Capt. C. E. Belknap, Grand Rapids; J. M. Whallon; L. L. Church; E. A. Crane; S. F. Dwight.

Minnesota—Gen. J. W. Bishop, St. Paul; Capt. J. R. Beatty, Mankato; Capt. A. H. Reed, Glencoe; Sergeant Thomas Downs, Minneapolis; Capt. W. A. Hotchkiss, Preston; Sergeant W. A. Spaulding, Minneapolis.

Mississippi—Gen. E. C. Walthall, Granada; Col. W. C. Richards, Columbus; Capt. J. S. McNeily, Greenville; Gen. E. S. Butts, Vicksburg; Col. T. Otis Baker, Natchez.

Missouri—Capt. H. M. Bledsoe, Pleasant Hill.

New York—Gen. Dan. Butterfield, New York; Col. L. R. Stegman, Brooklyn; Clinton Beckwith, Herkimer.

North Carolina—B. F. Baird, Valle Crucis; D. F. Baird, Valle Crucis; Isaac H. Bailey, Bakersville; J. G. Hall, Hickory; C. A. Cilley, Hickory.

New Jersey—Gen. E. A. Carman, Washington, D. C.; Col. John J. Toffey, Jersey City.

Ohio—Gen. John Beatty, Columbus; Gen. Aquila Wiley, Wooster; Gen. C. H. Grosvenor, Athens; Col. James Watson, Columbus; Capt. J. C. McElroy, Pomeroy; Capt. J. S. Gill, Delaware; Capt. Andrew Jackson, Cedarville; Frederick Wendel, Cincinnati; Gen. Ferd. Van Derveer, Cincinnati.

Pennsylvania — Private Joseph H. Adams, Lancaster; Capt. Wm. J. Alexander, Warren; Corp. Thomas G. Allen, Reading; Lieut. Theodore S. Baker, Philadelphia; Sergt. B. F. Balmer, Harrisburg; Sergt. George R. Beecher, Pittsburgh; Capt. John D. Bentley, Corry; Private A. W. Bergstresser, Harrisburg; Lieut.-Col. Charles M. Betts, Philadelphia; Lieut.-Col. Archibald Blakeley, Pittsburgh; Lieut. McEdwin Boring, Philadelphia; Capt. John M. Brinker, Buffalo, N. Y.; Capt. Wm. J. Byrnes, Philadelphia; Lieut. Steven S. Clair, Columbia; Lieut. George W. Clarke, Philadelphia; Sergt.-Maj. John F. Conaway, Philadelphia; Col. John Craig, Lehigh Gap; Maj. Charles C. Davis, Harrisburg; Capt. Samuel T. Davis, Lancaster; Lieut. Henry C. Deming, Harrisburg; Sergt. T. F. Dornblaser, Bucyrus, O.; Capt. Edward Edgerly, Lancaster; Capt. Robert D. Ellwood, Pittsburgh; Capt. John O. Foering, Philadelphia; Q.-M. Sergt. J. H. Friddy, Mountville; Lieut. J. B. Gettar, Shamokin; Sergt. Rev. J. T. Gibson, Pittsburgh; Capt. C. B. Gillespie, Freeport; Maj. Wm. E. Goodman, Philadephia; Lieut.-Col. Charles G. Green, Cincinnati, O.; Private E. L. Hambright, Roherstown; Lieut. Edward Hamman, Bethlehem; Maj. E. A. Hancock, Philadelphia; Sergt. A. B. Hay, Pittsburgh; Musician W. H. Hougendobler, Columbia; Gen. T. J. Jordan, Philadelphia; Bugler Frederick Kappler, Wilkesbarre; Lieut. Isaac Keith, St. Louis, Mo.; Corp. John W. Keller, Lancaster; Private Hugh Kennedy, Philadelphia; Capt. William W. Ker, Philadelphia; Lieut. I. D. Landis, Coatesville; Maj. August Ledig, Philadelphia; Private Thomas E. Lewis, Philadelphia; Maj. Wm. H. Longsdorf, Carlisle; Quartermaster N. W. Lowell, Erie; Capt. W. F. Lutje, Erie; Lieut. O. B. Macknight, Plaine; Corp. Henry Mank, Philadelphia; Lieut. J. H. Marshall, Lancaster; Capt.

Joseph Matchett, Catasauqua; Maj. Frank J. Miller, Berrysburg; Surgeon Geo. F. Mish, Middletown; Lieut. Thomas Monroe,. Gallitzin; Capt. Joseph A. Moore, Camp Hill; Lieut. Charles F. Muller, Chattanooga; Lieut. S. W. McClusky, Pittsburgh; Captain James D. McGill, Pittsburgh; Col. John P. Nicholson, Philadelphia; Private Harry Nissley, Mount Joy; Gen. J. S. Negley, Plainfield, N. J.; Private Hon. James W. Over, Pittsburgh; Gen. William J. Palmer, New York City; Gen. Ario Pardee; Wyncote; Maj. John M. Porter, New York City; Lieut. Jacob Pantz, Lancaster; Lieut. Henry Ransing, Lancaster; Col. Wm. Richards, Franklin; Quartermaster T. H. Rickert, Pottsville; Gen. Wm. A. Robinson, Pittsburgh; Gen. Thos. E. Rose, Lebanon, Ky.; Lieut.-Col. R. M. Russell, Hanover; Corp. Geo. Schaffner, Butler; Private Christian Scholder, Philadelphia; Capt. John Schuyler, Lock Haven; Capt. J. B. Schaeffner, Valley Falls, Kans.; Bugler Albert F. Shenck, Lancaster; Corp. H. C. Shenck, Lancaster; Corp. J. A. Shipp, Shamokin; Maj. Geo. A. Shuman, Landisburg; Capt. Geo. W. Skinner, Pittsburgh; Adjt. Geo. Stehlin, Orwigsburg; Sergt. J. H. R. Storey, Philadelphia; Capt. H. S. Thompson, *Pottsville; Hon. John Tweedale, Chief Clerk War Department; Capt. Joseph G. Vale, Carlisle; Capt. H. B. Waltman, York; Maj. Fred. F. Wiehl, Chattanooga; Lieut. E. S. Wisner, Marietta; James Rankin Young, Philadelphia.

South Carolina—Gen. H. L. Farley, Columbia; Capt. Perry Moses, Sumpter; Capt. R. F. McCaslan, Ninety-Six; A. C. Appleby, St. Georges; Col. C. I. Walker, Charleston; C. K. Henderson, Aiken; L. P. Harling, Hibler; E. J. Goggins, Leesville; J. D. McLucas, Marion; F. M. Mixon, Columbia; J. F. Culpeper, Timmonsville.

Tennessee—Gen. W. B. Bate, Nashville; Capt. Frank A. Moses, Knoxville; Capt. M. H. Clift, Chattanooga; Col. R. B. Snowden, Memphis; Capt. W. W. Carnes, Memphis; Capt. A. H. Buchannan, Lebanon; Maj. Jos. Vaulx, Nashville; Maj. H. J. Cheney, Nashville; Gen. G. P. Thruston, Nashville; Lieut. John Ruhm, Nashville; Col. John W. Morton, Nashville; J. P. Smartt, Chattanooga; John P. Hickman, Nashville. *Alternates*—Capt. D. D. Anderson, Knoxville; Col. W. L. Eakin, Chattanooga; Hon. Wm. Rule, Knoxville; Gen. A. J. Vaughn, Memphis; Gen. M. J. Wright, Washington, D. C.; Capt. Sam. Hawkins, Huntingdon; Maj. J. Minnick Williams, Nashville: Col. W. J. Hale, Hartsville; Maj. C. W. Anderson, Florence Station; Lieut. James M. Keeble, Nashville.

Texas—Gen. Roger Q. Mills, Washington, D. C.; Col. C. B. Kilgore, Wills Point; Capt. J. P. Douglas, Tyler; Capt. O. P. Bowser, Dallas; Capt. Travis Henderson, Paris.

Virginia—Hon. Geo. D. Wise, Richmond; Col. A. Fulkerson, Bristol; Maj. W. W. Parker, Richmond.

Wisconsin—Capt. Wm. A. Collins, Chicago, Ill.; Col. W. W. Watkins, Milwaukee; Gen. H. C. Hobart, Milwaukee.

Committees of Army Societies.

Army of the Cumberland—Gen. C. H. Manderson, Washington, D. C.; Gen. John M. Palmer, Washington, D. C.; Gen. J. J. Reynolds, Washington, D. C.; Gen. Absolom Baird, Washington, D. C.; Gen. C. H. Grosvenor, Athens, Ohio; Gen. E. A. Carman, Washington, D. C.; Gen. H. V. Boynton, Washington, D. C.

Army of the Tennessee—Gen. C. C. Walcutt, Columbus, Ohio; Gen. Willard Warner, Chattanooga, Tenn.; Gen. Green B. Raum, Chicago, Ill.; Maj. S. C. Plummer, Rock Island, Ill.; Maj. A. Willison, Creston, Iowa; Capt. E. H. Webster, Kansas City, Mo.; Capt. D. A. Mulvane, Topeka, Kas.; Maj. J. D. Fegan, Clinton, Iowa; Capt. B. M. Callender, Chicago, Ill.; Capt. J, G. Everest, Chicago, Ill.; Capt. S. S. Frowe, Chicago, Ill.; Capt. C. F. Matteson, Chicago, Ill.; Col. E. C. Dawes, Cincinnati, Ohio; Col. E. H. Hildt, Canal Dover, Ohio; Col. John Mason Loomis, Chicago, Ill.; Maj. W. L. B. Janney, Chicago, Ill.

Army of the Potomac—Gen. O. O. Howard; Gen. Wm. Cogswell, Washington, D. C.; Gen. E. A. Carman, Washington, D. C.; Capt. Cyrus E. Graves; Gen. Fred. Winkler.

The tables following show how each State and the Regular Army were represented at Chickamauga and Chattanooga:

CHICKAMAUGA.

ROSECRANS.

STATES.	Infantry.	Cavalry.	Artillery.	Total.
Indiana................	26	3	8	37
Illinois................	28	....	5	33
Kansas................	1	....	....	1
Kentucky..............	13	4	....	17
Michigan....	4	2	2	8
Minnesota.............	1	....	1	2
Ohio..................	42	3	10	55
Pennsylvania..........	3	2	1	6
Tennessee.............	....	2	....	2
United States.........	4	1	4	9
Wisconsin.............	5	1	3	9
Missouri..............	2	....	1	3
Total.............	129	18	35	182

BRAGG.

STATES.	Infantry.	Cavalry.	Artillery.	Total.
Alabama...............	23	5	8	35
Arkansas..	12	1	3	16
Confederate Regulars...	1	4	....	5
Florida...............	5	....	1	6
Georgia...............	12	5	7	24
Kentucky..............	5	2	2	9
Louisiana.............	4	1	3	8
Mississippi...........	17	....	4	21
Missouri..............	....	....	2	2
North Carolina........	4	1	....	5
South Carolina........	7	....	1	8
Tennessee.............	36	12	8	56
Texas.................	10	2	1	13
Virginia..............	2	....	1	3
Total.............	138	33	41	222

In addition to the above full organizations, Indiana and Illinois had each three regiments of mounted infantry, and Ohio had one company of sharpshooters, making the total number of separate organizations in Rosecrans army, 189.

Besides the above full organizations, Alabama had 7 battalions of infantry, Georgia 4, Louisiana 1, Mississippi 3, South Carolina 2, and Tennessee 5, and West Virginia had four full companies in one of the Virginia infantry regiments included above, and numerous representatives in the other companies of each of the regiments from Virginia. Alabama had 2 companies of cavalry, Georgia 1, Louisiana 2, Mississippi 1, and Tennessee 2, making the total number of separate organizations in Bragg's army, 251.

CHATTANOOGA.

GRANT.

STATES.	Infantry.	Cavalry.	Artillery.	Total.
Illinois	45		10	55
Indiana	31		3	34
Iowa	10		1	11
Kansas	1			1
Kentucky	11	1		12
Massachusetts	1			1
Michigan	4	1	1	6
Minnesota	2		1	3
Missouri	14		3	17
New Jersey	1			1
New York	14		2	16
Ohio	61	3	5	69
Pennsylvania	10		2	12
Tennessee			1	1
Wisconsin	7		3	10
U. S. Regulars	7		4	11
West Virginia	1			1
Total	220	5	36	261

BRAGG.

STATES.	Infantry.	Cavalry.	Artillery	Total.
Alabama	31	5	8	44
Arkansas	7	1	3	11
Florida	5		1	6
Georgia	36	5	9	50
Kentucky	5	3	1	9
Louisiana	4	1	2	7
Maryland			1	1
Missouri			2	2
Mississippi	15		4	19
North Carolina	2	1		3
South Carolina	13		2	15
Tennessee	36	11	7	54
Texas	6	2	1	9
Virginia	2		5	7
Confederate Regulars	1	4		5
Total	163	33	46	242

In addition to the above, Illinois and Indiana had each one regiment of mounted infantry, and Ohio had one battalion of sharpshooters.

The above represents Gen. Bragg's army before the detachment of forces to East Tennessee. Besides the complete organizations named, Alabama had five battalions of infantry, Georgia 6, Kentucky 1, Louisiana 2, Mississippi 2, South Carolina 2, and Tennessee 3. Kentucky had 3 battalions of cavalry, Tennessee 2, and Virginia 1. The Maryland Battery entered in the table was reorganized shortly before the battle of Chattanooga, and became a Georgia battery, giving the latter state 10 batteries, making the total number of separate organizations in Bragg's army, 269.

Besides the Union forces engaged in the battle the First Division of the Twelfth Corps kept open the lines of communication north of Bridgeport. While not in the battle it was one of the most essential forces of the campaign. In this division, Connecticut had two regiments, Indiana one, Maryland one, Massachusetts two, New Jersey one, New York four, Pennsylvania one, and Wisconsin one. The First Battalion of the Tenth Maine accompanied Gen. Hooker to the West, though it soon after returned to the East. The total number of separate organizations in Grant's army, counting this representative of Maine troops, was 278.

These figures suggest a comparison which will give eastern veterans a clearer idea of the magnitude of the military operations about Chattanooga.

The Army of the Cumberland at Chickamauga had only two infantry regiments less than the Army of the Potomac in the Seven Days' Battles; and Bragg had only three less than the Army of Northern Virginia in those battles, a total difference for the combined armies of only five regimants of Infantry. The losses of Rosecrans at Chickamauga in two days were 16,179, and of McClellan in the Seven Days' only 15,849, or 330 less than Rosecrans; of Bragg in two days, 17,804; of Lee in Seven Days', 19,749. Rosecrans' missing, notwithstanding the long-current exaggerations of the disaster to his right, were only 4,774, against 6,053 in the Seven Days' Battles. The total losses of both sides in the Seven Days' Battles were only 1,615 more than Rosecrans' and Braggs' for the two days' at Chickamauga.

The influential societies of the Army of the Cumberland and the Army of the Tennessee have each given most important aid to the project, and the Society of the Army of the Potomac has appointed a strong committee to assist. The Society of the Army of the Tennessee has been especially active and enthusiastic both in its annual meetings and in the work of its committee on the field. As has been seen, the Society of the Army of the Cumberland led in supporting the proposition to establish the Park. At each succeeding annual meeting since the project was broached it has received active encouragement, and the influence of this Society has been potent at every step.

The Grand Army of the Republic, through its commander, Gen. Lawler, has rendered and is still giving valuable aid.

At the last Annual Reunion of the Camps of Confederate Veterans the following was adopted:

"*Resolved*, That the thanks of Confederate Veterans are hereby tendered to the Congress of the United States for establishing the Chickamauga and Chattanooga National Military Park, where the history of the heroic fighting on both sides is being impartially preserved; and that the governors and legislatures of the Southern States, and especially our Senators and Representatives in Congress, be requested to actively co-operate with the Secretary of War, and the National Commission acting under him, in furthering the work of establishing the National Park."

The history set forth in these concluding chapters shows that the Military Park project is national in every element; that the interest in it is general and earnest; and that when the work now rapidly progressing is finished it will be the most complete field for military study that has yet been restored by any nation.

CHAPTER XX.

POINTS OF DISCUSSION AND DISPUTE.

An historical guide which assumes to set forth the salient points of campaigns and battles, would fall short of what might properly be expected, if it did not touch upon the various questions over which contentions have arisen on each side.

The Confederate authorities were much quicker than those at Washington in estimating the vital importance of Chattanooga, and strengthening their forces for its defense. Buckner's Corps was brought from East Tennessee. A large force was sent from Johnston's army in Mississippi. Gov. Brown furnished local State troops to relieve veterans in the rear, and the latter were sent to the front. For a time it was in contemplation to send General Lee to command against Rosecrans at the same time that Longstreet's Corps was sent south. Three brigades of this force reached Bragg in time for the first day's battle, and two more for the second day. The Confederates were every where prompt and active in devising and executing means of strengthening Bragg.

On the other hand Rosecrans was urged forward, in fact, almost driven forward into his mountain campaign by the most peremptory orders, and without any adequate measures for his support. He was at the time exerting all the energies of his army to prepare for an advance, and fortunately for those who were ordering him, he had independence enough to wait until he was ready to move. The only force directed to coöperate with Rosecrans, was Burnside's column of 12,000 then approaching Tennessee. It was very clear long before the battle that no attention was being given to these orders by Burnside; but the only consideration given the matter at

Washington was to issue other orders of a similar character which were treated with the same indifference. The cause is now known. If Gen. Burnside, who supposed he ranked Rosecrans, had entered the department of the latter, he would be serving under his junior. This was well understood at Knoxville, and Gen. Hartsuff, commanding the Twenty-third Corps, requested that as he did not rank Rosecrans, he might be sent. This request Burnside did not grant. At this time prompt action at Washington would have insured help of vital importance to Rosecrans at Chickamauga.

Gen. Grant had urged, soon after the fall of Vicksburg, that a considerable portion of his unemployed force be sent to Rosecrans to meet a probable concentration to strengthen Bragg. But this suggestion was not adopted. · And so when the battle came on Rosecrans had become weaker by necessary detachments, while Bragg had received abundant reenforcements.

The Transfer of Longstreet from Virginia.

Considering the condition of the Confederate railroads and their slim equipment, the movement of Longstreet from Richmond to Chickamauga properly ranks with the later transfer of Hooker's column from Alexandria to Bridgeport. The head of the latter force reached the Tennessee in five days, Longstreet's advance arrived at Ringgold by way of Atlanta in nine days.

There was no knowledge of the movement at Washington. Four days after Longstreet's troops had left Lee's front, a telegram from Gen. Halleck informed Rosecrans that it was important to ascertain the truth of a report that Bragg was reenforcing Lee. And yet the *New York Herald* of September 8th, had called editorial attention to a special dispatch from the front, printed over the signature of one of its well-known correspondents, announcing that Longstreet had gone south. The same paper also announced the order in which his column had moved. But Rosecrans was assured from Washington, four days before the battle opened, in reply to his own inquires, that no troops had gone south to Bragg, and the first knowledge Rosecrans obtained of Longstreet's presence was through the capture of prisoners.

Gen. Bragg's Troubles with Subordinates.

It is impossible to study the Confederate reports and correspondence without being convinced that Bragg had much just cause of complaint against a number of his subordinates; and further, that if his orders on three separate occasions had been executed, they would have caused Gen. Rosecrans much trouble, if not serious disaster.

A visit to the scene of operations in McLemore Cove from the 8th to the 13th of September, must satisfy any student that Gen. Bragg had strong grounds for dissatisfaction, first, because his orders to attack Gen. Thomas' column about Davis' Cross-roads were not carried out. The roads leading to the left flank of Negley's Division were numerous and in excellent condition, and even when Baird's Division had joined Negley, if the combinations ordered by Gen. Bragg had been effected, and the attacks vigorously made as directed, it now seems as if a serious check to Rosecrans' central column must have resulted.

In the same way, when Gen. Bragg, failing at the center, turned promptly toward Crittenden's Corps, then the left of Rosecrans and isolated, the chances for striking an effective blow in that quarter were excellent. Valid reasons appear to be entirely wanting for failure to obey Gen. Bragg's orders in this case also.

On the morning of the second day's battle at Chickamauga, the attack which Bragg ordered to be made at daylight was not delivered until 9:30 o'clock, and only made then upon orders which he personally transmitted without regard to the corps commander who had failed to attack.

While Gen. Rosecrans seems to have had various good grounds of complaint against his superiors, Gen. Bragg had the support and co-operation of these, but a lack of both from several of his subordinates.

Rosecrans' Leaving the Field.

Gen. Rosecrans, with Gens. McCook and Crittenden, were cut off with the extreme right of the army without fault of their own. Longstreet's penetration of the Union center did that. Gen. Crittenden was entirely without command, as each of his divisions in succession had been detached, Palmer's the first day, Wood's early the second, and Van Cleve's just before the break took place had been sent to the left of the point where it occurred. Stopping some distance in rear of the break, on one of the spurs of Missionary Ridge, Gen. Rosecrans, with Gen. Garfield, his Chief of Staff, and several other members, gave careful attention to the situation. As stragglers representing each of the corps had been found in the crowd on the roads, it was at first believed that the whole line had been routed. The sounds of battle showed that Thomas was holding his ground. It was, however, deemed not only prudent, but obligatory, that a new line should be selected about Chattanooga, on which the army could be rapidly formed in case it was driven from the field. There were, also, many orders to be given, looking to holding Chattanooga Valley, securing the supply trains, guarding the bridges at Chattanooga, and other similar matters necessary to hastily taking position at Chattanooga, if the results on the field demanded it. These things Gen. Rosecrans rapidly indicated to Gen. Garfield, asked him to attend to their execution, and said he himself would ride to Thomas. Gen. Garfield replied that this responsibility was great, especially that of selecting a new line. That, he argued, should be done by the general in command—that is, by the authority that could at once give orders regarding all contingencies that might arise in so grave an emergency. He much preferred to ride to Thomas with orders and information. To this argument Gen. Rosecrans yielded.

Gen. Garfield went to Thomas. and Gen. Rosecrans to Chattanooga.

Union Forces Involved in the Break.

The popular impression which prevailed long after the war, that McCook's and Crittenden's Corps left the field in a body, while the Fourteenth alone remained with Thomas, did great injustice to the first named organizations, and awarded too much credit to the last. Johnson's Division of the Twentieth Corps and Palmer's of the Twenty-first fought unflinchingly both days with Thomas. This subject is most clearly presented in Van Horne's History of the Army of the Cumberland, Vol. I, page 361 :

"As the statement appears in many histories of the war, and even in some of recent publication, that Gen. Thomas with his single corps saved the army at Chickamauga, it is imperative to refute this error, as it does great injustice to the officers and men of the other corps. The preceding narrative gives an indirect refutation, but this prevalent mistake should be explicitly corrected. Gens. Crittenden and McCook had each eight brigades on the field, and Gen. Granger had three. And of these nineteen brigades, twelve were with Gen. Thomas in the final conflict. Five brigades of McCook's Corps were cut off on the right, but not more than two from Crittenden's, counting fragments. Palmer's Division of Crittenden's Corps, and Johnson's from McCook's, were with Gen. Thomas throughout the battle, and Gen. Wood of the former corps, with two brigades of his own division, and one from Van Cleve's, went to him on the second day. Granger's three large brigades constituted nearly one-fourth of the entire force on the final line. More men left the field from Gen. Thomas' own corps, the Fourteenth, than from Gen. Crittenden's. Four regiments of Wilder's Brigade of Reynold's Division were on the right of the breach; a large portion, more than a moiety, of Negley's Division was led or driven from the field (Beatty's Brigade, through the emergencies of battle and orders of Gen. Negley's Adjutant-General, joined the divisions on the right, and at night were found by Gen. Beatty at Rossville), and Brannan lost a portion of one of his brigades through orders of a general who left the field before the final crisis of the battle."

The impression, which still exists in many quarters, that a large part of Rosecrans' army fell back in disorder to Chattanooga, is altogether erroneous. The army was withdrawn to Rossville by Gen. Thomas, under orders received between 4 and 5 o'clock from Gen. Rosecrans to take a strong position there, sending all unorganized forces to Chattanooga. The withdrawal was by McFarland's Gap, as Gen. Bragg's plan of battle had succeeded so far as to obtain control of the La Fayette Road beyond the Union left. The withdrawal began at 5:30 o'clock with the line around the Kelly Field. Each of the corps was re-organized at Rossville, and was in strong position there soon after daylight. These lines were maintained throughout the 21st of September, the enemy feeling them, but making no attack, and during the night of that day the army marched on to Chattanooga.

Rosecrans' Concentration before Chickamauga.

There has been wide criticism of Gen. Rosecrans for not withdrawing at once over Lookout Mountain when he found that Chattanooga was evacuated, and proceeding along its western base to the occupation of that city.

His own answer is, that with Bragg concentrated within easy reach, and so situated that the movements of each of Rosecrans' columns were accurately known by him, the first signs of withdrawal over the mountains would have brought the precipitation of Bragg upon Crittenden, and the probable forcing back of the latter and enabling Bragg to re-occupy Chattanooga. The concentration along the eastern base of Lookout was also along the shortest and on supporting lines.

Confederate Criticism of Gen. Bragg.

After the battle of Chickamauga, there was considerable criticism of Gen. Bragg for not crossing the Tennessee above Chattanooga, marching on Rosecrans' line of supplies, and thus compelling him to give up the city and retire on Nashville. After the battle of Chattanooga, this criticism gained wider currency. Gen. Bragg thus disposed of it in his report:

"The suggestion of a movement by our right immediately after the battle to the north of the Tennessee and thence upon Nashville, requires notice only because it will find a place on the files of the department. Such a movement was utterly impossible for want of transportation. Nearly half our army consisted of re-enforcements just before the battle, without a wagon or an artillery horse, and nearly, if not quite, a third of the artillery horses on the field had been lost. The railroad bridges, too, had been destroyed to a point south of Ringgold, and on all the road from Cleveland to Knoxville. To these insurmountable difficulties were added the entire absence of means to cross the river, except by fording at a few precarious points too deep for artillery and the well-known danger of sudden rises, by which all communication would be cut, a contingency which did actually happen a few days after the visionary scheme was proposed. But the most serious objection to the proposition was its entire want of military propriety. It abandoned to the enemy our entire line of communication, and laid open to him our depots of supplies, while it placed us with a greatly inferior force beyond a difficult and at times impassable river, in a country affording no subsistence to men or animals. It also left open to the enemy; at a distance of only ten miles, our battle field, with thousands of our wounded and his own, and all the trophies and supplies we had won. All this was to be risked and given up for what? To gain the enemy's rear and cut him off from his depot of supplies by the route over the mountains, when the very movement abandoned to his unmolested use the better and more practicable route, of half the length, on the south side of the river. It is hardly necessary to say, the proposition was not even entertained, whatever may have been the inferences drawn from subsequent movements."

Thomas' Success at Missionary Ridge.

The declaration was current at the time of the battle, and has been persistently maintained in various histories since, that the successful storming of Missionary Ridge by Gen. Thomas' Corps was made possible because Gen. Sherman's attack at the north end of the Ridge had drawn large forces from Thomas' front, and so enabled him to break through. As a matter of fact, not a soldier or a gun left the Confederate center to go to their right after Sherman's assault began. The movements on the Ridge which led to this belief were those of the troops which had abandoned Lookout and were on their way to the Confederate right. Most of these reached their destination by 9 A. M. The exact opposite is true, that soon after Gen. Thomas moved against the Confederate center, that is, about an hour before sunset, Brown's, Cumming's, and Maney's Brigades were dispatched by Gen. Cleburne from Tunnel Hill to the assistance of the forces opposing Thomas, Cleburne himself accompanying them. Brown's Brigade reached Cheatham's line before the close of the action, and, supported by Cumming's, participated in the effort to check Baird's northward advance along the crest of the Ridge.

Bragg's Holding on to Missionary Ridge.

Many Confederate officers criticized Gen. Bragg for establishing his line on Missionary Ridge, after the Union army had carried Lookout Mountain, instead of withdrawing to Dalton, where he could have protected his flanks. With the road to the Confederate left flank at Rossville open to

Hooker, and Gen. Sherman's army on the right flank at Tunnel Hill, the Missionary Ridge line was practically turned on both flanks. So strong was the expectation of withdrawal at Gen. Hardee's Headquarters, that Gen. Cleburne sent his artillery and ordnance stores across the Chickamauga during the evening of the 24th, recalling them upon learning that it had been decided to give battle on Missionary Ridge.

ARMY OF THE TENNESSEE.

MAJ.-GEN. WILLIAM T. SHERMAN

[Nov. 25, 1863.]

1st Division, Fifteenth Corps—BRIG.-GEN. PETER J. OSTERHAUS.
2d Division, Fifteenth Corps—BRIG.-GEN. MORGAN L. SMITH.
4th Division, Fifteenth Corps—BRIG.-GEN. HUGH EWING.
2d Division, Seventeenth Corps—BRIG.-GEN. JOHN E. SMITH.

General Sherman's forces, excepting Osterhaus' Division which was engaged with Hooker at Lookout Mountain and Rossville, crossed the Tennessee north-west of this point the night of the 23d. The afternoon of the 24th, supported by Davis' Division of the Fourteenth Corps, and Bushbeck's Division of the Eleventh Corps, the column advanced and took possession of the detached range north of this point without opposition. Early on the 25th the rest of the Eleventh Corps reported to General Sherman.

Lightburn's, Alexander's, and Cockerill's Brigades were left in position on the detached hills. The main assault on the Ridge began about 10 A. M. Corse's Brigade ascended the north point; Giles A. Smith's, assisted by three regiments from Lightburn's, assaulted on Corse's left; Loomis Brigade on his right, with Bushbeck's Brigade supporting, the latter opposite the Tunnel. Corse effected a lodgment about the Moon house, and held the point until toward sunset. About 1 o'clock Matthies' Brigade, with Raum's in support, assaulted the slope between Tunnel Hill and the north point in aid of Loomis. They reached the crest, but after severe fighting were forced to withdraw. A general assault of the attacking forces was made at the same time, continuing until after 3 o'clock.

General Hardee's forces opposed General Sherman, being posted around the high point of Tunnel Hill, and thence south along the crest to the high ground south of the Tunnel. The main attack ended about an hour before sundown, the Confederates retaining their morning positions. At night they withdrew to Chickamauga Station.

TABLET AT NORTH END OF MISSIONARY RIDGE.

CLEBURNE'S DIVISION—HARDEE'S CORPS.

MAJ.-GEN. PATRICK R. CLEBURNE.

[Nov. 25, 1863.]

Liddell's Brigade—Col. DANIEL C. GOVAN.
Smith's Brigade—Brig.-Gen. JAMES A. SMITH.
Polk's Brigade—Brig.-Gen. LUCIUS E. POLK.
Lowrey's Brigade—Brig.-Gen. MARK P. LOWREY.

This Division reached the eastern base of Missionary Ridge from Chickamauga Station the evening of November 23d. At dawn of the 24th, it began to throw up earthworks along the crest of the Ridge from Bragg's Headquarters to the Shallow Ford Road. At 2 P. M., it was dispatched in haste to Tunnel Hill to confront Gen. Sherman's forces, reaching that point at 2:30. The Division was established about Tunnel Hill during the night, Smith's Brigade held the central knoll north of the Tunnel, three regiments consolidated under Col. R. Q. Mills being posted along the crest facing west, and the rest of the brigade facing north-west, Col. H. B. Granbury and Maj. W. A. Taylor commanding. This was the central point of the battle and the brunt of Gen. Sherman's attacks was sustained here. Gen. Polk's Brigade was posted on a hill at the extreme right overlooking the bridge over the Chickamauga, with Wright's Brigade of Cheatham's Division and Lewis' Brigade of Bate's Division in support. Govan's Brigade was posted on the spur jutting out to the east. Lowrey's Brigade was en echelon 200 paces in front of Govan. On the line were the batteries of Calvert (Key) directly over the Tunnel, Douglas' Battery (Bingham) on Govan's line, and Swett's (Shannon) with Smith's Brigade. The Union attacks were concentrated on Tunnel Hill, and were vigorous from 10 o'clock in the morning of November 25th until about 4 P. M. Cumming's, Pettus', and Brown's Brigades of Stevenson's Division and Maney's of Walker's took part in repelling the final assaults. During the night the forces which held the position withdrew with their guns and material to Chickamauga Station, Cleburne's Division being the rearguard.

TABLET AT TUNNEL HILL.

# HOOKER'S COLUMN.

MAJ.-GEN. JOSEPH HOOKER.

[Nov. 25, 1863, 3 P. M.]

Osterhaus' Division, 15th Corps—Maj.-Gen. PETER J. OSTERHOUS.
Cruft's Division, 4th Corps—Brig.-Gen. CHARLES CRUFT.
Geary's Division, 12th Corps—Brig.-Gen. JOHN GEARY.

This column, descending from Lookout Mountain at 10 A. M., November 25th, and marching in the order named, reached this point about 3 P. M., after having been delayed about three hours by the destruction of a bridge over Chattanooga Creek. Osterhaus' Division pushed through the Gap to the eastern base of Missionary Ridge driving back a small force of Stewart's Division, first turned northward in rear of the Confederate line which occupied the crest of the Ridge, and after proceeding over a mile, assaulted and carried the Ridge from the east.

Cruft's Division moved into the Gap and pushed northward with its center on the summit of the Ridge.

Geary's Division moved along the western base of the Ridge gradually nearing the crest and first reaching it about a mile to the north of this point and about three-quarters of a mile to the south of Johnson's Division of the 14th Corps.

All three divisions were sharply engaged by Stewart's troops, but the latter being largely outnumbered and nearly surrounded, were obliged to withdraw with heavy loss of men and material.

TABLET AT ROSSVILLE.

INDEX.

APPROACHES of the Park, length of, 1, 2.
Army societies, committees of, 281.
Armies, Union and Confederate, at opening of the Chickamauga campaign, 15.
Artillery battalions, Confederate, at Chattanooga: Maj. Austin Leyden, 156; Col. E. P. Alexander, 156; Maj. Melancthon Smith, 157; Maj. T. R. Hotchkiss, 158; Capt. William W. Carnes, 159; Maj. Robert Martin, 160; Capt. H. C. Semple, 161; Capt. C. H. Slocomb, 162; Maj. S. C. Williams, 163; Maj. A. R. Courtney, 164; Reserve, Maj. Felix H. Robertson, 166.
Artillery reserve, Union, at Chattanooga, 147.

BARNES' brigade at Viniard's, 38; on Kelly Field line, 69.
Battery H, Fifth U. S. Artillery, captured, 177, 178
Battery locations, how marked, 11.
Belknap, Capt. C. E., at Widow Glenn's, 194.
Boulevard, the central, 2.
Boundaries, legal, 1, 2.
Bragg, evacuates Chattanooga, 19; concentrates at La Fayette, 20; orders attack on Rosecrans' center in McLemore's Cove, 21; orders attack on Crittenden, the Union left, 23; general order for battle of Chickamauga, 26; crosses the Chickamauga and forms for battle, 27, 170, 184; attacked on right and in rear by Rosecrans, 27; movements into action, 186; headquarters on Missionary Ridge, 2; investment of Chattanooga, 89; movements from Chickamauga, 92; lines around Chattanooga, 92.
Brock Field, 179, 182, 183.
Brown's brigade at Missionary Ridge, 216.
Brotherton House, battle lines about, 176; to Snodgrass Hill, 189.
Brown's Ferry affair, 99–104.
" Burning House "—Poe's, 176.

CAPTURE of Union regiments: 22d Michigan, 21st and 89th Ohio, 56.
Cavalry, Union, 169.

Chattanooga, battle of, 109; Grant's order of battle, 109, positions of the opposing armies, 112; advance on Orchard Knob, 113; battle of Lookout Mountain, 116; Sherman's Crossing, 120; Confederate movements, night of November 24, 122; battle of Missionary Ridge, 123; Sherman's assault on Tunnel Hill, 123; Confederate defense of Tunnel Hill, 126; Confederate withdrawal from Lookout, 129; Thomas' storming of Missionary Ridge, 132; Hooker at Missionary Ridge, 215; Union artillery at Chattanooga, 136; Union losses, 137; post of Chattanooga, 147.

Chickamauga campaign—Rosecrans' strategy, 15; plan of campaign, 16; its objective, 15; position of armies at opening of, 15; composition of the armies, 15; feint on the left, 16; crossing the Cumberlands, the Tennessee river, the Raccoon and Lookout ranges, 16–19; evacuation of Chattanooga, 19; movements of Crittenden's feint on the left, 17, 19; movements of Bragg's army from Chattanooga to La Fayette, 20; Union forces in Chattanooga, 19, 20.

Chickamauga campaign skeletonized, 95; successive moves of each army, 95–98.

Chickamauga—first day's battle, 29; Bragg's plan, 24; fields cleared since the battle, 29; first Confederate troops on the field, 31; Minty at Reed's Bridge, Wilder at Alexander's, 31; Bragg's formation for battle, 32; Thomas' and McCook's Corps by night march gain Bragg's right and rear, 32; Brannan opens the battle near Jay's Mill, 34; Negley's Division confronts Breckinridge's at Glass Mill, 34; main features of first day's operations, 34–40; position of the opposing forces, 32;

Engagements about—Jay's Mill, 34; Winfrey's (E. C. Reed) House, 35, 36, 39; on extreme left, 36; Brock Field, 36; Brotherton's 37; Poe's, 37; Viniard's, 38; at night of 19th September, 39, 40; night engagement of Johnson's and Baird's divisions, with Cleburne's and Cheatham's, 39, 40.

Chickamauga from Chattanooga via Missionary Ridge; via of Rossville, 195.

Chickamauga—second day's battle, 41; re-arrangement of the lines, 41, 42; Bragg's fresh troops, 41; Bragg's order for an early attack not executed, 44; Breckinridge opens the battle, 44; reaches the Kelly Field, 45; is finally repulsed, 45, 47; Longstreet breaks through the Union center, 49; cause of the gap in the Union lines, 48, 49; Brannan swings back to Snodgrass Hill, 49; Wood rallies there, 49; Negley leaves the field, 52; Davis and Sheridan forced off the field, 52; Rosecrans cut off with them, 52; Forrest's Cavalry captures Cloud Hospital, 53; Confederate assault on the Kelly Field line, 57; Longstreet assaults on Snodgrass Hill, 55, 56; arrival of Granger's reserve to the relief of Thomas, 55; Kershaw's, B. Johnson's, Hindman's, and Preston's Divisions assault Snodgrass Hill, 55, 56; capture of three Union regiments by Kelly's and Trigg's brigades, 56; Thomas' withdrawal to Rossville, 57; takes position there, 58; strength and losses, 58, 59, 227-229.

Clayton's brigade reaches the Tanyard, 37.

Clearings and woods as they were in 1863, 29.

Confederate army, roster of, at Chickamauga, with movements of each division in both days' battle, 72-87; the same for the battles at Chattanooga, 155-166.

Confederate right, and Union left, Sunday, September 20th, from about McDonald's, 198, 199.

Consolidation of 20th and 21st Corps at Chattanooga, 93.

Crawfish Springs, roads from, 167; old wheel and mill, 169; view from, 170; Union army arrives at, 170; night march through, 170; Union hospitals, 169.

Crest Road—to La Fayette Road by the cut-off, 195; the drive upon, 214.

Crittenden's Corps—feint on Union left, 16; at Lee and Gordon's Mill, 173; its moves from Lee and Gordon's into action, 175; its lines at Lee and Gordon's, 173.

Croxton and Forrest open first day's battle, 34.

Davis' Cross Roads, Confederate movement against Negley's and Baird's divisions, 21-23.

DeLong Place, Missionary Ridge, 2, 3.

Distances, table of, 12; length of Park approaches, 1.

Divisions, Confederate, movements into battle at Chickamauga first day: Cheatham, 35, 73; Cleburne, 39, 75; Breckinridge, 34, 76; Hood (Law), 37, 83; Bushrod Johnson, 37, 38, 84; Liddell, 35, 78; Preston, 38, 80; Stewart, 37, 79; Walker (Gist) 34, 77; Forrest's Cavalry, 34, 85; Wheeler's Cavalry, 86.

Divisions, Confederate, movements at Chickamauga, second day: Cheatham, 43, 73; Cleburne, 43, 45, 75; Breckinridge, 41, 43, 44, 45, 47, 76; Hindman, 41, 43, 52, 53, 55, 74; Hood (Law), 43, 49, 83; Bushrod Johnson, 43, 53, 55, 84; Liddell, 43, 53, 78; McLaw (Kershaw) 41, 43, 49, 53, 55, 56, 82; Preston, 41, 43, 56, 80; Stewart, 43, 49, 79; Walker (Gist), 41, 43, 53, 77; Forrest's Cavalry, 43, 45, 53, 85; Wheeler's Cavalry, 86.

Divisions, Confederate, positions and movements in the battles about Chattanooga: Breckinridge (Bate), 113, 123, 133, 136, 162; Buckner (Johnson), 113, 114, 133, 163; Cheatham, 113, 114, 117, 122, 128, 129, 133, 136, 157; Cleburne, 113, 114, 122, 123, 127, 126-129; Hindman (Patton Anderson), 113, 114, 133; Hood, 113, 156; McLaw, 113, 155; Stevenson, 113, 117, 122, 126, 128, 129, 159; Stewart, 113, 122, 129, 133, 161; Walker (Gist), 113, 122, 129, 160; Cavalry, Wheeler's, 164.

Divisions, Union, movements into battle at Chickamauga, first day: Baird, 32, 35, 39, 60; Brannan, 32, 34, 37, 62; Davis, 38, 64; Johnson, 35, 36, 39, 65; Granger (D. McCook's brigade), 32, 70; Negley, 34, 37, 61; Palmer, 35, 36, 37, 68; Reynolds, 36, 37, 63; Sheridan, 39, 66; Steedman, 32, 34, 70; Van Cleve, 37, 69; Wood, 38, 39, 67; Cavalry divisions, 71.

Divisions, Union, movements at Chickamauga, second day: Baird, 43, 44, 45, 57, 60; Brannan, 47, 49, 52, 55, 57, 62; Davis, 43, 49, 52, 64; Johnson, 43, 57, 65; Morgan (D. McCook's brigade), 70; Negley, 47, 52, 61; Palmer, 43, 57, 68; Reynolds, 43, 57, 63; Sheridan, 52, 66; Steedman, 55, 56, 70; Van Cleve, 43, 58, 69, 290; Wood, 43, 47, 49, 67; Cavalry divisions, 71.

Divisions, Union, positions and movements at the battles about Chattanooga, 112; Baird, 112, 113, 125, 133, 136, 138, 145; Cruft, 112, 116, 117, 119, 131, 132, 137, 140; Davis, 112, 121, 122, 126, 138, 144; Ewing, 112, 120, 121, 123, 126, 138, 153; Geary, 112, 116, 117, 119, 120, 129, 131, 132, 137, 150; Johnson, 112, 120, 132, 133, 134, 138, 143; Osterhaus, 112, 116, 117, 119, 131, 132, 137, 151; Schurz, 113, 125, 137, 138, 149; Sheridan, 112, 113, 114, 133, 134, 138, 141; Smith, John E., 112, 120, 121, 123, 138, 154; Smith, Morgan L., 112, 120, 121, 123, 138, 152; Steinwehr, 113, 125, 137, 138, 148; Williams, 150; Wood, 112, 113, 114, 133, 134, 137, 138, 142; Cavalry (Eli Long), 112, 146.

Dodge's Brigade, on north line Kelly Field, 44.

Dyer Fields, 173.

ENGINEER troops at Chattanooga, 146.

FIGHTING ground at Chickamauga of Union organizations: Baird's division, 172, 182; Baldwin's brigade, 181; Beatty's, John, brigade, at Glass' Mill, 34, 169; Beatty, Samuel, 183; Brannan's division, 172, 177, 178; Connell's brigade, 177; Croxton's brigade, 177, 178, 179; Cruft's brigade, 182; Davis' division, 172; Dicks' brigade, 183; Dodge's brigade, 181; Grose's brigade, 182; Hazen's brigade, 68, 182, 194; Johnson's division, 172, 182; King's, E. A., brigade, 183; McCook's brigade, 198, 200; Negley's division, 173; Palmer's division, 182; Reynold's division, 172, 183; Scribner's brigade, 179; Stanley's brigade, 34, 169; Starkweather's brigade, 182; Turchin's brigade, 183, 200; Van Cleve's division, 69, 183; Van Derveer's brigade, 177, 178, 179, 203, 204; Willich's brigade, 181.

Fighting ground at Chickamauga of Confederate organizations: Bate's brigade, 183; Breckinridge's division, 34, 169, 198, 199, 200; Brown's brigade, 183, 291; Cheatham's division, 181, 182; Clayton's brigade, 183; Cleburne's division, 45, 182; Ector's brigade, 177, 179; Forrest's cavalry, 177, 178, 179; Govan's brigade, 181, 200; Jackson's brigade, 181; Law's brigade, 37, 183; Liddell's division, 177, 178, 200; Maney's brigade, 181; Smith's, Preston, brigade, 181; Stewart's division, 45, 183; Strahl's brigade, 181; Walker's division, 177, 178; Walthall's brigade, 177, 178, 181, 200; Wilson's brigade, 178; Wright's brigade, 181.

First day's battle lines, best route around, 176.

Forrest and Croxton open the first day's battle, 34.

Forrest at Union hospitals, Cloud's, 198.

Fulton's Brigade attacks Van Cleve south of Brotherton's, 176.

GLASS' Mill, affair at, between Breckinridge's and Negley's troops, 34, 169; affair between Crook's and Wheeler's Cavalry, 169; John Beatty's and Stanley's Brigades, Helm's Brigade, Eli Long's Cavalry Brigade, 169.

Gracie's Brigade carries a salient on Snodgrass Hill, 56.

Granger, Gordon, at Cloud's, moves from Cloud's to Snodgrass Hill, 198; at Snodgrass Hill, 190, 192.

Grant arrives at Chattanooga, November 23d, 101.

Guide to Chattanooga Field, 207; Lookout Mountain, cars to, 207; views from, 207; Wauhatchie, Brown's Ferry, Moccasin Point, Chattanooga, Orchard Knob, and Missionary Ridge, seen from, 207–213; to Orchard Knob, Sherman Heights, and Bragg's Headquarters by street cars, 213.

Guide to the Chickamauga Field, 167; approaching from Crawfish Springs, 167; Crawfish Springs and vicinity, 167; composition of the line the second day, 186–189; Confederate forces, movements of, into Saturday's battle, 183; Brannan's, Baird's, and Johnson's Divisions, movements of, into Saturday's battle, 172; Davis', Wood's, and Sheridan's attack at Viniard's, 175; Glass Mill position, 167; Harker's Brigade, vital stand of, 190; night attack of Cleburne and Cheatham on Baird and Johnson, 182; night march of Rosecrans' army, 170; Palmer's and Van Cleve's division in action at the center, 175; Reynolds' division in action at Poe's, 172; routes to the field, 167; Snodgrass Hill—Confederate attack, 192, 193; Union line on, 189; Thomas arrives at Kelly Field, 170.

Guide to the Chickamauga Field, approaching from Chattanooga, 195; approaching by Missionary Ridge, 195; Cloud House and hospitals, 198, Kelly Field, lines and movements about, 201, 204; Snodgrass Hill from Kelly's, 201; from Brotherton's, 201; Union left and Confederate right, Sunday, 198; Saturday's line, how best to visit, 201; withdrawal from Snodgrass Hill, 206; from Kelly Field, 204.

HARKER's brigade gains rear of Bushrod Johnson, 176.

Hazen's brigade on Snodgrass Hill, 68.

Historical tablets, 4; specimens of, 5–10, 296, 297, 298.

Hooker arrives at Bridgeport, September 30th, with 11th and 12th Corps, 93; his column at Rossville, 215; see chapters IX, X, and p. 116.

JACKSON's brigade at Missionary Ridge, 216.

Jay's Mill and vicinity, 178.

KELLY's brigade, captures by, 57.

Kelly Field, Confederate attacks upon, 202–204; John Beatty's, Stanley's, and Van Derveer's brigades in, 203; lines around, September 20, 202; occupation by Confederates, 204; operations

about, 202-204; Stovall and Adams' brigades gain the Union rear in, 203; Sunday's line about, 186.
Kelly House to Snodgrass Hill, 201.

LEE and Gordon's Mill line, 173.
Lee Mansion, Rosecrans' Headquarters, 169.
Lines of battle about Snodgrass Hill, 189-193.
Lines of battle at Chickamauga, September 20, morning, Union and Confederate, 186-189.
Losses at Chattanooga: Orchard Knob, 137; Lookout Mountain, 137, 138; Missionary Ridge, 137, 138.
Losses, Union and Confederate at Chickamauga, 227-229; compared with European battles, 257.
Lytle, Gen. W. H., killed, 173.

McAFEE's Church, 197, 198.
McCook's, D., brigade (Morgan's division), at Jay's Mill, 178, 179.
McDonald's to Snodgrass Hill, 201.
McLemore's Cove, movements in, 21; Bragg orders attack on Rosecrans' center, 21; Negley at Davis' Cross Roads, 21; failure to execute Bragg's orders, 23; Bragg orders attack on Union left, 23; another failure to carry out orders, Bragg's disappointment, 24; Rosecrans hastens concentration of his army, 24, 25; concentration accomplished, 25.
Missionary Ridge, positions of Confederate divisions upon, 215.
Missionary Ridge, position of Union divisions on Thomas' line, 215, 216.
Monuments of 8-inch shells where general officers were killed, 11, 31, 173, 175, 182, 187. (For E. A. King's monument, see List of Illustrations.)
Moore's brigade at Missionary Ridge, 216.

NATIONAL Park, general description of, 1; approaches of, 1, 2; boundaries of, 1, 2; main boulevard, 2; minor purchases, Bragg's Headquarters, De Long spur, Orchard Knob, Tunnel Hill. 2, 13; restoring the fields, 3; observation towers, 3; historical tablets, 4; specimen tablets, 5-10; marking battery locations, 11; restoring works, 11; marking lines, 11; table of distances, 12; pyramidal monuments to general officers killed, 11.
National Park, work of establishing it, 272; Secretary Proctor organizes the work, 272; commission appointed, 272; Major Frank G. Smith, U. S. A., succeeds Col. S. C. Kellogg, U. S. A., 273; subsequent support of Secretaries Elkins and Lamont; 273; Assistant Secretaries Grant and Doe active friends, 273; engineers of the Park and their work, 273; the assistant in Confederate work, 274.

INDEX. 305

Night march of Union army September 18th, and movements into battle, 19th, 170-175.
Ninth Ohio, recaptures regular battery, 35.

OATES, W. C., attacks near Brotherton, 176.
Observation Towers. See List of Illustrations, 3, 175, 177, 192, 211.
Occupation of Chattanooga, first Union troops to enter, 19, 20.
Opening of the battle of Chickamauga, Brannan, Forrest, Walker, 177.
Orchard Knob, 2, 213, 214.

PARK Project, history of, 219; suggestion of the scheme first indorsed by Society Army of the Cumberland; committee of the Society meets in Washington. 220; Joint Memorial Association agreed upon, 221; meeting of Union and Confederate veterans at Chattanooga to consider, 222; addresses by Gen. Rosecrans, Gov. Marks, and W. A. Henderson, 222, 232, 239; project explained by Gen. Boynton, 223-232; indorsement of Confederate Veterans, 242; barbecue at Crawfish Springs, 243; addresses of Gov. Gordon and Gen. Rosecrans, 243-247; organization of Chickamauga Memorial Association, 248; incorporators, directors, and officers elected, 248-250.
Park Project, plan changed to a National Military Park, 251; the matter before Congress, 251; bill to establish the Park, 251; Gen. C. H. Grosvenor introduces it, 251; favorable report by House Committee on Military Affairs, 252-259; bill passed unanimously by both houses, 260; signed by President Harrison, 260; text of bill establishing the Park, 261-266; active friends of the measure in Congress, 267-268; friends in the press at Washington, 268-269; in the War Record Office, 268; bill for the national dedication of the Park, 269; regulations for monuments, tablets, and markers, 270.
Plan of battle, Bragg's for Chickamauga, 25, 26.
Plan of Chickamauga campaign, Rosecrans', 16; of battle of Chattanooga, Grant's, 109.
Poe House, 176; Reynolds' operations about, 176.
Points of discussion and dispute, 287; prompt re-inforcement of Bragg, 287; delay in aiding Rosecrans, 287; Grant urges sending troops to Rosecrans, 288; transfer of Longstreet from Virginia, 288; Bragg's troubles with subordinates, 289; Rosecrans forced off the field, 290; Union troops involved in Sunday's break, 291; stopped at Rossville, 292; Rosecrans' concentration east of Lookout, 292; Confederate criticism of Bragg, 293; Thomas' success at Missionary Ridge, 294; Bragg's holding on to Missionary Ridge, 294.

REED's Bridge, Confederate crossing at, 31, 184; Bushrod Johnson's division, Robertson's brigade, 31, 184; Minty's Cavalry, Wilder's Mounted Infantry, 184; Wilder assists Minty at, 31.

Regulars, at Chickamauga, 282; at Chattanooga, 283.

Regular Battery II, 5th U. S. captured, 35; recaptured by Ninth Ohio, 35.

Re-opening the Tennessee River: battle of Wauhatchie, 105; Hooker arrives at Brown's Ferry, 105; Geary halts at Wauhatchie, Longstreet makes a night attack on Geary, 105; Hood's division the assaulting force, 106; Union troops successful and the line of supplies by the river and adjacent roads opened, 108.

Re-opening the Tennessee River: the Brown's Ferry affair, 99; Rosecrans ready to execute his plan upon Hooker's arrival, 99; Hooker delayed by non-arrival of his trains, Rosecrans relieved, 101; his plan carried out by Thomas, 103; Gen. W. F. Smith executes it, 101; Hazen's brigade moves in boats to Brown's Ferry, Turchin's, by land, 103; the Michigan Mechanics and Engineers, 103; Hooker co-operates from Bridgeport, 104; Law's brigade defends the ferry, 104.

Restoring the fields, 3.

Restoring works, 11.

Reynolds' division, charge of, September 20th, 200.

Rosecrans crosses the Cumberland, 17; crosses the Tennessee River and Mountains beyond to McLemore's Cove, 16-19; concentrated in McLemore's Cove, 25; interposes by night march between Bragg and Chattanooga, 27; attacks right and rear of Bragg at Jay's Mill, opening battle of Chickamauga, 27; takes position at Chattanooga, September 22, 90; relieved October 19, 101; Thomas put in command, 101.

Rossville Gap, Rosecrans' lines, September 20th, midnight, and September 21st, 89, 90, 197.

SHELL Monuments, to whom erected, 11.

Sherman's column reaches Lookout Valley, November 18, 94.

Sherman Heights, 213.

Snodgrass Hill, base of, positions of Confederate lines, 193.

Snodgrass Hill, crest of, position of Union lines, 193-194.

Society Army of the Cumberland, first to indorse Park project, 220.

State Commissions, 275, 277.

State troops, 183, 184.

THOMAS' Headquarters at Kelly's Field, 171.

Thomas in command on the field at Chickamauga, 52.

Thomas succeeds Rosecrans, October 19, 101.

Thomas' withdrawal from Kelly's Field, 204.

Thomas' withdrawal from Snodgrass Hill, 206.

Trigg's brigade, captures by, 56.
Troops of the states at Chickamauga, 283; at Chattanooga, 284.
Tunnel Hill, 13.
Turchin's brigade, charge of, September 20, 200.

UNION army reaches Chattanooga, 89; formation of the lines, 90.
Union army, roster of, at Chickamauga, with movements of each division in both days' battles, 60-72.
   The same for the battles at Chattanooga, 140-154.
Union hospitals at Cloud House, Church and Spring, 198; at Crawfish Springs, 169.

VIDITOE House, 173.
Viniard's, battle lines about, 175.

WALTHALL, opposes Hooker at Lookout Mountain, 117, 209; opposes Baird on Missionary Ridge, 136, 21
Wauhatchie, battle of, 105-108.
Widow Glenn's, Rosecrans' Headquarters, 173.
Wilder's brigade, in front of Hood, September 18th, 31, 32; at Viniard's, September 19th, 38, 184; at Widow Glenn's, 173, 188.
Winfrey House (E. C. Reed's), 181.
Withdrawal, Union troops from Snodgrass Hill, 193; Kelly's, 204.
Woods and clearings as they were in 1863, 29.

www.ingramcontent.com/pod-product-compliance
Lightning Source LLC
Chambersburg PA
CBHW030010240426
43672CB00007B/893